CHEESES OF THE WORLD

by

THE U. S. DEPARTMENT OF AGRICULTURE

Dairy Products Laboratory
Eastern Utilization Research and Development Division
Agricultural Research Service

DOVER PUBLICATIONS, INC.
New York

Published in Canada by General Publishing Company, Ltd., 30 Lesmill Road, Don Mills, Toronto, Ontario.

Published in the United Kingdom by Constable and Company, Ltd., 10 Orange Street, London WC 2.

This Dover edition, first published in 1972, in an unabridged republication of *Cheese Varieties and Descriptions,* first published by the U. S. Department of Agriculture in 1953 and revised in 1969.

International Standard Book Number: 0-486-22831-2
Library of Congress Catalog Card Number: 73-188947

Manufactured in the United States of America
Dover Publications, Inc.
180 Varick Street
New York, N. Y. 10014

Preface

The publication was prepared to answer the questions of many people who ask USDA for general information on the characteristics of different cheeses, and the methods of production. The descriptions of the cheeses were derived from many sources. Information came from a study of the literature and from cheese manufacturers and research workers. Although every effort has been made to get complete and accurate information, in many cases, only fragmentary information was obtained.

Several new names of cheese and modifications of established varieties have become available since the 1953 edition. For example, the established names such as Swiss, Roquefort, and Gouda have been changed in the new Danish nomenclature system to Somsoe, Donablu, and Fynbo, respectively. Pizza cheese is an example of a new variety in the United States. Market changes and consumer demands have been responsible in part for many of the changes and new varieties. Descriptions of these new cheeses and an updating of the old varieties will be forthcoming in the next revision which is now underway.

Authentic information on any type of cheese for use in the planned revision of this handbook will be greatly appreciated.

Tribute should be paid to the authors who contributed to the publication in the past. They were: C. F. Doane, K. J. Matheson, H. W. Lawson, and G. P. Sanders.

HOMER E. WALTER
ROBERT C. HARGROVE

CONTENTS

Introduction

Cheese is a highly nutritious and palatable food. It is of value in the diet because it contains in concentrated form almost all the protein and usually most of the fat, as well as essential minerals, vitamins, and other nutrients, of milk.

Cheese is made wherever animals are milked and produce more milk than the people use in fluid form. Most cheese is made from cow's milk, simply because cows are milked more generally throughout the world than other animals. Smaller quantities are made from the milk of goats and ewes. Cheese is also made in some countries from the milk of other animals, such as camels, asses, mares, buffaloes, and reindeer.

People all over the world like and eat cheese. People in the United States are no exception. Although we do not eat nearly so much cheese per capita in the United States as do people in some countries, we eat nearly twice as much now as 20 years ago, or about 14 pounds (all kinds) per capita per year. This increased consumption is the result, at least in part, of improvements made in recent years in the quality and uniformity of many kinds of cheese.

No one knows who made the first cheese, but according to an ancient legend it was made accidentally by an Arabian merchant. The merchant put his supply of milk into a pouch made of a sheep's stomach when he set out on a long day's journey across the desert. The rennet in the lining of the pouch combined with the heat of the sun caused the milk to separate into curd and whey. He found at nightfall that the whey satisfied his thirst and the cheese (curd) satisfied his hunger and had a delightful flavor. Thus, according to the legend, the making of one of our most useful foods was begun.

According to ancient records, cheese was used as a food more than 4,000 years ago. It was made and eaten in Biblical times. Travelers from Asia are believed to have brought the art of cheesemaking to Europe. Cheese was made in many parts of the Roman Empire when it was at its height. Then cheesemaking was introduced to England by the Romans. During the Middle Ages—from the decline of the Roman Empire until the discovery of America—as well as later, cheese was made and improved by the monks in the monasteries of Europe. Gorgonzola was made in the Po Valley in Italy in 879 A. D. and Italy became the cheesemaking center of Europe in the 10th century. Roquefort was mentioned in the ancient records of the monastery at Conques, France, in 1070. The Pilgrims included cheese in the ship's supplies when they made their famous voyage to America in the Mayflower in 1620.

Until the middle of the 19th century, however, cheesemaking was a local farm industry. Housewives made cheese from the surplus milk produced on the farm. In 1851 the first cheese factory in the United States was built by Jesse Williams near Rome, Oneida County, N. Y. Herkimer County, which adjoins Oneida County, was the center of the cheese industry in the United States for the next 50 years. For many years during this period the largest cheese market in the world was at Little Falls, N. Y.; there cheese from about 200 factories was sold, in addition to farmmade cheese. As the population increased in the East, and there was a corresponding increase in the demand for market milk, the industry gradually moved westward, centering in the rich farm lands of Wisconsin. Cheesemaking in the United States and in the other leading cheese-producing countries of the world is now largely a factory industry, only small amounts being made on farms for home use.

Almost 2 billion pounds of cheese is now made in the United States each year. About 15 percent of the annual milk production is used in making this cheese.

"Natural" cheese is made directly from milk (or whey, in some instances). It is made by coagulating or curdling milk, stirring and heating the curd, draining off the whey, and collecting or pressing the curd. Desirable flavor and texture are obtained in many cheeses by curing the cheese, that is, holding it for a specified time at a specific temperature and humidity. Process cheese is made from a combination of one or more batches or kinds of natural cheese heated to pasteurization temperatures and packaged.

This bulletin contains descriptions of more than 400 cheeses, arranged in alphabetical order (pp. 4–143). Many cheeses are named for the town or community in which they are made, or for a landmark of the community. Hence, many cheeses with different local names are practically the same in their characteristics. On the other hand, several different kinds are known by the same local name. More than 800 names are indexed (pp. 145–151).

A typical analysis, based on data in the literature, is given for most cheeses. In some instances, the analysis includes figures of composition prescribed by the Federal Government (see Selected Reference 30, p. 141). It was not possible to obtain analytical data for all the cheeses.

It is difficult, if not impossible, to classify the different cheeses satisfactorily in groups. Attempts to do so by other writers have not been entirely successful. There probably are only about 18 distinct types or kinds of natural cheese. No two of these are made by the same method; that is, the details of setting the milk, cutting, stirring, heating, draining, pressing, and salting the curd, and curing the cheese are varied to produce characteristics and qualities peculiar to each kind of cheese. The following cheeses are typical of the 18 kinds: Brick, Camembert, Cheddar, Cottage, Cream, Edam, Gouda, Hand, Limburger, Neufchâtel, Parmesan, Provolone, Romano, Roquefort, Sapsago, Swiss, Trappist, and whey cheeses (Mysost and Ricotta).

Such a grouping, though informative, is imperfect and incomplete. Cheeses can be also classified as very hard (grating), hard, semisoft, or soft; and as ripened by bacteria, by mold, by surface micro-organisms, or by a combination of these, or as unripened. Following are examples of cheeses in these classifications:

1. Very hard (grating):
   (*a*) Ripened by bacteria: Asiago old, Parmesan, Romano, Sapsago, Spalen.
2. Hard:
   (*a*) Ripened by bacteria, without eyes: Cheddar, Granular or Stirred-curd, and Caciocavallo.
   (*b*) Ripened by bacteria, with eyes: Swiss, Emmentaler, and Gruyère.
3. Semisoft:
   (*a*) Ripened principally by bacteria: Brick and Münster.
   (*b*) Ripened by bacteria and surface micro-organisms: Limburger, Port du Salut, and Trappist.
   (*c*) Ripened principally by blue mold in the interior: Roquefort, Gorgonzola, Blue, Stilton, and Wensleydale.
4. Soft:
   (*a*) Ripened: Bel Paese, Brie, Camembert, Cooked, Hand, and Neufchâtel (as made in France).
   (*b*) Unripened: Cottage, Pot, Bakers', Cream, Neufchâtel (as made in the United States), Mysost, Primost, and fresh Ricotta.

Accidental modifications or changes in one or more steps of the cheesemaking process throughout the centuries were largely responsible for the development of the different kinds of cheese. These changes were little understood and difficult to duplicate because scientific knowledge of bacteriology and chemistry was lacking. As a result, cheesemaking was considered an art, and the making process was a closely guarded secret passed down from father to son.

With increased scientific knowledge, especially since 1900, has come an understanding of the bacteriology and chemistry involved in the making of many cheeses. Thus it has become possible to control more precisely each step in the making process and to manufacture a uniform product. Now, cheesemaking is becoming a science rather than an art.

DESCRIPTIONS OF CHEESES

Abertam

Abertam is a hard cheese made from ewe's milk in the region of Carlsbad, Bohemia.

Alemtejo

Alemtejo is a rather soft cheese made in the Province of Alemtejo, Portugal. It is cylindrical in shape and is made in 3 sizes, weighing about 2 ounces, 1 pound, and 4 pounds, respectively. It is made mostly from ewe's milk, but goat's milk is often added, especially for the smaller sizes. Warm milk is curdled, usually with an extract prepared from the flowers of a kind of thistle. The cheese is ripened for several weeks.

Analysis: Moisture, 30 to 50 percent; fat, 25 to 38 percent; protein, 11 to 25 percent; and salt, 1 to 3 percent.

Allgäuer Rundkäse

Allgäuer Rundkäse or Allgäuer Emmentaler is a type of Swiss cheese named for the district of Allgäu in the Alps in southwestern Bavaria. It is from 5 to 5¾ inches thick and weighs usually between 150 and 175 pounds. (See Swiss.)

Alpin

Alpin cheese, a variant of Mont d'Or cheese, is made in the Alpine region of France. It is known also as Clérimbert. The milk is coagulated with rennet at a temperature of 80° F. in about 2 hours. The curd is dipped into molds 3 or 4 inches in diameter and 2½ inches deep, and the whey is drained off. The cheese is turned several times the first day, after which it is salted and then ripened for 8 to 15 days.

Altenburger

Altenburger is a goat's-milk cheese made in Germany, especially in Thüringen in central Germany, where it is known as Altenburger Ziegenkäse. It is 8 inches in diameter, 1 or 2 inches thick, and weighs about 2 pounds.

Ambert

Ambert cheese, known also as Fourme d'Ambert, is a cylindrical Roquefort-type cheese made to a limited extent in central France, from cow's milk. It is said to differ from other Roquefort-type cheeses made in southeastern France in that the salt is mixed with the curd instead of being rubbed on the surface of the cheese. It is cured for at least 3 months. (See Roquefort.)

American

American and American-type cheeses are descriptive terms used to identify the group which includes Cheddar (i. e., American Cheddar), Colby, Granular or Stirred-curd, and Washed- or Soaked-curd cheeses. Sometimes Monterey or Jack cheese is included in this group. A description of each kind is given under its specific name.

Ancien Impérial

Ancien Impérial is a French cheese about 2 inches square and ½ inch thick that may be sold and consumed either fresh or after it has cured. The fresh cheese is known also as Petit Carré and the cured cheese as Carré Affiné. The curd is prepared in the same way as for Neufchâtel, and the curing process is not essentially different. (See Neufchâtel.)

Appenzeller

Appenzeller cheese, which is similar to Swiss, is made from cow's milk in the Canton of Appenzell, Switzerland, and also in Bavaria and Baden. It is made usually from skim milk, but sometimes from whole milk, and soaked in cider or white wine and spices.

Appetitost

Appetitost is a Danish cheese made from sour buttermilk. Some is imported, and a small quantity is made in the United States.

Armavir

Armavir, a sour-milk cheese that resembles Hand cheese, is made in the western Caucasus from ewe's whole milk. Sour buttermilk or whey is added to heated milk. The cheese is pressed in forms and is ripened in a warm place.

Asadero

Asadero, also called Oaxaca, is a white, whole-milk Mexican cheese. It melts easily when heated, which accounts for the name Asadero (fit for roasting). It is named Oaxaca for the State of Oaxaca, although it is now made for the most part in the State of Jalisco. The curd is heated, and the hot curd is cut and braided or kneaded into loaves of various sizes, ranging from 8 ounces to 11 pounds in weight.

Asiago

Asiago cheese originated in the commune of that name in the Province of Vicenza, Italy. It is made also in Carnia, Venetia, Trentino, Lombardy, and nearby areas. It was made originally from ewe's milk and was called Pecorino di Asiago. It is now made from cow's milk and is a sweet-curd, semicooked, Grana-type cheese with a pungent aroma. It is round and flat and weighs usually between 16 and 22 pounds. Like other grating cheeses, it may be used as a table cheese when not aged. Table cheese of this kind that can be sliced is called Asiago di taglio (slicing cheese).

In Italy, Asiago is made from partly skimmed milk, which is curdled with rennet at a temperature of 92° to 96° F. The curd is cut into particles the size of wheat grains, and the temperature is raised to approximately 108° or as high as 118°. After about 15 minutes the greater part of the whey is run off. The curd is dipped into circular hoops and pressed. The cheeses are salted in brine for several days, after which they are ripened. After curing 4 to 10 months, the cheese is at its best for eating, resembling Battelmatt; after 12 to 20 months, it is strong and sharp in flavor and is suitable for grating, resembling Romano and Grana. The yield of cured cheese is about 7½ pounds per 100 pounds of milk containing 3.5 percent of fat.

In the United States, three modifications of Asiago are made, namely, fresh (soft), medium, and old. The method of manufacture is much the same for all three and is similar to that used for other Italian cheeses, such as Fontina, Parmesan, and Romano.

A bacterial starter is added to warm milk that may be standardized to adjust the fat content. Rennet (preferably in the form of rennet paste) or rennet extract plus a lipase enzyme preparation is diluted with water and mixed with the milk. When the curd is sufficiently firm, it is cut and then heated gradually and stirred continuously. The heating and cutting are continued until the particles of curd are about the size of wheat grains. After further stirring and heating, the curd is allowed to settle to the bottom of the kettle and then is removed by dipping with a cloth. It is then pressed in hoops.

When the cheeses are removed from the hoops, they are salted in a brine bath and cured on shelves. While curing, they are washed and turned frequently and sometimes are rubbed occasionally with vegetable oil. Sometimes they are coated with paraffin, either clear or colored black or brown.

Asiago fresh cheese is cured for not less than 60 days (some authorities say at least 4 months); Asiago medium is cured for at least 6 months; and Asiago old, which is used mostly as grated cheese, is cured for not less than a year.

Analysis: Asiago fresh—moisture, 40 to 45 percent; fat, not less than 50 percent in the solids. Asiago medium—moisture, not more than 35 percent; fat, not less than 45 percent in the solids. Asiago old—moisture, not more than 32 percent; fat, not less than 42 percent in the solids.

Asin

Asin cheese, which is also called Water cheese, is a sour-milk, washed-curd, whitish, soft, buttery, more or less ripened cheese that is made on farms and in small dairies in the mountainous regions in northern Italy.

It contains a few large eyes. It is made mostly in spring, while the cows are grazing on green pasture, and is consumed in summer and autumn. It is popular as a dessert cheese and frequently is eaten with honey and fruits.

The cheeses are cylindrical and flat, about 8 inches in diameter and 6 inches thick, and weigh about 14 pounds.

The method of manufacture is quite different from that of any other cheese. Fresh, warm cow's milk is put into a vat without rennet and is curdled by souring. The curd is cut and stirred until the pieces are the size of wheat grains. Then hot water (at a temperature of 185° to 195° F.) is added slowly, with stirring—as much as 1 part of water to 3 parts of curd and whey. This heats the curd to a temperature of approximately 105° to 110°. To avoid excessive washing, some hot whey may be added with the water. For 35 to 40 minutes after the curd is cut, whey is expelled from the granules, and they shrink and acquire firmness. A sample of the curd is squeezed in the hand, then rubbed, and when the granules can be rubbed apart readily the curd is permitted to settle for about 10 minutes and then is dipped with a cloth. The curd is pressed by hand to expel more whey, is placed in a circular hoop, pressed lightly overnight, and then—still in the hoop—is placed in a moderately warm room. After a few days the hoop is removed. The cheese is turned, and may be salted lightly, each day. After 10 to 15 days a whitish mold growing on the surface becomes visible, and the rind gradually turns pale yellow.

The cheese has a mild flavor and is ready to eat when it is 1 to 2 months old. After an additional 2 or 3 months of ripening in a special salt brine it has more flavor, and is called Salmistra.

The yield is about 11 pounds of cheese per 100 pounds of milk.

Backsteiner

Backsteiner cheese, which is made to a limited extent in northern Germany, is similar to Stangenkäse; that is, it is a modified Limburger-Romadur-type cheese. Backsteiner means brick, and the cheese is so called because of its brick-like shape. However, it is not like the Brick cheese made in the United States but is more like Limburger that is made from partly skimmed milk, except that Backsteiner is smaller and is cured for a shorter time. When made in squares, it is known as Quadratkäse. (See Limburger and Romadur.)

Analysis: Moisture, 35 to 70 percent; fat, 3 to 38 percent; and protein, 20 to 25 percent.

Bagozzo

Bagozzo or Grana Bagozzo, which is also known as Bresciano, is a Parmesan-type cheese similar to but smaller than Reggiano and Parmigiano. It has a hard, yellow body and a rather sharp flavor. The surface often is colored red.

Bakers'

Bakers' is a skim-milk cheese that is softer, more homogeneous, and contains more acid than Cottage cheese. Bakers' cheese usually is used commercially in making such bakery products as cheese cake, pie, and pastries. Usually it is not offered in retail trade. However, it may be creamed and eaten like Cottage cheese.

The milk is pasteurized, cooled to a temperature of 90° F. and inoculated with lactic starter and rennet. After 4 to 6 hours the sour coagulated mixture is stirred, or broken without cooking or washing. It is drained or pumped into special draining bags, which are tied and piled to allow whey drainage. The bags are piled several times to form a drier cheese. Crushed ice may be placed between the bags to retard acid development during overnight drainage. The salted or unsalted curd may be packed in polyethylene bag-lined cans for storage. It will keep for several months if stored frozen at a temperature below 0° F. but preferably it is kept at 32° F. Yields of 15–18 pounds of cheese are obtained per 100 pounds of skim milk.

Bakers' cheese may be made from spray-dried nonfat milk solids. Reconstituted milk, containing 11 percent solids, is warmed to 90° F. and 8 pounds of lactic starter and 0.2 millimeters of rennet (which has to be diluted in water) are added. In 4 to 6 hours the coagulated curd is bagged and drained by the same method as described above for regular skim milk. The yield is 19 to 22 pounds of cheese.

Continuous centrifuges have been used successfully to recover the cheese solids instead of the bag method. The centrifuged curd is cooled under pressure and packaged directly into a polyethylene-lined tin can. Control of the acid development is maintained and the keeping quality is extended considerably.

Analysis: Moisture, 68 to 75 percent (not more than 80); fat, 0.5 percent or less; and salt, 1 percent.

Banbury

Banbury, a soft, rich cheese, was very popular in England in the early part of the 19th century. It is cylindrical in shape and is about an inch thick.

Barberey

Barberey, a soft cheese resembling Camembert, derives its name from the village of Barberey, near Troyes, France. It is also commonly known as Fromage de Troyes. Fresh warm milk is coagulated with rennet, usually in about 4 hours. The uncut curd is put into a wooden mold with a perforated bottom to drain. About 3 hours later the cheese is put into an earthenware mold, and after 24 hours the mold is removed. The cheese is salted, dried in a well-ventilated room, and may be ripened for about 3 weeks, usually in an underground curing room. However, in summer the cheese often is sold without ripening. It is about 5½ inches in diameter and 1¼ inches thick.

Battelmatt

Battelmatt is a small Swiss-type cheese made from cow's milk in the Canton of Tessin, Switzerland, when the quantity of milk is insufficient for making the large "wheels." It is cylindrical and flat, 18 to 24 inches in diameter, 3¼ to 4 inches thick, and 40 to 80 pounds in weight. It has a softer body than Swiss and contains a greater percentage of moisture; the eyes are smaller; and it ripens more rapidly, being marketed within 3 to 4 months. Its flavor is more like Tilsiter than Swiss.

Analysis: Moisture, 44 to 50 percent; fat, 20 to 30 percent; and protein, 21 to 25 percent.

Belgian Cooked

Belgian Cooked cheese is made by a method similar to that used for Cooked cheese (Kochkäse). Skim milk is allowed to curdle, and the curd is heated to between 135° and 140° F. and then drained in a cloth. When drained it is kneaded thoroughly by hand and then allowed to ripen, usually for 10 to 14 days in winter and 6 to 8 days in summer. When the flavor has developed sufficiently, cream and salt are added and the mixture is heated slowly to approximately 180°, stirred until it is blended completely, and then put into molds to ripen for several days. The cheese usually weighs about 3½ pounds. (See Cooked cheese.)

Analysis: Moisture, approximately 70 to 75 percent; not more than 80 percent.

Bellelay

Bellelay, also called Tête de Moine and Monk's Head, is a soft, blue-veined, whole-milk cheese that resembles Gorgonzola. It was made originally in the 15th century by monks in the Canton of Bern, Switzerland, and now is made exclusively in that locality. (See Gorgonzola.)

Sweet milk is set at about 90° F. with sufficient rennet to coagulate it in 20 to 30 minutes. The curd is cut comparatively fine and is stirred while being heated slowly to a temperature of 110°. It is cooked until it is much firmer than for Limburger but not so firm as for Swiss.

The curd then is dipped into wooden hoops lined with cloth. The cheeses are pressed a few minutes at a time in rotation, one press being used for a number of cheeses. After the cheese is pressed it is wrapped in bark and left for 2 weeks or until firm enough to require no support. It is cured in a moist cellar at a comparatively low temperature so there will be no eye development. It ripens in about 12 months, but it will keep for 3 or 4 years if it is kept cold. When ready for market the cheese is 7 inches in diameter and weighs from 9 to 15 pounds. It has a soft, buttery consistency and can be spread on bread.

Analysis: Moisture, 37 to 40 percent; fat, approximately 30 percent; protein, 25 to 28 percent; and salt, approximately 3 percent.

Bel Paese

Bel Paese, which means "beautiful country," is the trade name of one of the best known and most popular of a group of Italian table cheeses. They are uncooked, soft, sweet, mild, and fast-ripened. Bel Paese was first made about 1920 in Melzo, upper Lombardy, Italy, although cheese of this general type has been made in Italy for approximately 60 years. A similar cheese called Königskäse is made in Robbio, near Pavia, Italy. Others in the group are Bella Alpina, Bella Milano, Bel Piano Lombardo, Bel Piemonte Fior d'Alpe, Savoia, and Vittoria. Similar cheese is marketed in other European countries under such names as Schönland and Fleur des Alpes, and the group is also referred to as Butter cheese, especially in Germany; a similar so-called Butter cheese is made in Canada.

Production of a soft cheese of the Bel Paese type was introduced in the United States by the U.S. Department of Agriculture in 1938 and the cheese which is now being made commercially is said to be of as high quality in every respect as that made in Italy. Innovations made here in the method include pasteurization of the milk and the use of a uniformly active lactic starter, which improve the quality and uniformity of the cheese and practically eliminate defects. Because of the Italian trademark, cheese of this type made in the United States is sold under various other names.

A small percentage of an active lactic starter (usually 0.25 percent or slightly more) is added to cow's whole milk (which should be strictly fresh and pasteurized), at a temperature of 104° to 110° F. Enough rennet is added so that the curd will be firm enough for cutting in 15 to 20 minutes—usually from 10 to 20 milliliters of rennet (diluted with water) per 100 pounds of milk is sufficient.

The curd is cut into ⅜-inch cubes and is stirred carefully, at first by hand and then with a rake, to prevent matting and to insure rapid expulsion of the whey. During this period the setting temperature is maintained. When the curd particles have firmed sufficiently, the whey is drawn off and the curd is dipped into forms placed on reed mats on a draining table. The forms are preferably square or round perforated metal forms but square wooden forms are also used. A follower, or cover, is placed on the curd in each form. In Italy the curd may be transferred to the forms within 30 minutes after the rennet is added. The cheeses are drained in the forms for 5 to 7 hours and are turned frequently during this period. The room temperature should be about 80° F. A box cover may be placed over the forms to aid in maintaining the temperature of the cheese.

The cheeses are salted by placing them in a 16- to 18-percent salt solution at 55° F. for 14 to 18 hours. Then they are dried and placed on shelves in the curing room in which the temperature is 38° to 42° and the relative humidity is 80 to 90 percent. Some fine salt may be sprinkled on the surface of the cheeses.

Soon after curing is begun a nearly colorless or slightly gray or brownish slime appears on the surface, and this is desirable for characteristic ripening. The cheeses are washed with dilute salt brine and are turned 2 or 3 times each week, to keep the slime coating thin and the rind firm and clean.

After 3 or 4 days the outer surface of the cheeses may be colored with dilute cheese color. After 3 weeks in the curing room the cheeses are cleaned thoroughly, dried, and wrapped in tinfoil. They may be paraffined before wrapping. The wrapped cheeses are placed in individual cartons and are cured for 2 to 3 weeks or even 6 weeks longer, at the same temperature, after which they are ready for market.

In some sections in Italy, the cheeses weigh about 4½ pounds and are 5¼ to 6 inches in diameter. The yield is 11 to 15 pounds of cheese per 100 pounds of milk.

Analysis: Moisture, 44 to 47 percent; fat, 28 to 29 percent; protein, 21.9 percent; salt, 2.3 to 2.5 percent.

Bergkäse

Bergkäse is the name of a group of Alpine cheeses, chiefly of the Swiss type. The group includes Battelmatt and Piora, which are made in the Canton of Tessin, Switzerland; Gruyère, made in Switzerland and France; Fontina, made in the Aosta Valley in Italy; Montasio, made in Carinthia and nearby areas; Walliser, made in the Canton of Wallis, Switzerland; and several others. A type of soft cheese known as Vacherin, which is made in the Canton of Fribourg, Switzerland, is also classed in the Bergkäse group. A description of each cheese is given under its specific name.

Bergquara

Bergquara is a Swedish cheese resembling Gouda. It was made in Sweden as early as the 18th century.

Bernarde

Bernarde or Formagelle Bernarde, an Italian cheese, is made from cow's whole milk to which about 10 percent of goat's milk is added for flavor. The milk is ripened for 3 or 4 hours. It is colored lightly with saffron. Sufficient rennet is added to coagulate the milk in about 45 minutes at a temperature of 93° to 95° F., after which the curd is turned and then left to settle for 5 minutes. It is then broken with a harp until the pieces are the size of hazelnuts. The temperature is increased slightly and the curd is allowed to settle for about 10 minutes. It is placed in hoops and cured in a highly humid room at a temperature of 50° to 59°. After 3 days in the curing room salting is begun. In the following 18 days about 2.5 to 3 percent of salt is added by rubbing dry salt on the surface of the cheese 3 or 4 times. The cheese is ready to eat after curing for 2 months.

Bgug-Panir

Bgug-Panir cheese, sometimes called Daralag, is made in Armenia from partly or entirely skimmed ewe's milk. Rennet is used to coagulate the milk, and the curd is put into a rack to drain after which it is broken up. Salt and herbs are added, and the cheese is pressed. After pressing, it is put into a salt bath for 2 days or more, after which it is cured.

Bitto

Bitto is a firm, semicooked cheese of the Swiss group, made originally in Friuli and now made also in Lombardy, in northern Italy. It is similar to Fontina and Montasio. It is made from cow's milk, from ewe's milk, or from a mixture of goat's milk and cow's milk, and from whole, slightly skimmed, or skim milk. It is heated to a temperature of 93° to 98° F., and sufficient rennet is added to coagulate the milk in 30 to 35 minutes. The curd is then subdivided and heated in about 30 minutes to a temperature between 113° and 122°. The curd is dipped and pressed; the cheese is dry-salted over a period of 25 to 40 days and is cured—sometimes for as long as 2 years. The cheese weighs between 35 and 75 pounds. It has small eyes. When made from whole milk and not fully cured, it is used as table cheese. When made from skim milk and fully cured, it is grated and used as a condiment.

Bleu

Bleu (or Fromage Bleu) is the French name for a group of Roquefort-type (blue-veined) cheeses made in the Roquefort area in southeastern France from milk other than ewe's milk. It applies also to Roquefort-type cheeses made elsewhere in France (that is, outside the Roquefort area), regardless of the kind of milk used. Because of the mottled, marbled, or veined appearance of the curd they are also called Fromage Persillé. Other cheeses in this group are Bleu d'Auvergne, Laguiole, Gex, Gex Bressans (goat's-milk Gex), Mont Cenis, Sassenage, Septmoncel, and St. Flour. Some of these are described under their specific names. Roquefort-type cheese made in the United States is called Blue cheese. (See Roquefort and Blue.)

Blue

Blue, Blue-mold, or Blue-veined cheese is the name for cheese of the Roquefort type that is made in the United States and Canada. It is made from cow's or goat's milk, rather than ewe's milk. The French word for this type of cheese is Bleu. (See Roquefort and Bleu.) Considerable quantities of Blue cheese are made in the United States, and cheese of this type is imported from Argentina, Canada, Denmark, France, Finland, and Sweden. Danish cheese of the Roquefort type is called Danablu. Blue cheese is about 7½ inches in diameter and weighs from 4½ to 5 pounds; it is round and flat like Gorgonzola, but smaller.

It was not until about 1918 that attempts to make Roquefort-type cheese in the United States met with success, primarily because prior to that time information was not available on methods of manufacture and curing, including isolation, identification, and use of the blue-green *Penicillium roqueforti* mold and means for maintaining the correct temperature and humidity in the curing room to prevent excessive drying. Caves which simulate the temperature and humidity of the Roquefort caves of France are now used successfully by many factories. The U.S. Department of Agriculture and the California Agricultural Experiment Station developed a method for making Blue cheese from goat's milk, and the USDA and the Iowa, Minnesota, and Washington stations have published information on making it from cow's milk. A brief description of the process for making Blue cheese follows:

Lactic starter is added to fresh clean milk, which may be pasteurized and may be homogenized, and it is set with rennet at a temperature of 84° F. From 1 to 1½ hours later the coagulated curd is cut, then the whey is drained off and the curd is placed in perforated metal hoops that are about 7½ inches in diameter and 6 inches deep. Blue-mold powder is mixed with the curd, either while it is still in the vat or while it is being put into the hoops. Some salt may be mixed with it. The hoops are turned frequently and the curd is held in the hoops at least 24 hours. Salting may be started either when the cheeses are removed from the hoops or several days later. The cheeses are dry-salted over a period of 7 to 10 days in a room which is maintained at a temperature of 46° to 48° and a relative humidity of about 95 percent. About a week after salting, each cheese is pierced with 40 or more ⅛-inch holes to permit air to reach the interior of the cheese; this is essential for mold growth. Then the cheeses are placed on their edges on racks in the curing room. They are cured for 3 months at a temperature of 48° and a relative humidity of 95 percent and are scraped or cleaned at regular intervals—usually every 3 or 4 weeks—to reduce slime formation and growth of foreign molds on the surface. Then they are wrapped in tinfoil and stored 2 or 3 months at a temperature of about 40° in a moist room. The total curing period must be at least 60 days. The yield of cured cheese is 10 to 11 pounds per 100 pounds of cow's whole milk.

Analysis: Moisture, not more than 46 percent (usually 40 to 42 percent); fat, 29.5 to 30.5 percent (not less than 50 percent in the solids); protein, 20 to 21 percent; and salt, 4.5 to 5 percent.

Bondon

Bondon is a small, unripened, whole-milk, French cheese of the fresh Neufchâtel type. A lactic culture and rennet are added to fresh milk at a temperature of 60° to 65° F. From 18 to 24 hours later, when the curd is firm, it is transferred to a cloth which has been stretched over a tub. The curd is stirred frequently, and when it has drained sufficiently it is transferred to a clean cloth and pressed between boards with a weight on top. Salt is mixed in, and the curd is placed in molds that are lined with wax paper. The molds are 2¾ inches deep and 1¾ inches in diameter.

Analysis: Moisture, 54.3 percent; fat, 23 percent (50.3 percent in the solids); protein, 16.1 percent; and salt, 2.5 percent.

Bondost

Bondost is a Swedish, farm-type, cow's-milk cheese that has been made also in a few factories in the United States, chiefly in Wisconsin, for more than 30 years. It is cylindrical in shape, about 5 inches in diameter and 3 to 4 inches thick, and weighs 2½ to 3 pounds.

Either raw or pasteurized milk may be used. Lactic starter and color may be added, and the milk is warmed to a temperature of 84° to 88° F. Enough rennet is added so that the curd will be ready to cut in about 20 to 30 minutes. The curd is cut into ¼-inch or ⅜-inch cubes and is heated, with stirring, until it is firm enough to press. To aid in firming the curd, part of the whey may be removed and salt, which has been dissolved in warm water, may be sprinkled over the surface of the curd at the rate of ½ to 1 pound of salt per 100 pounds of curd; the curd must be well stirred to prevent matting. When the curd is firm enough to press, the forms should be filled as quickly as possible. Sometimes cumin or caraway seed is mixed with the curd just before it is put into the forms.

The cheese is pressed for 15 to 18 hours; then it is immersed in salt brine at a temperature of 50° to 60° F. for 24 to 48 hours, the time depending on the condition of the curd when it was put into the forms and the amount of salt, if any, that was added earlier. After the cheese is taken out of the brine, it is cured on shelves for 2 or 3 days in a reasonably well ventilated room, at a temperature of 50° to 60°. After the surface of the cheese is well dried and a light rind has formed, it may be paraffined, and it is packed for storage at a temperature of 50° to 60°. It is ready to eat in 6 to 8 weeks.

If cheese with more pronounced flavor and better keeping quality is desired, it is left in the curing room for 2 or 3 weeks and is washed or rubbed with a salt brine solution every other day, after which it may be paraffined, and it is then packed for storage at a temperature of 40° to 50° F.

Analysis: Moisture, 42.8 percent; fat, 29.7 percent; fat in the solids, 51.9 percent; and salt, 1.3 percent.

Borelli

Borelli is a small cheese made in Italy from buffalo's milk.

Boudanne

Boudanne is a French cheese made from cow's milk. Either whole or skim milk is heated to about 85° F. and sufficient rennet is added to coagulate the milk in an hour. The curd is then cut to the size of peas, stirred, and heated to 100° or above. After settling for 10 or 15 minutes, the curd is pressed by hand and put into molds 8 inches in diameter and 3 inches deep. The cheese is drained, turned frequently, salted, and ripened for 2 or 3 months.

Bourgain

Bourgain is a type of fresh Neufchâtel cheese made in France. However, the fat content is low, the cheese is not salted, it contains a relatively high percentage of moisture, and it is very soft. It is perishable and is consumed locally.

Box (Firm)

Box (firm), a German cheese, is known in different localities as Hohenburg, Mondsee, and Weihenstephan. It has a mild but piquant flavor and is similar to the Brick cheese made in the United States. Cow's whole milk is heated in a kettle to a temperature of 90° or 93° F., colored with saffron, and set with sufficient rennet to curdle it in 20 or 25 minutes. The curd is cut to the size of peas, then heated slowly, with stirring, to 105°. Heating is then discontinued and 5 minutes later the whey is removed. The curd is enclosed in a cloth, then placed in hoops, and light pressure is applied. The hoops of curd are turned after 15 minutes, and turning is repeated frequently for several hours. When the cheeses are removed from the hoops they are placed in a well-ventilated room at 60° for 3 to 5 days and then are taken to the curing room where they are cured for 2 to 3 months. They are salted by rubbing salt on the surface. Each cheese weighs between 1 and 4 pounds.

Box (Soft)

Box (soft) is a cheese of minor importance made from partly skimmed cow's milk in the small village of Hohenheim, in Württemberg, Germany. It is often called Hohenheimer cheese and is also known locally as Schachtelkäse.

Skim milk is mixed with an equal volume of whole milk. The milk is warmed in a copper kettle to a temperature of 110° F., colored with saffron, and rennet is added. After a coagulation period of 1 to 1½ hours, the curd is cut into rather large pieces. A few minutes after cutting, the whey is dipped off, a small handful of caraway seed is added for every 200 pounds of milk used, and the curd is broken into smaller pieces. It is then dipped into perforated tin hoops, 6½ inches in diameter and 6½ inches deep, where it remains for 10 or 12 hours during which time it is turned frequently. Then it is transferred to wooden hoops only half as deep, where it remains an additional 12 hours. The cheeses are then removed from the hoops, salted on the surface, and placed in the ripening cellar, where they are cured for about 3 months.

Fromage de Boîte, which is a soft cheese of this type and which is similar to Pont l'Évêque, is made in the fall in the mountains of Doubs, France.

Bra

Bra cheese is named for the village of Bra in Piedmont, Italy, where it was first made by nomads. It is a hard, nearly white cheese with a compact texture and sharp and salty flavor. Partly skimmed milk is heated to a temperature of about 90° F., and sufficient rennet is added to the milk to coagulate it in 30 to 40 minutes. The curd is cut as small as rice grains, and after about 30 minutes the whey is drained off. The curd is placed in forms about 12 inches in diameter and 3 inches deep and pressed for 12 to 24 hours. It is removed from the forms several times in the early stages of pressing, broken into coarse pieces, and repacked in the forms. The cheese is salted by immersion in brine and also by sprinkling salt on the surface, after which it is cured. The yield is from 6¼ to 7¼ pounds per 100 pounds of partly skimmed milk. Each cheese weighs about 12 pounds.

Brand

Brand is a German Hand cheese made from sour-milk curd that is heated to a somewhat higher temperature than usual. The curd is salted and allowed to ferment for a day. It is then mixed with butter, pressed, dried, and finally placed in kegs to ripen. While ripening, it is moistened occasionally with beer. Each cheese weighs about 5 ounces.

Brick

Brick cheese, one of the few cheeses of American origin, is made in considerable quantities in numerous factories, particularly in Wisconsin. It is a sweet-curd, semisoft, cow's-milk cheese, with a mild but rather pungent and sweet flavor, midway between Cheddar and Limburger but not so sharp as Cheddar and not so strong as Limburger. The body is softer than Cheddar but firmer than Limburger, is elastic, and slices well without crumbling. Brick has an open texture with numerous round and irregular shaped eyes (holes). Although the exact derivation of the name is unknown, it may refer to its brick-like shape or to the bricks used in pressing.

High-quality whole milk, preferably pasteurized, is warmed to a temperature of 88° to 92° F. Lactic starter is added, and enough rennet so the curd will be firm enough to cut in about 30 minutes. After the curd is cut into cubes and stirred gently for 15 to 25 minutes, it is warmed in about 45 minutes to a temperature of 106° to 110°, or even as low as 96° and as high as 115° in some cases (depending on the size of the cubes and the rate of acid development). The final cooking temperature is maintained until the curd is transferred to the forms. Part of the whey is removed, and the curd either is stirred in the remainder of the whey or warm water (at the cooking temperature) is added and stirring is continued. When the curd reaches the desired degree of firmness, the curd-whey mixture is dipped into the forms.

The forms, which are made of wood or perforated metal and have no top or bottom, are rectangular (10 inches long, 5 inches wide, and 5½ inches deep). They are placed on a mat or metal screen on a drain table.

A flat-sided pail or scoop is used to transfer the curd to the forms. As soon as the curd settles, a cover (10 by 5 inches) is placed on each form, if necessary, to reduce loss of heat. The forms are turned about five times at 30-minute intervals, and about the second or third time a 5-pound weight (usually a brick) is placed on each. Draining continues under this pressure overnight; the forms are kept covered if the room is cold.

The next morning the forms are removed, and either dry or brine salting is begun. For dry salting, the cheeses are rubbed with salt and laid on one of their broad sides on a salting table. Salting is repeated daily for 3 days.

Then the cheeses are scraped smooth and placed on shelves in the curing room. For brine salting, the cheeses are floated in a saturated salt solution at a temperature of 55° to 60° F. for a day, and salt is sprinkled on the upper surface. After 24 hours, they are turned and left in the brine for another day, or 48 hours in all.

The cheese is cured at a temperature of 60° F. and a relative humidity of 90 percent. The bricks are placed close together for 10 to 12 days to prevent drying and cracking of the rind. Micro-organisms grow on the surface and produce a reddish-brown color. This is desirable in normal curing. The cheeses are washed frequently with salty water. After about 12 days, they are separated so the air can circulate around them and dry them, or they are removed to a cooler, drier room to dry; then they are dipped in paraffin or cheese wax, wrapped in parchment and an overwrapper of heavy paper, and packed in boxes. The cheese usually is stored for further curing for 2 to 3 months at 40° to 50° F. If the cheese is made from raw milk, it is cured for at least 60 days at not less than 35° F. unless it is to be used for manufacturing and is designated "Brick cheese for manufacturing."

Brick cheese that measures about 10 inches long, 5 inches wide, and 3 inches thick, will weigh aproximately 5 pounds. The yield is about 9.5 pounds of cheese per 100 pounds of milk containing 3.5 percent of fat.

Analysis: Moisture, not more than 44 percent (usually 39 to 42 percent); fat, 31 percent (not less than 50 percent of the solids); protein, 20 to 23 percent; and salt, 1.8 to 2 percent, or slightly more.

Brickbat

Brickbat cheese, which was made in Wiltshire, England, as long ago as the eighteenth century, is made from fresh milk to which a small portion of cream is added. The milk is set with rennet at a temperature of about 90° F. After a coagulation period of 2 hours, the curd is cut into coarse pieces, dipped into wooden forms, and light pressure is applied. The cheese is said to be good to eat for as long as a year after being made.

Brie

Brie, which was first made several centuries ago in the Department of Seine-et-Marne, France, is a soft, surface-ripened cheese made usually from cow's whole milk but also at times from skim milk or partly skimmed milk. The quality varies with the kind of milk used. Melun, Coulommiers, and Meaux are noted for the production of Brie, which also is known locally as Fromage de Melun and Coulommiers. Brie-type cheese is made also in other parts of France and in other countries, including the United States.

Brie is made in three sizes: Large (about 16 inches in diameter and 1½ to 1⅔ inches thick, weighing about 6 pounds); medium (about 12 inches in diameter and slightly thinner than the large size, weighing about 3½ pounds); and small (5½ to not more than 8 inches in diameter and

1¼ inches thick, weighing about a pound). According to some authorities, the small size is the same as Coulommiers or Petit Moule.

Brie is similar to Camembert. Both are ripened partly by molds and bacteria, and probably yeasts, that grow on the surface of the cheese. However, because of differences in the details of manufacture, the internal ripening and characteristic flavor and aroma differ.

The cheesemaking process is complicated and exacting. Fresh milk, or evening milk which is cooled, held overnight, and mixed with morning milk, is used. About 10 percent of slightly ripened skim milk is sometimes added. The milk is warmed to a temperature of 85° to 90° F., and enough rennet is added so the curd will be firm enough to dip in 2 or 3 hours. A ladle is used to transfer large, thin, horizontal slices of curd to round metal hoops, each of which has a rim that fits snugly in the top. The hoops rest on straw or rush drain mats on a drain board. The temperature of the room should be about 65°.

When the curd has settled sufficiently, the metal rims are removed. The hoops of cheese are piled several high on a draining table, and a drain board and clean mat are placed under each cheese. The hoops are turned frequently, and the mats are changed at each turning. The clean mats are placed at right angles to those used previously, which results in a checked pattern on the surface of the cheese.

About 24 hours after the curd was placed in the hoops, the hoops are removed and a tinned metal strap is fitted around each cheese. The cheeses are turned and the mats are changed as before for another 24 hours. Then the straps are removed, and fine dry salt is rubbed on the surface and sides of the cheeses. They are turned and salted daily for 2 or 3 days.

Then the cheeses are taken to a well ventilated drying room where they are held at a temperature of 55° to 60° F. for about 8 days. A felty layer of white mold grows rapidly on the surface, and the curd softens rapidly and becomes slightly yellow and translucent during this period. Then the cheeses are moved to a curing cellar or cave in which the temperature is about 52°, the relative humidity about 85 percent, and there is little ventilation. The primary layer of white mold is gradually superseded by a secondary growth of yellow mold that changes to red as ripening continues and the cheese becomes less acid and the curd becomes yellower and creamier. Regulating the growth of desirable molds on the surface of the cheese is essential for successful production. Some manufacturers inoculate the milk with the desirable micro-organisms to insure their growth.

The cheese may be shipped before curing is completed, in which case the retailer places the cheese in a cellar for final ripening. Brie is perishable and must be kept under refrigeration. Before sale the cheeses may be cut into pie-shaped segments, each of which is wrapped separately. However, it ripens more normally if it is not cut.

About 14 pounds of cheese is obtained from 100 pounds of whole milk.

Analysis: Moisture, 45 to 52.5 percent; fat, 25 to 28 percent when the cheese is made from whole milk, and 20 to 22 percent when it is made from partly skimmed milk; protein, 21.6 percent; and salt, 1.5 to 4 percent.

Brioler

Brioler and Woriener, which are named for the localities in East Prussia where they are made, are similar to Limburger cheese. Cow's whole milk is curdled with rennet at a temperature of about 91° F. The curd is cut in about 20 minutes. It is not subjected to additional heating and is not pressed while in the forms. The room is kept comparatively warm while whey drains from the curd, and the cheese is cured in cellars that are comparatively dry. The curing period is from 4 to 6 weeks. Each cheese is 3 to 4 inches square, 2 to 3 inches thick, and weighs about 2¼ pounds. (See Limburger.)

Broccio

Broccio cheese, which is also called Brouse, is similar to Ricotta and Ziger. Fresh and sour whey are mixed, and the mixture is heated to nearly the boiling point. The coagulum that forms on the surface is removed with a skimmer and drained on a fine mat or in a basket. This cheese will keep for a day in summer or 2 days in winter. If salted, it can be kept for longer periods. (See Ricotta and Ziger.)

Burgundy

Burgundy cheese, known in France as Fromage de Bourgogne, is a soft, white, loaf-shaped cheese that weighs about 4 pounds.

Analysis: Moisture, 29.5 percent; fat, 38.6 percent; and protein, 28.8 percent.

Burmeister

Burmeister is the trade name of a soft, ripened Brick-type cheese made in Wisconsin.

Buttermilk

Buttermilk cheese is made from the curd of buttermilk and is somewhat finer grained than cottage cheese, which it closely resembles. Buttermilk with an acidity of 0.5 or 0.6 percent is run into a steam-heated vat or starter can, or into a pail which can be heated in a tub of hot water. The buttermilk is stirred, heated to a temperature of 75° to 78° F., covered, and left for 1½ to 2 hours. The temperature is then raised to 140°, and in about an hour the curd settles to the bottom. The whey is removed and the curd is transferred to a cloth to drain for about 10 hours. It should be stirred occasionally while draining. When dry, the curd is salted, put into small packages, and wrapped in parchment paper. The cheese contains about the same amount of moisture as, but more fat than, cottage cheese. (See Danish Export, which is a buttermilk cheese.)

In an attempt to utilize sweet buttermilk in cheesemaking, sometimes about 10 percent of sweet buttermilk is added to milk used in making cheese by the Cheddar method. Cheese made in this way is said to ripen faster than Cheddar cheese. It is illegal to add buttermilk to Cheddar cheese milk in some countries.

Caciocavallo

Caciocavallo, an Italian plastic-curd (pasta filata) cheese, was made first in southern Italy but now is made also in Sicily and in summer in northern Italy. In northern Italy it is made chiefly for export. It is especially suitable for making in warm climates, as it keeps well. The cured cheese has a smooth, firm body, and preferably the interior of the cheese is white.

Caciocavallo and Provolone are made by almost identical methods. However, Caciocavallo contains less fat than Provolone and usually is not smoked, and each is molded in distinctive shapes. Typically, Caciocavallo is spindle-shaped, with a pointed bottom and with a neck and head at the top. One theory of the origin of the name is that the cheeses, which are tied in pairs and hung over poles to cure, look as if they were hung over a saddle; hence, cheese on horseback, or "cacio a cavallo."

Caciocavallo is made usually from cow's milk, but sometimes from a mixture of cow's and ewe's milk. Evening milk is skimmed and mixed with whole morning milk in a vat or wooden tub. Starter may be added; whey from the previous day, containing lactobacilli and thermophilic streptococci, may be used. The milk is set at a temperature of about 96° F. with rennet, preferably rennet paste. The curd is cut in 20 to 30 minutes, with a metal skimmer and then with a stirrer, into pieces about the size of a pea. After the curd settles, the whey is removed and the curd is pressed.

The compressed curd is transferred to a wooden tub in a warm room and covered with hot whey. An energetic fermentation occurs. As soon as a sample of the curd will stretch into a tough, elastic fiber when it is immersed in very hot water, it is ready for draining and molding (this may be from 5 to 8 hours or as long as 20 hours after fermentation begins).

The curd is transferred to a special table to drain; then it is cut into long thin slices which are placed in a tub and covered with very hot water. The slices are worked with a paddle and by hand until they are very elastic; then they are drawn into rope-like pieces of uniform size and draped on a pole. These rope-like pieces are molded into the typical Caviocavallo shape. While being molded they are immersed occasionally in very hot water to keep them hot. Molding while hot expels whey from the curd and produces cheese with a compact curd, free of openings, and with a properly sealed surface.

The cheeses are placed in a vat of cold water—on a cloth stretched under the water or in forms—for 3 or 4 hours, to cool and harden. Then they are salted in brine at about 50° F. for 3 or 4 days, after which they are dried, tied in pairs, and hung over poles in a curing room at a temperature of 62° to 65° and a relative humidity of 80 to 85 percent. They are cleaned when they become moldy, and then are oiled.

Cheese cured for 2 to 4 months is suitable for table use, and that cured for 6 to 12 months or longer is suitable for grating. The yield is 7¾ to 8¾ pounds of uncured cheese, or about 6¾ pounds of cured cheese, per 100 pounds of partly skimmed cow's milk. The cheeses usually weigh between 4½ and 5½ pounds.

Analysis: Moisture, not more than 40 percent (usually 28 to 38 percent); fat, 19 to 30 percent (not less than 42 percent in the solids); protein, 32 to 38 percent; and salt, 2 to 6 percent.

Caciocavallo Siciliano

Caciocavallo Siciliano, a plastic-curd (pasta filata) cheese like the Italian Provolone and Caciocavallo, is essentially a pressed Provolone. Although small quantities are made in the United States, it is made chiefly in Sicily, usually from cow's whole milk, but sometimes from goat's milk or a mixture of the two. According to some authorities, it is always made in the shape of an oblong block. Each cheese weighs between 17½ and 26 pounds.

The method of making Caciocavallo Siciliano is similar to the method of making Caciocavallo and Provolone, except for the following: The curd is not placed in cold water to firm it, but is pressed in forms. Although according to some authorities it may be salted in brine, it usually is salted with dry salt over a period of about 20 days. It is not smoked and may be paraffined. It is cured for at least 3 months and is used both as a table cheese and for grating. (See Caciocavallo and Provolone.)

Analysis: Moisture, not more than 40 percent; fat in the solids, not less than 42 percent.

Cacio Fiore

Cacio Fiore, also called Caciotta, is a soft, yellowish, Italian cheese with a delicate, buttery flavor. It has a soft and delicate curd similar to Bel Paese and the Stracchino and Crescenza cheeses of Lombardy. It is made from ewe's or goat's milk, usually in the cold winter months.

Whole milk is colored with saffron and is set at a temperature of 95° F., preferably with vegetable rennet extract (caglio fiore). Use of this extract, which is prepared from salt water and wild artichoke flowers (fiore), produces the soft, delicate curd. After a coagulation period of 25 minutes, the curd is broken into comparatively large pieces and is dipped into rectangular or round wooden forms that are lined with linen cloth; the forms are placed on straw mats on an inclined table to drain. After draining, the cheese is salted with dry salt and is kept on a straw mat and turned daily. It is ready to eat about 10 days after it is made. The average yield is 25 to 30 pounds of cheese per 100 pounds of milk. Each cheese weighs between 2 and 4½ pounds.

Cacio Fiore Aquilano is a similar cheese that usually is made in winter (January and February). It is a rectangular, fast-ripening, Stracchino (Lombardy) type cheese made from ewe's milk, preferably with vegetable (fiore) rennet, although good results can be obtained also with calf rennet.

Fresh milk is colored with saffron and is set with rennet at a temperature of 95° F. After a coagulation period of 50 minutes, the curd is cut, drained, placed in the forms, and salted in the same way as in making Crescenza. (See Crescenza.) This cheese should be eaten within a month after it is made.

Caerphilly

Caerphilly is a semisoft, cow's milk cheese made in Wales, and is especially popular among Welch miners. It is circular and flat, about 9 inches in diameter and 2½ to 3½ inches thick, and weighs about 8 pounds. The cheese is white and smooth, lacks elasticity, and is granular rather than waxy when broken.

Fresh whole milk is inoculated with starter and ripened slightly. The milk is heated to 84° or 90° F., and rennet is added. After a curdling period of 40 to 60 minutes, the curd is cut into small pieces, stirred carefully for 10 minutes, and (if the rennet was added at 84°) warmed gradually to 90° in another 20 minutes. Then the whey is drained off, and the curd is ladled into small cloth bags which are hung up for draining or pressed lightly. After about an hour the curd is broken up or it may be cut into small cubes, and it is repressed. Again the curd is broken up, and salt is mixed in at the rate of 1 ounce of salt to 3 pounds of curd. The curd is then placed in cloth-lined forms and again pressed. The cheeses are redressed and repressed after several hours, and then daily, with gradually increasing pressure, for about 3 days. They are cured on shelves in a damp curing room at 65° to 70°, for 2 to 3 weeks. During that time they are kept clean and are inverted frequently. A thin, white layer of mold forms on the surface, which is considered desirable in proper ripening. The cheese is perishable and must be eaten soon after curing. The yield is relatively high.

Analysis: Moisture, 37.0 percent or more; fat, 30.4 percent; and protein, 37.2 percent.

Calcagno

Calcagno, a hard cheese made in Sicily, is classed as a pecorino (ewe's-milk) cheese suitable for grating.

Cambridge

Cambridge cheese, which is known also as York cheese, is a soft cheese made in England. Cow's whole milk is set at a temperature of 90° F. with enough rennet to coagulate it in an hour. The uncut curd is dipped into molds, and it is ready to eat after standing for 30 hours.

Camembert

Camembert, a soft, surface-ripened, cow's-milk cheese, was first made in 1791 by Marie Fontaine (Madame Harel) at Camembert, a hamlet in the Department of Orne, France. It is said that Napoleon was served this cheese, which was as yet unnamed, and he thereupon named it Camembert. The industry soon extended from Orne to the Department of Calvados, and these two Departments are still the principal centers of production. However, Camembert-type cheese is made also in other parts of France and in other countries, including the United States.

Each cheese is about 4½ inches in diameter, 1 to 1½ inches thick, and weighs about 10 ounces. The interior is yellow and waxy, creamy, or almost fluid in consistency, depending on the degree of ripening. The rind is a thin, felt-like layer of gray mold and dry cheese interspersed with patches of reddish yellow. Camembert is made in much the same way as Brie, but it is smaller and the characteristic flavor differs.

The method of making Camembert is in general as follows: Good-quality whole milk or milk standardized to a fat content of 3.5 percent is put in small vats or in flat-bottomed, conical metal cans that hold about 200 pounds. Lactic starter is added, and the milk is warmed to a temperature of approximately 85° F. A little color may be added, and enough rennet is added so the curd will be firm enough to dip in 1 to 1½ hours. The curd may be cut before it is put into the hoops to hasten drainage of the whey, but usually it is hooped without cutting.

The curd is ladled carefully—a slice at a time and with as little breaking as possible—into perforated, circular hoops that rest on rush mats on drain boards on a draining table. The hoops are about 4½ inches in diameter and 5 inches deep and are open at both ends. In some factories half hoops just large enough to slip over the deeper hoops easily (4⅝ inches in diameter and 2½ inches deep) are used, and in some factories heavy metal disks are placed on the curd to aid in settling it evenly. The temperature of the room should be about 70° F.

The hoops are turned and the mats are changed after a few hours, and this procedure is repeated frequently for about 2 days. At the end of the first day, the cheeses will have settled to a thickness of 1½ to 1¾ inches, and the deeper hoops may be removed. At the end of the second day, the cheeses are removed from the hoops, salted with fine dry salt, and may be inoculated with a culture of mold and bacteria. The culture either is mixed with the salt and rubbed on the surface of the cheeses, or it is dissolved in water and sprayed on. Then the cheeses are moved to the curing room.

Curing the cheese is the most difficult part of the manufacturing process for there must be a uniform and progressive development of the ripening agents and at the same time the curd must dry gradually but not too rapidly. The cheeses are cured on open board frames or shelves at a temperature of about 55° F. and a relative humidity of 85 to 90 percent for about 3 weeks; then at a temperature of 48° to 50°. In the United States, if the cheese is made from raw milk it is cured for at least 60 days. Cheeses are turned frequently. A primary surface growth of a grayish-white felt-like layer of mold is followed by a secondary fermentation that produces a trace of sliminess and changes the surface to show spots of yellow and finally a reddish or russet color; at the same time the interior of the curd becomes creamy and somewhat yellow.

The cheeses are wrapped in paper, parchment, or cellophane and may be covered with metal foil; they usually are packed in round, flat, wooden or plastic boxes. Sometimes they are cut in pie-shaped segments for marketing, but they are said to cure more normally if they are not cut. From 13 to 15 pounds of Camembert cheese is obtained per 100 pounds of whole milk.

Analysis: Moisture, 52.3 percent in domestic Camembert, and 43 to 54.4 percent in imported; fat, 24 to 28 percent (at least 50 percent in the solids); protein, 17 to 21 percent; and salt, 2.6 percent.

Camosun

Camosun is a semisoft, open-textured cheese that is said to resemble Gouda and Monterey. The method of making Camosun, which was developed in 1932 by the Extension Service of Washington State College as a means of utilizing surplus milk on farms, is similar to but less time consuming than the Granular or Stirred-curd process. The drained curd is pressed in hoops about 6 inches in diameter and 7 inches deep. The cheese is salted in brine for 30 hours, then coated with paraffin and cured for 1 to 3 months in a relatively humid room at 50° to 60° F. (See Granular or Stirred-curd.)

Canned

Canned cheese refers to a method of packaging, not to a kind of cheese, although cheese so packaged usually is American Cheddar cheese. The cheese curd is pressed in special forms the size and shape of the can, either round or rectangular, and is sealed and cured in the can. Between 1933 and 1940, the U.S. Department of Agriculture developed a method for curing cheese in a special valve-vented can which permits the escape of gases but prevents the entrance of air and hence prevents the development of mold. Later, the New York (Geneva) and Washington experiment stations developed methods for sealing the cheese in cans under vacuum. The properties and composition of canned cheese are like those of the same cheese not canned except that there is no loss of moisture and no loss in weight while curing. Early work on curing cheese in cans developed information on the conditions necessary for curing cheese in packages and thus helped to pave the way for the present large-scale production of packaged natural rindless loaf cheese. (See Natural Rindless Loaf.)

Canquillote

Canquillote, also called Fromagère and Tempête, is a skim-milk cheese made in eastern France. The milk is curdled by souring, after which it is heated slowly and the whey removed. The curd is pressed and then broken up and allowed to ferment at a temperature of about 70° F. for about 2 or 3 days, with frequent stirring. After the characteristic flavor has developed, the curd is warmed and stirred. Water, salt, eggs, and butter are mixed with the curd, and it is pressed in molds of various shapes.

Cantal

Cantal, also known locally as Fourme, is a hard, rather yellow cheese with a piquant flavor and firm, close body. It has been made for centuries in the region of the Auvergne Mountains in the Department of Cantal, France. The cheeses are about 14 inches in diameter and usually weigh about 75 pounds, but may vary in weight from 40 to 120 pounds.

The method of manufacture has remained rather primitive. Rennet is added to cow's whole milk, either fresh or slightly ripened, at a temperature of 86° F., and about an hour later the curd is cut fine and the whey is drained off. The curd is pressed to remove as much whey as possible and then is ripened for 24 hours, which is considered very important. The curd then is broken up and 3 to 4 percent of salt is added. It is kneaded thoroughly, placed in hoops, and pressed for 36 to 48 hours; it is turned 2 or 3 times during the first 24 hours. The cheeses then are removed from the hoops, dried, and placed in the curing cellar. They are cured usually for 3 to 4 months but sometimes for as long as 6 months. While curing they are washed with salty water and turned frequently. The yield of cured cheese is about 10 percent of the weight of the milk.

Analysis: Moisture, 39.9 to 44.8 percent; fat, 28 to 34 percent; protein, 20.5 to 25 percent; and salt, 2 to 3.1 percent.

Caraway

Caraway cheese is a so-called Spiced cheese that contains caraway seed. (See Spiced cheese.)

Carré

Carré or Carré Frais, known also as Double Crème Carré and Fromage Double Crème, is a small, rich French Cream cheese of the Neufchâtel type. Usually it is about 2 inches square, less than an inch thick, and weighs less than 4 ounces. However, it is also made in a larger size—about 4½ to 5 inches in diameter, 1 to 1½ inches thick, and 10 to 12 ounces in weight—similar to Camembert and Coulommiers. It is made from a rich milk-and-cream mixture, which is coagulated with rennet. The curd is placed in a cloth to drain; when the whey has drained completely, the curd is salted, mixed thoroughly, and then put into molds to form the cheeses. It is eaten fresh.

Cheese made in a similar way, with considerable salt added to act as a preservative, is called Demisel.

Analysis: Fat in the solids, 60 percent; salt, 2 percent.

Carré de l'Est

Carré de l'Est is a Camembert-type cheese made in France from either raw or pasteurized cow's whole milk. In fact, the method used for making Camembert in some factories in the United States is like the French method for making Carré de l'Est rather than true Camembert. The chief difference in the making process is that the curd is cut before dipping in making Carré de l'Est, which accelerates early drainage of whey, and the cheese is said to be softer. (See Camembert.)

Analysis: Moisture, 50 to 55 percent; fat in the solids, 45 to 50 percent.

Casigiolu

Casigiolu, also called Panedda and Pera di vacca, is made in Sardinia. It is a plastic-curd cheese and is made by the same method used in making Caciocavallo. (See Caciocavallo.)

Castelmagno

Castelmagno is a blue-mold, Gorgonzola-type cheese made in Italy.

Champoléon

Champoléon, also known as Queyras, is a hard cheese similar to Canquillote. It is made from skim milk in the Hautes-Alps region in France.

Chantelle

Chantelle is the trade name of a semisoft, ripened cheese that is made in Illinois from cow's fresh, whole milk. It is made and cured in a manner similar to Bel Paese. Micro-organisms growing on the surface of the cheese are partly responsible for the characteristic ripening. However, Chantelle is coated with red cheese wax when the surface ripening is at an earlier stage of development than in Bel Paese; it is cured at somewhat higher temperatures; and it does not soften so much in ripening. It may be shipped about 3 weeks after it is made, in which case it undergoes further ripening while it is being transported and marketed. It is somewhat similar to Trappist cheese; that is, it has a characteristic mild flavor, a rather open texture, and a smooth, waxy body suitable for slicing. It is round and flat, about 8 inches in diameter, and weighs about 5 pounds.

Analysis: Moisture, 48.9 percent; fat, 26.7 percent; fat in the solids, 52.5 percent; and salt, 2.4 percent.

Chaource

Chaource, which is named for the village of Chaource in the Department of Aube, France, is a soft, whole-milk cheese that resembles Camembert. It is about 4 inches in diameter and 3 inches thick.

Chaschol

Chaschol, or Chaschosis, is a hard cheese made in the Canton of Grisons in eastern Switzerland from cow's skim milk. It is from 17 to 20 inches in diameter, from 2¾ to 4 inches thick, and weighs from 22 to 45 pounds.

Cheddar

Cheddar cheese is named for the village of Cheddar in Somersetshire, England, where it was first made. The exact date of origin is not known, but it has been made since the latter part of the 16th century.

Colonial housewives made the first Cheddar cheese in America; and the first cheese factory in the United States was a Cheddar-cheese factory, established in 1851 by Jesse Williams, near Rome, Oneida County, N. Y.

Production increased rapidly with the establishment of the factory system. At present, nearly 1.3 billion pounds of Cheddar (and Cheddar-type) cheese is made in the United States each year, which is about 67 percent of all the cheese made. In fact, it is made and used so widely that it often is called American cheese, or American Cheddar cheese, and cheeses similar to Cheddar but made by a slightly modified process are called American-type cheeses. (See American.)

In addition to being the name of the cheese, Cheddar is the name of a step in the manufacturing process and also the name of the most common style, which is about 14½ inches in diameter, 12 inches thick, and weighs between 70 and 78 pounds. Other styles are: Daisy, which is about 13¼ inches in diameter, slightly more than 4 inches thick, and weighs 21 to 23 pounds; Flat or Twin, which is 14½ inches in diameter, slightly more than 5 inches thick, and weighs 32 to 37 pounds; Longhorn, which is 6 inches in diameter, 13 inches long, and weighs 12 to 13 pounds; Young American, which is 7 inches in diameter, 7 inches thick, and weighs 11 to 12 pounds; Picnic or Junior Twin, which is 9¾ inches in diameter, 5 inches thick, and weighs 11 to 12 pounds; and rectangular blocks or prints, which usually are 14 inches long, 11 inches wide, 3¼ inches thick, and weigh 20 pounds. However, they are made in barrel sizes that weigh up to 600 pounds. The blocks are often cut into prints and packaged (see Natural Rindless Loaf). In many stores, the 1-pound print is most popular.

Cheddar is a hard cheese, ranging in color from nearly white to yellow. It is made from sweet, whole cow's milk, either raw or pasteurized. (If it is made from partly skimmed or skim milk, it must be so labeled.)

Research has shown that pasteurizing the milk improves the quality of the cheese; and that cheese of uniformly good quality can be made from pasteurized milk by the so-called time-schedule method. Use of the time schedule systematizes the cheese-making operations and makes it possible to control the amount of acid that develops and the rate of its development during the making process. More than 90 percent of the Cheddar cheese made in the United States is now made from either heat-treated or pasteurized milk.

The pasteurized milk is cooled to the setting temperature (86° to 88° F.) and run into the cheese vat. Starter is added and the milk is agitated (stirred) usually for about an hour as the milk ripens (develops acidity). The amount of starter and the length of the ripening period are adjusted so that acid will develop at the desired rate during the making process. Then rennet and color are mixed in thoroughly and stirring is stopped. When the curd is sufficiently firm, usually about 30 minutes after setting, it is cut with curd knives into ¼-inch or ⅜-inch cubes. It is stirred continuously from cutting to dipping (draining the whey). About 15 minutes after cutting is completed, the curd is heated gradually (in about 30 minutes) to a temperature of about 100°.

About 2¼ hours after the rennet was added, the curd is pushed back from the gate end of the vat, and the whey is drained. Draining should be completed in 15 minutes; then a ditch is made down the middle of the vat and the curd is packed about 7 or 8 inches deep on each side. When it is firm enough to be turned without breaking it is cheddared or matted, that is, it is cut into slabs 5 or 6 inches wide which are turned frequently and, finally, when firm enough, piled in layers. Then the curd is run through a curd mill and spread evenly over the bottom of the vat and stirred. About 2½ to 3½ pounds of salt for each 1,000 pounds of milk is mixed in; and the curd is piled on either side of the vat while the whey drains.

When the salt has dissolved completely, the curd is transferred to cloth-lined metal hoops and pressed for about 30 minutes. Then the hoops are removed from the press, the cheeses are dressed, pressed again for 12 to 24 hours, and then removed from the hoops and dried for 3 or 4 days at a temperature of 50° to 60° F. before dipping in paraffin or wax.

When rindless cheese is made the press cloths are removed after pressing and the cheese wrapped in a heat-sealing plastic film.

Cheeses are cured usually at a temperature between 40° and 50° F., but it may be as low as 35° or as high as 60°. They are cured for at least 60 days, usually for 3 to 6 months, and in some instances for as long as a year. Between 9½ and 11 pounds of cheese is obtained per 100 pounds of milk.

Analysis: Moisture, 37 to 38 percent (not more than 39 percent); fat, 32 percent (fat in the solids, not less than 50 percent); protein, 25 percent; and salt, 1.4 to 1.8 percent.

Cheshire

Cheshire, which is also called Chester, ranks with Cheddar as the oldest and most popular of English cheeses; both were well known as early as the reign of Queen Elizabeth I. Cheshire was first made in the village of Chester on the river Dee; it is said that it was molded originally in the form of the famous "Cheshire Cat."

Cheshire is a firm cheese, but it is more crumbly and not so compact as Cheddar. It is cylindrical in shape, like Cheddar; the cheeses are about 14 inches in diameter and usually between 50 and 70 pounds in weight. The curd may be nearly white but more often it is colored deep yellow with annatto.

There are three general types of Cheshire cheese: (1) Early-ripening, which is made from early spring until May and which usually is marketed locally; (2) medium-ripening, which is made in May and June and in the autumn and which is the most common type; and (3) late-ripening, which is made in summer, is cured more fully, and is sold in more distant markets. The three types differ slightly in the details of manufacture, such as the setting temperature, the rate of development of acidity, the cutting of the curd, and the cooking temperature. Following is a general description of the method of making medium-ripening Cheshire:

Evening and morning milk are mixed in a cheese vat, color usually is added, and the milk is set with lactic starter and rennet at a temperature of 86° F. After a coagulation period of an hour, the curd is stirred carefully and cut gradually to fine particles with a curd breaker or curd knives. In the next hour, part of the whey is removed and the curd settles in the remaining whey and then is stirred and warmed to 88°. In the next 30 or 40 minutes the curd settles again in the whey, after which the whey is drained off. Then the loosely matted curd is rolled up to one end of the vat and is pressed with a lightly weighted curd rack to hasten drainage, after which the curd is cut into rather large cubes and is spread on a curd cloth on a drain rack. After it has drained for 2 to 3 hours, during which time it is turned occasionally, it is cut into small cubes. It is kept warm while it continues to drain. Then it is put through a curd mill, salt is mixed in at the rate of 3 to 4 pounds per 100 pounds of curd, and it is placed in forms. There are holes in the sides of the forms through which skewers (pegs) are inserted to make holes in the cheese to facilitate the drainage of whey. The forms, which may be turned occasionally, are kept overnight in a cheese oven or other warm place at a temperature between 75° and 80°. The next morning the cheese is removed from the forms, dressed in cloth, and placed in a press. It is pressed for about 4 days and turned daily while in the press; the pressure is increased gradually until finally it reaches about 2,000 pounds. The cheese is removed from the press, scalded in hot water, and dressed in a bandage. It is cured on shelves in a curing room at a temperature of 60° to 65°.

The early-ripening type may be cured for as short a time as 3 weeks, the medium-ripening type is cured for about 2 months, and the late-ripening type is cured for at least 10 weeks and often for 8 to 10 months. The longer curing period improves the cheese.

The yield of cured cheese is 9 to 11 pounds per 100 pounds of whole milk.

Analysis: Moisture, 37 to 43 percent; fat, 28 to 31 percent; and salt, 2 to 2.5 percent.

Cheshire-Stilton

Cheshire-Stilton is an English cheese that combines the characteristics of the Cheshire and Stilton varieties. The method of making, size, and shape are similar to Cheshire, and mold peculiar to Stilton develops during curing. The mold is propagated by mixing a small portion of fresh curd every day with older curd in which the mold is growing well. (See Cheshire and Stilton.)

Chhana

Chhana is a sour-milk cheese made in Asia from cow's whole milk.

Chiavari

Chiavari is a sour-milk cheese made from cow's whole milk in the region of Chiavari, in the Province of Genoa, Italy.

Christalinna

Christalinna is a hard cheese made from cow's milk in the Canton of Grisons, Switzerland.

Christian IX

Christian IX is a Danish cheese that differs from Kuminost principally in size and shape. It is cylindrical and flat and weighs less than 35 pounds. It contains spices, such as caraway seed. The surface is coated with yellow paraffin or wax.

Analysis: At least 45 percent of fat in the solids.

Colby

Colby cheese, which is similar to Cheddar, may be made from either raw or pasteurized milk. It is made in the same way as Cheddar except that (as in Granular or Stirred-curd cheese) the curd is not matted and milled. However, in making Granular or Stirred-curd cheese, water is not added to the curd to cool it as is done in making Colby.

After the curd has been cut, stirred, and heated (as in the Cheddar process) the whey is drained to the level of the curd. Then the vat gate is closed and rather cool water (about 60° F.) is added with continuous stirring until the temperature of the curd has been reduced to about 80°. Stirring is continued for 10 to 20 minutes, then the curd is pushed to the sides of the vat and stirred enough to prevent matting as the whey drains. About an hour after the whey is drained, salt is added to the curd in 2 or 3 applications, each application being mixed thoroughly with the curd (as in the Cheddar process). The curd is again pushed to the sides of the vat to drain while the salt is dissolving, which requires at least 20 minutes. Then the curd is hooped and pressed (as in the Cheddar process). The cheese is cured for a somewhat longer period than washed-curd cheese, but not so long as Cheddar. If it is made from raw milk, it must be cured for at least 60 days unless it is to be used for manufacturing.

Colby has a softer body and more open texture than Cheddar cheese, and it contains more moisture. For these reasons, it does not keep as well as Cheddar.

Analysis: Moisture, not more than 40 percent (usually 38 percent); fat in the solids, not less than 50 percent; and salt, 1.4 to 1.8 percent.

Cold-pack

Cold-pack cheese, known also as Club or Comminuted cheese and which is said to have originated in the United States, usually is an excellent product with a sharp cheese flavor. It is prepared by grinding very fine and mixing without heating one or more lots of the same or different varieties of cheese to which vinegar or lactic, citric, acetic, or phosphoric acid, water, salt, color, and spices may be added. The acid or vinegar should not reduce the pH of the cheese below 4.5.

It usually is made from carefully selected and well aged Cheddar cheese. Other Cheddar types (such as Washed-curd, Colby, or Granular), Roquefort (or Roquefort-type), Gorgonzola, Gruyère, and Limburger are also used in various combinations. Soft, unripened cheese (such as Cream, Neufchâtel, and Cottage), and semisoft, spiced, part skim-milk, skim-milk, and hard, grating cheeses are not used. It is made from pasteurized-milk cheese or from cheese that has been held for at least 60 days at a temperature of not less than 35° F. It may be made from smoked cheese, or it may be smoked as a part of the making process.

The ground cheese mixture is packed in various types of containers, all of which are designed to keep out air. Some of the common types are: Transparent sausage-shaped casings; waxed cardboard cups; metal foil; transparent, flexible wrappers in cardboard cartons; and porcelain or glass jars or crocks with airtight covers. When marketed in the latter type of package, the cheese sometimes is called Potted cheese.

This type of product can be made at home; however, grinding and mixing the cheese changes its texture and the product is inclined to be "mealy." The housewife can make the product richer and increase its smoothness by adding butter. When made for sale commercially, however, adding the butter makes the product subject to the Federal law that restricts the manufacture and sale of "filled" cheese. (See Filled cheese.)

Analysis: Moisture, not more than the maximum legal limit for the variety of natural cheese from which it is made, or the average of the maximum legal limits if more than one variety is used, but in no case more than 42 percent (or 39 percent if made from Cheddar or Cheddar-type cheeses). Fat in the solids, not less than the minimum legal limit for the variety of natural cheese used, or the average of the minimum legal limits if more than one variety is used, but in no case less than 47 percent (or 45 percent if made from Swiss or Gruyère).

Cold-pack Cheese Food

Cold-pack cheese food is prepared by grinding very fine and mixing without heating one or more lots of the same or different varieties of cheese with one or more so-called optional dairy ingredients, to which may be added one or more of the following: An acidifying agent, water, salt, color, spices, and a sweetening agent.

Cold-pack cheese food is made from pasteurized-milk cheese or from cheese that has been held for at least 60 days at a temperature of not less than 35° F. Cheddar cheese and the Cheddar types (such as Washed-curd, Colby, and Granular), Roquefort (or Roquefort-type), Gorgonzola, Gruyère, and Limburger are used in various combinations. Soft, unripened cheese (such as Cream, Neufchâtel, and Cottage), and semisoft, spiced, part skim-milk, skim-milk, and the hard, grating cheeses are not used. It may be made from smoked cheese, or it may be smoked as a part of the making process.

The optional dairy ingredients used are cream, milk, skim milk, cheese whey, or any of these from which part of the water has been removed; and albumin from cheese whey. They are pasteurized or are made from products that have been pasteurized.

The acidifying agents used are: Vinegar, lactic acid, citric acid, acetic acid, and phosphoric acid. The pH of the cheese food should not be reduced below 4.5.

The sweetening agents used are: Sugar, dextrose, corn sugar, corn sirup, corn-sirup solids, glucose sirup, glucose sirup solids, maltose, malt sirup, and hypdrolyzed lactose.

Fruits, vegetables, or meats may be added.

Analysis: Moisture, not more than 44 percent; fat, not less than 23 percent. If fruits, vegetables, or meats are added, the milk-fat content must be at least 22 percent.

Commission

Commission cheese is made in the Provinces of North Holland and Friesland, in the Netherlands. It is made from slightly skimmed milk in the same way as Edam and is the same shape, but each cheese weighs about 8 pounds, which is twice as much as the average Edam. (See Edam.)

Analysis: Fat in the solids, at least 40 percent.

Comté

Comté cheese, made in eastern France, is similar to Gruyère. Each cheese weighs between 100 and 120 pounds. (See Gruyère.)

Cooked

Cooked cheese (German, Kochkäse, literally Cook cheese) is so named because it is made by heating or "cooking" cheese curd. It is made not only in the United States but also in many foreign countries, and in the home as well as in the factory. The method of making differs somewhat in different countries and in different localities within a country, and the cheese is known by different local names. In the United States, the local names include Cup cheese and Pennsylvania Pot cheese; in northern Germany, it is called Topfen; and in Sardinia, Fresa. When properly made, Cooked cheese has an agreeable flavor and a smooth buttery consistency similar to Camembert.

The fresh cheese curd which is the basic ingredient of Cooked cheese is made from skim milk, or reconstituted concentrated skim milk or nonfat dry milk solids, or a mixture of any of these. The curd usually is prepared in the same way as ordinary Cottage-cheese curd and preferably should be rather dry. (See Cottage cheese.)

The fresh curd is either stirred thoroughly or ground in a meat grinder, after which it is placed in a container, such as a crock or pot, covered, and kept warm until it ripens. It is stirred once or twice a day while it ripens. Usually it will ripen sufficiently in 3 or 4 days at a temperature of 80° to 85° F., in about 5 days at 75°, and in a week at 70°. The length of the ripening period depends on the softness and moisture content of the original curd, the temperature at which it is held, and the flavor desired in the finished cheese. The curd is ripened to a lesser extent if cheese with a mild flavor is desired.

Sometimes soda is added to the curd before it is cooked, at the rate of ¼ teaspoon of soda per pound of curd or 1 pound per 100 pounds of curd. The soda aids in softening the curd; when it is added the ripening period is shortened or may even be omitted.

When ripe the curd consists of two layers. On the top is a layer of particles of curd covered with a wrinkled, gelatinous, viscous mass of mold mycelia, beneath which is a layer of semiliquid curd with a characteristic strong flavor and odor. It may be slightly yellow throughout.

Sometimes flavoring materials, such as butter or cream, salt, caraway seed, egg, pimentos, or olives, are added either just before the curd is cooked or just before it is poured into the glasses.

The entire mass is heated to 180° F., with continual stirring, until it is melted and smooth and has a honey-like consistency when dropped from a ladle. This usually requires about 30 minutes. Skim milk or water may be added to replace the loss by evaporation. It is poured into clean molds, cups, or glasses, covered, and cooled. When cool, it is ready to eat. However, it will keep several days under refrigeration; the flavors blend and there is some ripening during the holding period.

Analysis: Not more than 80 percent of moisture (usually 70 to 75 percent).

Coon

Coon cheese is a Cheddar cheese that is cured by a special patented method. There are two characteristic features in the curing process: Cheese containing 36 to 40 percent of moisture is cured at a temperature of 55° to 70° F., and at a relative humidity as high as 95 percent; both temperature and humidity are higher than usual. High-quality cheese is required for these curing conditions. Mold grows readily on cheese when the temperature and relative humidity are high. Cheddar usually is cured at a temperature of 40° to 50° and at a relative humidity of 70 to 75 percent.

The surface of Coon cheese is colored very dark; the body is short and crumbly; and the flavor is very sharp and tangy. It is a favorite with some consumers who prefer fully cured, extremely sharp Cheddar cheese.

Analysis: Moisture, 36 percent; fat, 33 percent; and salt, 2 percent.

Cornhusker

Cornhusker cheese was introduced by the Nebraska Agricultural Experiment Station about 1940. It is similar to Cheddar and Colby, but has a softer body, contains more moisture, and takes less time to make. (The making process, up to the hooping stage, takes only about 2 hours.) Like Brick cheese, Cornhusker contains numerous mechanical openings.

Lactic starter is added to whole milk; the milk is coagulated firmly with rennet; and the curd is cut, heated, and stirred until it is firm. Then the whey is drained off, and the curd is washed with water, salted, hooped, and pressed. The pressed cheese is coated with two layers of wax. The cheese is cured in a moist room at a temperature of 65° F. for 1 to 2 months or at 45° for 6 to 12 months. The yield is 10.7 pounds per 100 pounds of milk containing 3.7 percent of fat.

Analysis: Moisture, 40 to 45 percent; and fat, 28 to 32 percent.

Cotherstone

Cotherstone, known also as Yorkshire-Stilton, is a blue-veined cheese made on a small scale in the valley of the Tees, in Yorkshire, in northern England, from cow's milk. It is similar to Stilton but is less well known than either Stilton or Wensleydale, other blue-veined cheeses made in England.

Analysis: Moisture, 38 percent; fat, 30 percent; protein, 24 percent; and salt, 2.5 percent.

Cotronese

Cotronese is a ewe's milk cheese similar to Moliterno. Both originated in Calabria and Lucania, Italy. They are said to be seasoned at times with pepper.

Cottage

Cottage cheese, sometimes called Pot cheese and also Dutch cheese or Schmierkäse, is a soft, uncured cheese made from skim milk or from reconstituted concentrated skim milk or nonfat dry milk solids.

Large-grained, low-acid cheese is made by adding rennet to the milk, cutting the curd into large cubes, and washing the curd thoroughly to reduce the acid flavor. It is known as sweet-curd Cottage cheese, flake-type Cottage cheese, and low-acid rennet-type Cottage cheese. The large particles of curd resemble kernels of popped corn, and in some localities this kind of cheese is called Popcorn cheese. Small-grained Cottage cheese sometimes is called country-style or farm-style cheese.

Usually some cream is mixed with the cheese curd before it is marketed or consumed. If the cheese contains 4 percent or more of fat, it is called Creamed Cottage cheese. Flavoring materials, such as peppers, olives, and pimientos, may be added also.

Large quantities of Cottage cheese are made and consumed in the United States; it is highly nutritious and palatable and is used as a table cheese and in salads. It is easy to make both in the home and in the factory. In the home, about 1 pound of cheese is obtained from 1 gallon of skim milk; in the factory, from 12 to 15 pounds of curd is obtained from 100 pounds of skim milk and this makes from 14 to 18 pounds of Creamed Cottage cheese.

Cottage cheese may be made by either the short-setting method or the long-setting method. In the short-setting method, more lactic starter is added to the milk than in the long-setting method; the milk is set at a higher temperature; and the coagulation period is shorter. In both methods, the milk is pasteurized and cooled to the setting temperature. Lactic starter is added; rennet may be added; and the milk is held at the setting temperature until it curdles.

The curd is ready to cut when it is firm but not hard and brittle. It is cut into cubes, the size determining to some extent the size of the curd particles in the finished cheese. Then the curd is heated, with careful stirring. The temperature to which the curd is heated and the length of the heating period depend on the characteristics of the curd and the acidity of the whey. When the curd has attained the proper firmness, the whey is drained off and the curd washed first with cool tap water, then with ice water. Then the water is drained off. When the curd is firm and dry, it is salted. It may be creamed and packed in consumer-size cartons. However, it is customary for the manufacturer to pack the curd in tubs or tins that hold as much as 50 pounds for shipping to the distributor, who creams and packs it in consumer-size cartons to supply his daily needs. The curd may be held for several days at a temperature of 32° to 35° F.

Analysis: Moisture, not more than 80 percent (usually 70 to 72 percent).

Coulommiers

Coulommiers cheese, first made in the vicinity of Coulommiers, in the Department of Seine-et-Marne, France, is a soft, mold-ripened, unwashed cheese. According to some authorities, Coulommiers and the smallest (1-pound) Brie are identical; according to other authorities, Coulommiers is similar to Brie and to Camembert, but is ripened for a shorter period. (See Brie for a description of the making process.)

A modified Coulommiers cheese is made in the United States and Canada. It is suitable for making in the home as the process and equipment are simple. It usually is eaten fresh or when only a few days old. If mellower cheese with a stronger flavor is desired, it may be held for a week or two, although by that time the surface of the cheese may be moldy. The cheeses are round and flat, about 5½ inches in diameter and 1 to 1½ inches thick, and they weigh between ¾ and 1 pound. The yield is 1⅓ to 2 pounds of cheese per gallon of milk.

Cow's fresh, whole milk, or a mixture of evening and morning milk, is warmed to 86° F. (some authorities recommend 80°), in a vat or other container. Lactic starter and rennet are added, the amount depending on the condition of the milk and whether it is desired to have the curd firm enough to cut in 30 minutes, in 1 to 1½ hours, or in 2 to 3 hours. After the rennet is added, the surface of the mixture is stirred gently for a few minutes to keep the cream from rising, but stirring is discontinued before coagulation begins. The temperature of the milk should not go below 80°. While the curd is still soft, large ladlefuls are removed and set aside to be placed on the cheeses later to form smooth tops.

The coagulated curd may be cut into ½- or ¾-inch cubes and ladled carefully into the hoops about 15 minutes after cutting; or it may be cut into thin slices with a sharp-edged ladle and transferred to the hoops without breaking. The set-aside curd is put into the hoops last.

The hoops are metal, open at top and bottom, and perforated on the sides to permit drainage of the whey. They are about 5 inches in diameter and consist of two fitted sections—a lower section about 2 inches deep and an upper collar 3 inches deep. Two to four hoops are placed on a drain mat which is spread on a movable board on a grooved drain table.

The temperature of the room should be at least 68° F. so the curd will drain and firm properly, and the hoops are covered to reduce loss of heat. The hoops are turned frequently at first, then less often, as the curd settles and drains. When the curd has settled into the lower half of the hoops, the top half is removed and a drain mat is placed over the hoops with a drain board over the mat, and the hoops together with the board are turned together.

The cheeses may be sprinkled with fine salt after each turning the first day; they are turned and salted again in the hoops the morning of the second day, and are removed from the hoops the morning of the third day. Or salting may be delayed until the cheeses are removed from the hoops, when they are placed in strong salt brine for an hour or longer, then dried.

The cheeses are wrapped in parchment, usually with an outer tinfoil wrapper. Usually they are eaten fresh, but they may be held a week or two at a temperature of about 52° F., and no higher than 60°. Some people prefer this cheese after it has cured several weeks. While curing, it should be held at a somewhat lower temperature either in a moist place or covered to prevent drying, turned frequently, and kept clean and free of excess mold.

Analysis: Moisture, 55 to 60 percent; fat, 22 to 24 percent; protein, 13 to 15 percent; and salt, 2 to 2.5 percent.

Cream

Cream cheese is a soft, mild, rich, uncured cheese made of cream or a mixture of cream and milk, and used as a spread for bread, in sandwiches, and with salads. It is similar to unripened Neufchâtel but has a higher fat content. It is one of the most popular soft cheeses in the United States and is made in many factories throughout the country, especially in New York and Wisconsin. In addition, there are several French Cream cheeses. (See Carré and Fromage a la Crème.)

The method of making Cream cheese varies in the different factories in the United States; following is a general description:

The cream, or milk-and-cream mixture, which usually is homogenized, is pasteurized, cooled to a temperature of 75° to 85° F., and lactic-acid culture, with or without rennet, is added. After the curd forms, it is stirred until it is smooth and then is heated by one of two methods. In one method, the curd is heated in the vat, with stirring, to a temperature of 115° to 125° and held at that temperature until the whey begins to separate from the curd. Then the curd is ready to drain. It may be placed in draining bags immediately or it may be cooled before it is placed in the bags. In the other method, the curd is stirred until it is smooth, and stirring is continued as hot water (equal to the volume of curd) is added. The temperature of the water should be about 170° to 180°. When the curd-water mixture reaches a temperature of 120° to 130°, it is poured into the draining bags.

When whey has practically stopped draining from the curd, the cheese is packaged by either the cold-pack method or the hot-pack method. In the cold-pack method, the curd is pressed and chilled, and salt is added; it is then mixed until it is smooth, and flavoring materials—such as pimientos, olives, pineapple, or relish—may be added. Usually cream cheese is packed in metal foil or in glasses sealed with metal tops.

In the hot-pack method, the curd is stirred and salted, and any one of several dairy ingredients may be added. Then the mixture is pasteurized, it may be homogenized, flavoring material may be added, and it is packed immediately (while it is in a semifluid condition) in the final package.

Analysis: Moisture, not more than 55 percent (usually 48 to 52 percent); fat, not less than 33 percent (usually 35 to 38 percent); protein, 10 percent; and salt, 0.8 to 1.2 percent.

Creole

Creole is a soft, rich, unripened, Cottage-type cheese, made by mixing about equal quantities of Cottage-type curd and rich cream. It is made in Louisiana and considerable quantities are produced for the New Orleans market.

Crescenza

Crescenza, also known as Carsenza, Stracchino Crescenza, and Crescenza Lombardi, is an uncooked, soft, creamy, mildly sweet, fast-ripening, yellowish cheese of the Bel Paese type. It is made from September to April in Lombardy, in northern Italy, from cow's whole milk. A similar cheese called Raviggiolo is made in Tuscany, Italy, from ewe's milk.

The milk is coagulated with rennet extract at 87° F. The curd is cut and dipped into rectangular wooden forms which are laid on straw mats to drain for a day. The cheese is held at 68° for another day; then it is salted with dry salt and ripened in a cold, moist room for 10 to 15 days. The cheeses weigh from ½ to 3½ pounds.

Analysis: Fat in the solids, exceeds 50 percent.

Creuse

Creuse is a skim-milk cheese made on farms in the Department of Creuse, France. Enough rennet is added to the milk to coagulate it in approximately 12 hours, or it may be warmed and curdled by souring. The curd is stirred and warmed, then dipped into earthenware molds, about 7 inches in diameter and 5 or 6 inches deep. The molds are perforated on the bottom and sides so that the whey can drain off. After several days the cheese is removed from the molds, and it is turned and rubbed with salt at regular intervals. It may be aged for a year or more, in which case it becomes very dry and firm; or it may be put into tightly closed containers lined with straw to ripen, in which case it becomes soft and yellow and acquires a very pronounced flavor.

Damen

Damen, sometimes called Gloire des Montagnes, is a soft, uncured cheese made in Hungary from cow's milk.

Danish Export

Danish Export cheese is made in some of the creameries in Denmark to furnish an outlet for skim milk and buttermilk. The cheese is small, flat, and cylindrical, about the size and shape of Gouda. As much as 15 percent of fresh buttermilk is mixed with skim milk and set at 98° F. with enough rennet to coagulate it in 25 minutes. The curd is cut carefully, stirred, dipped into forms having rounded bottoms, kneaded, pressed down, and finally covered with a board on which a weight is placed. After 12 hours, the cheeses are placed in a brine tank. They are taken out of the brine after 24 hours, covered with salt for a short time, and then transferred to the curing room where the temperature is about 55°. They are turned and wiped with a cloth every day during the ripening period of 5 weeks.

Analysis: Moisture, 39 to 50 percent; fat, 9 to 24 percent; protein, 28 to 34 percent; and salt, 1 to 3 percent.

Delft

Delft is a spiced cheese made in the Netherlands from partly skimmed cow's milk. It is almost exactly like Leyden. (See Leyden.)

Derby

Derby, or Derbyshire, is a hard, sweet-curd cheese made in Derbyshire, England, from cow's whole milk. It is similar to Cheddar but is not so firm and solid, is more flaky when broken, has a higher moisture content, and ripens more rapidly. Gloucester, Leicester, Warwickshire, and Wiltshire are other English cheeses that are very similar to Derby.

Factory production of cheese in England began in 1870 with the establishment of two factories for making Derby cheese. This made it possible to produce cheese more uniform in quality and size than was made in farm dairies. The cheeses are circular, about 15 inches in diameter and 5 inches thick, and weigh about 30 pounds.

A mixture of evening and morning milk is warmed to a temperature of 80° to 85° F. Lactic starter and rennet are added, and color is added for certain markets. About an hour after the milk is set, the curd should be very firm. It is then cut, heated with stirring to a temperature of 96° in 50 minutes, and the whey is drained off. Sometimes the curd is placed on a cloth on a drain rack to drain, and sometimes the whey is expelled by pressing the curd lightly, then more heavily, in the vat. The matted curd is cut into large blocks which are kept warm and are turned occasionally as the whey continues to drain and then develops firmness.

When the curd is sufficiently firm—usually in about 40 minutes—it is put through a curd mill. Sometimes it is salted at this time (as in making Cheddar and Cheshire), and it is put in the hoops and pressed.

When the cheeses have been in the press an hour, they are removed and immersed in hot water (at a temperature of 150° F.) for about a minute; then they are dressed in cloth and pressed again. About 5 hours later, they are removed from the press again. If the curd was not salted earlier, the cheeses are salted on the surface before they are redressed and returned to the press. This procedure is repeated at intervals and the pressure is increased gradually, until the final pressure is about a ton.

Usually the cheeses are taken to the curing room on the third day. They are cured at a temperature of approximately 60° F. for at least a month, but more often for 3 or 4 months as the flavor and quality improve with age.

Analysis: Moisture, 35 to 39 percent; fat, 28 to 30.5 percent; and salt, 2 percent.

Devonshire Cream

Devonshire Cream cheese is made in England. Cream is allowed to rise on the milk, then the milk with the layer of cream is heated to the boiling point, without stirring. After this it is set aside for a short time until the layer of cream becomes firm. The cream is put into small molds, which are placed on straw mats to drain. When the cheeses are hard enough to retain their shape, they are ready to market.

Domiati

Domiati, a so-called pickled cheese and one of the most popular Egyptian cheeses, is made also in some of the other tropical countries where Arabic is spoken. It is made from whole or partly skimmed cow's or buffalo's milk. It is a soft, white cheese with no openings, mild and salty in flavor when fresh and cleanly acid when cured. When it is held for prolonged periods (a year or more) it darkens in color and develops a strong flavor. The cheeses usually are 1½ inches thick and about 3⅛ inches square; but sometimes they are cylindrical in shape, either 2½ or 5 inches in diameter.

The principal characteristic that distinguishes Domiati from other cheeses is that salt is added to the milk at the beginning of the cheese-making process, before rennet is added. Usually from 5 to 15 percent of salt is added to two-thirds of the milk, and the rest is heated to a temperature of 170° F.; then the two portions are mixed, and rennet is added at 105° to 115°. However, if the cheese is made in a jacketed vat so a constant temperature can be maintained, a setting temperature of 95° to 100° is preferable. After a coagulation period of 2 to 3 hours, the curd is ladled into metal hoops or wooden forms lined with mosquito netting. If a large quantity of cheese is being made, a form may be made by fastening planks to a drain table. The forms vary in size. The smallest are the size of a single cheese, a large wooden form may hold 100 pounds of curd, and a form made of planks may hold as much as a ton.

The curd in the small hoops or forms is inverted frequently; that in the large forms is pressed and then cut into suitable sizes for marketing. If it is to be marketed as fresh cheese, it is wrapped in waxed paper. If it is to be cured, it is pickled in salt-whey or salt-milk brine. For local markets, the cheese is cured for 4 to 8 months in the brine solution in earthenware containers. For shipping, the cheese in the brine solution is sealed in tin containers.

About 25 pounds of cheese can be made from 100 pounds of cow's whole milk and 33 pounds from 100 pounds of buffalo's whole milk, to which 7.5 percent of salt is added.

Analysis (whole-milk, cured cheese): Moisture, 52 to 55 percent; fat 20 to 25 percent; and salt, 4.8 percent.

Dorset

Dorset cheese, known also as Dorset Blue, Blue Vinny, and Blue Veiny, is one of the hard, blue-veined cheeses made in England; however, it is not so well known as Stilton and Wensleydale, other English blue-veined cheeses. The name Dorset refers to the County Dorset in England where the cheese was first made at least 200 years ago, and the other names refer to the blue mold that develops in the open-textured curd during the curing process. The cheese is circular and flat and weighs from 14 to 16 pounds. It usually is hard, dry, and crumbly, with a sharp and frequently acid flavor; it is white with blue veining throughout.

Dorset is made from partly skimmed cow's milk. The milk, often highly acid, is warmed to a temperature of 80° F. and curdled with rennet. When the curd is very firm, it is cut into cubes and stirred for several minutes, after which it settles in the whey; then it is stirred again. When the curd is sufficiently acid and firm, the whey is drained off and the curd collected in cloths. The curd, in the cloths, is either hung up or placed on a draining rack to drain further. It is kept warm, and inverted and repacked occasionally as it drains. When it has acquired the desired texture, it is broken up and salted at the rate of about 5½ ounces of salt to 10 pounds of curd. Then it is placed in forms and pressed overnight, lightly at first and later with gradually increasing pressure. The following morning the cheese is inverted, and it is pressed another day with a pressure of 300 pounds. The cheeses may be bandaged before they are placed in the curing room.

Analysis: Moisture, 41.5 percent; fat, 8.8 to 27.6 percent; and salt, 2.9 percent.

Dotter

Dotter cheese is said to have been made in Nuremberg, Germany, by mixing egg yolk with skim milk and then making this mixture into cheese in the usual way.

Dry

Dry cheese, known also as Sperrkäse and Trockenkäse, is made in small dairies in the eastern part of the Bavarian Alps and in the Tyrol. It is made for home consumption and only in winter when the milk cannot be used profitably for other purposes. The method is simple. Skim milk is put into a large kettle, heated, and kept warm until it has thickened thoroughly by souring. It is then broken up and cooked until it is quite firm. A small quantity of salt is added, and sometimes some caraway seed, and the curd is then put into forms of various sizes. It is placed in a drying room to dry until it becomes very hard; it is then ready to eat.

Duel

Duel cheese is a soft, cured, cow's milk cheese made in Austria. It is 2 inches square and 1 inch thick.

Dunlop

Dunlop, a rich, white, pressed cheese made in Scotland, formerly was considered the national cheese of Scotland. However, it has been largely superseded by Cheddar which it resembles.

Analysis: Moisture, 38 percent; fat, 32 percent; and protein, 26 percent.

Edam

Edam cheese was first made in the vicinity of Edam in the Province of North Holland, Netherlands. It is known in the Netherlands by various local names, such as Manbollen, Katzenkopf, and Tete de Maure. Like Gouda, it is a semisoft to hard, sweet-curd cheese made from cow's milk. Originally it was made from whole milk but now the fat content of the milk is usually reduced to about 2.5 percent. When the cheese is made for export, the fat content is indicated on the label, according to Government specifications. Edam is made also in the United States.

Edam has a pleasingly mild, clean, sometimes salty, flavor and a rather firm and crumbly body, free of holes and openings. It usually is shaped like a flattened ball, but in the United States it is made also in a loaf shape. The cheeses usually weigh from 3½ to 4½ pounds but sometimes weigh as much as 14 pounds. In the United States, they sometimes weigh only about ¾ to 1 pound.

High-quality milk should be used in making Edam; if the milk is pasteurized, as is common in the United States, lactic starter is added. Color may be added and the milk is set with rennet extract. About 15 minutes later the curd is cut into ⅜-inch cubes, then stirred and heated to a temperature of 90° to 95° F. When the curd is sufficiently firm, part of the whey is drained off. When enough whey has drained so that the curd is exposed, the curd is pushed to the side of the vat and more whey pressed out. The curd is stirred and may be salted. The temperature of the curd should be at least 88° when it is put into the molds for pressing.

Special pressing molds, preferably metal but sometimes hardwood and lined with cheesecloth, are used. Each has a round lower section about 6 inches deep and 6 inches in diameter, with holes in the bottom for drainage, and a round cover. In the United States the cheese sometimes is pressed in rectangular loaf-shaped molds.

The molds are filled with curd, covered, and then pressed for about 30 minutes with a pressure of 20 to 30 pounds. Then the cheeses are removed from the molds and dipped in warm whey (at a temperature of 125° to 130° F.). The rough edges of curd are trimmed off, and the cheeses are bandaged and again pressed for 6 to 12 hours with a pressure of 60 to 120 pounds.

The cheeses then are rubbed with fine salt and placed in salt in special salting molds that are the same shape as the pressing molds but have no covers. Salting is continued for 5 or 6 days, and the cheeses are turned daily. In the United States, and less commonly in the Netherlands, the cheeses are salted by immersion in a salting bath for about a week; however, dry salting is preferable as it aids in producing a smooth rind.

The cheeses are scrubbed with a brush in warm water or whey, wiped dry, and then cured on shelves at a temperature of 50° to 60° F. and a relative humidity of 80 to 90 percent. They are piled in layers on the shelves to aid in flattening the top and bottom surfaces. They are washed, dried, and turned daily for a week or two, then less frequently. In some factories they are washed in a churn-like machine, and the surfaces may be smoothed by rotating the cheeses in a machine that resembles a lathe.

In the Netherlands, cheese for export is colored red, rubbed with oil, and wrapped in some transparent material; the red coating is an identifying characteristic of Edam cheese. However, cheese made for consumption within that country is rubbed with oil but not colored.

In the United States, Edam cheese is covered with red paraffin or some other tightly adhering red coating.

The cheeses are packed usually 8 to 12 in a box; for export to warm climates they may be sealed in tins. Between 8 and 9 pounds of cured cheese is obtained per 100 pounds of milk.

Analysis: Moisture, not more than 45 percent (usually 35 to 38 percent); fat, 26.5 to 29.5 percent (not less than 40 percent in the solids); protein, 27 to 29 percent; and salt, 1.6 to 2 percent.

Egg

Egg cheese, first made in the Province of Nyland, Finland, is made from fresh milk to which fresh eggs are added at the rate of 2 to 12 eggs for each 6 quarts of milk. Usually the eggs and starter are mixed and then added to the milk, but sometimes only half the eggs are added with the starter and the other half are added after the whey has drained from the curd. Best results are obtained with a cream starter.

Emiliano

Emiliano, a very hard cheese of the Italian Grana or Parmesan type, is the same as Reggiano, according to some authorities. The cheese is cylindrical and the sides may be either straight or slightly convex. It is 12 to 16 inches in diameter, 6 to 8½ inches thick, and weighs from 44 to 66 pounds. The surface is colored dark and is oiled; the interior is light yellow. The flavor varies from mild to rather sharp, and the texture is granular. Usually there are no eyes, but some cheeses have a few small eyes, unevenly distributed. The curing period usually is about a year, but it may be as long as 20 months for cheese made in the winter and 2 years for cheese made in the spring. The aged cheese is used for grating. (See Parmesan.)

Analysis: Moisture, 30 to 35 percent at 1 year; 20 to 30 percent at 2 years; fat in the solids, 32 to 39 percent.

Engadine

Engadine cheese is made in the Canton of Grisons, Switzerland, from cow's whole milk.

Analysis: Moisture, 47.30 percent; fat, 11.40 percent; and protein, 36.34 percent.

English Dairy

English Dairy cheese is a very hard cheese that is made in the same general way as Cheddar except that it is cooked much longer. It was made some years ago, mostly in the United States, and was used in cooking.

Époisse

Époisse is a soft cheese made from whole or partly skimmed milk in the Department of Côte-d'Or, France.

Eriwani

Eriwani cheese, also known by different local names such at Karab, Tali, Kurini, Elisavetpolen, and Kasach, is made from fresh ewe's milk, principally in the Caucasus. The milk is set at about 95° F. with enough rennet to coagulate it in 20 minutes. The curd is broken up, put into a sack to drain, and then pressed with stones until the whey stops running. The cheese is salted in brine.

Ervy

Ervy, a soft cheese resembling Camembert, is named for the village of Ervy in the Department of Aube, France, where it is made. It is about 7 inches in diameter and 2½ inches thick, and weighs about 4 pounds.

Farm

Farm cheese as originally made on farms in France is essentially the same as Cottage cheese. It is known by several different names, including Fromage à la Pie, Mou, Maigre, and Ferme. The making process is simple. Whole or skim milk is curdled by souring, and the whey is poured off. Sometimes the curd is enclosed in cloth on which a board and weight are placed, to hasten drainage. The curd is kneaded to further expel whey. Then salt and sometimes sweet cream are mixed with the curd, and it is molded into various sizes and shapes. The cheese usually is consumed locally, either while fresh or after curing.

In the United States, Farm cheese, which is known also as Farmer cheese and Pressed cheese and, erroneously, as Cream cheese, is a firm, pressed cheese made on farms. There is considerable variation in the cheese because the method of making differs in different localities and may not be uniform on all farms in one locality. Usually whole milk is used, but sometimes the milk is partly skimmed. Starter (which may be buttermilk of good flavor) is added to the milk at room temperature or at a temperature as high as 86° F. Rennet may be added, or the milk may be coagulated by souring. The coagulation period may be as long as 5 or 6 hours, or overnight. The curd is cut into coarse particles and stirred, and it may be heated to about 90°. The whey is drained off and the curd is stirred and salted. Then the curd is placed in bags or in cloth-lined metal hoops and pressed overnight. The next morning the cheese is removed from the bag or hoop and wrapped in parchment if it is to be eaten without much curing. If it is to be cured, the pressed cheese is dried and then coated by dipping in hot paraffin. It is cured in a moist cellar at a temperature not over 60°. The cheese should have a clean, mild flavor and should slice without crumbling. The yield is about 10 pounds per 100 pounds of whole milk and about 9 pounds per 100 pounds of partly-skimmed milk.

Feta

Feta, a white, so-called pickled cheese, is the principal soft cheese made by the shepherds in the mountainous region near Athens, Greece. It usually is made from ewe's milk but is sometimes made from goat's milk. In the United States it is made from cow's milk.

The fresh milk is poured into large containers, heated to about 95° F., and rennet is added. When firm, the curd is cut or broken. It is dipped into bottomless wooden forms—about 4 feet long, 2½ feet wide, and 8 inches deep—that have been placed on a coarse cloth on a drain table or rack. When the curd is sufficiently firm, it is cut into blocks and dry salt is rubbed on the surface. Later the same day the blocks are turned and salted again. The next morning the blocks are cut into slices about an inch thick, and these are salted and then packed either in paraffined wooden kegs that hold from 100 to 170 pounds, or in smaller tin containers. The cheese is ready to eat in about a month.

When made on a smaller scale, the curd may be dipped into a cloth bag after the milk coagulates. The bag is twisted and worked to expel most of the whey from the curd and then hung up to drain for a few hours. The curd is then taken out of the bag and cut into slices about an inch thick. The slices are sprinkled liberally with dry salt. About 24 hours later the curd is packed in wooden kegs. The cheese is ready to eat in 4 or 5 days.

Filled

Filled cheese is made from milk or skim milk to which foreign fat has been added. The foreign fat is added either by stirring it vigorously into the milk and using enough rennet to coagulate the milk quickly, or by incorporating the fat into the milk by homogenization. The cheese then is made in the usual manner. Filled cheese, whether made in the United States or imported, is a taxable product, subject to various Federal and State laws that define the conditions under which it can be manufactured and sold.

Fiore Sardo

Fiore Sardo, a hard, Italian cheese made from ewe's milk, is used as a table cheese when immature and as a condiment when fully cured. (See Sardo.)

Fløtost

Fløtost (Flø in Norwegian indicates cream) is a boiled-whey cheese made in Norway. It is like Mysost except that it contains more fat—usually not less than 20 percent of fat in the solids. (See Mysost.)

Flower

Flower cheese is a soft, cured cheese made in England from cow's whole milk. It contains the petals of various kinds of flowers, such as roses or marigolds, which accounts for its name.

Foggiano

Foggiano cheese, which resembles Cotronese and Moliterno, is made from ewe's milk in Apulia, Italy.

Fontina

Fontina is a cooked-curd, whole-milk, semisoft to hard, slightly yellow cheese with a delicate, nutty flavor and a pleasing aroma. It is made from ewe's milk in the Aosta Valley in Piedmont, Italy (it is said to be made also from cow's milk in summer), and from cow's milk in the United States. It is round and flat, like a Daisy (Cheddar), and weighs between 25 and 75 pounds—usually 33 to 44 pounds. A smaller style is called Midget Fontina.

According to Italian authorities, Fontina is similar to Montasio and Bitto, and it is said to be similar also to Battelmatt.

Fontina is made by a method similar to that used in making Gruyère. Color may be added to the milk, which is set with either rennet paste or rennet extract. The cheese is salted in brine and cured for at least 2 months. It may have a few small, round eyes. The surface may be oiled. When partly cured, it is used as a table cheese (it is frequently melted); when fully cured, it is hard and is used for grating.

Analysis: Moisture, not more than 42 percent (usually 38 percent); fat, 28 to 31.5 percent (not less than 50 percent in the solids).

Forez

Forez cheese, sometimes called d'Ambert, is made in central France. It is cylindrical in shape, about 10 inches in diameter and 6 inches thick. The making process is said to be very crude, and the cheese is cured in a very unusual way. It is placed on the floor of a cellar and covered with dirt, over which water is permitted to trickle. Frequently the cheese is spoiled by the undesirable molds and bacteria that grow on it. Good-quality Forez is said to resemble Roquefort in flavor.

Formagelle

Formagelle is a small, soft cheese made from ewe's or goat's milk in the mountains of northern Italy. It is made only in the spring or autumn; it may or may not be salted; and it is eaten while fresh.

Formaggi di Pasta Filata

Formaggi di Pasta Filata (cheese from plastic curd) refers to a group of Italian cheeses that are made by curdling the milk with rennet, warming and fermenting the curd, heating it until it is plastic, drawing it into ropes and then kneading and shaping it while it is hot and plastic. This unusual manipulation of the curd while it is being drawn and shaped results in cheese that is free of holes or pockets of air and whey and that keeps well even in warm climates. Some plastic-curd cheeses are eaten as table cheese when fresh or after curing only a few months; others are used for grating after long curing which makes them hard and sharp in flavor.

Among the best known plastic-curd cheeses are: Provolone, Caciocavallo, Moliterno, Mozzarella, Provatura, and Scamorze. Others are Katschkawalj and Kaskaval, which are made in the Balkans; Oschtjepek and Parenica, made in Slovakia; and Panedda, made in Sardinia. Many of these are known locally by other names. A description of most of the different kinds is given under its specific name.

Formaggini

Formaggini (small cheese) is a descriptive term applied to several kinds of small, Italian cheeses.

Formaggini di Lecco is a small, cylindrical, dessert cheese that is made in the vicinity of Lecco, in Lombardy, from cow's milk to which some goat's milk may be added. It may be eaten while fresh and sweet or at any stage of ripening. When fully cured, it is very piquant. It is made by a method similar to that used in making other soft cheeses. Rennet is added to the warmed milk, which is then held at a temperature of 55° F. for 24 hours. Then, with as little breaking of the curd as possible, the whey is drained off; this takes 3 or 4 hours. Salt is added to the curd, sometimes pepper, sugar, and cinnamon, and occasionally oil and vinegar. The curd is put into cylindrical molds about 1¼ inches in diameter and 2 inches deep. Each cheese weighs about 2 ounces.

Formaggini di Montpellier is another soft, Italian cheese. It is made by curdling milk with a rennet paste containing white wine, thistle blossoms, and flavoring materials.

Fresa

Fresa is a mild, sweet, soft, cooked cheese made in Sardinia from cow's milk. (See Cooked.)

Fribourg

Fribourg, made originally in Switzerland and now also in the Po valley in Italy, is a hard cheese made by a method similar to that used in making Swiss. It is a cooked-curd cheese, the curd being heated to 120° F. or slightly higher. According to some authorities Fribourg is the same as Spalen (or Sbrinz). (See Spalen.)

Friesian Clove

Friesian Clove is a spiced cheese made in the Netherlands from cow's milk that may be partly skimmed. Cloves are added to the curd before it is hooped. The cheeses are round and flat and weigh between 20 and 40 pounds. (See Spiced cheese.)

The cheese is similar in analysis to Leyden, the moisture and fat content depending on the extent to which the milk is skimmed. (See Leyden.)

Fromage à la Crème

Fromage à la Crème (French Cream Cheese) is a soft, rich cheese that is consumed without ripening. Rennet is added to fresh whole milk, or milk with cream added, and it is coagulated at a temperature of 70° F. The coagulated curd is held for 20 to 24 hours; then the free whey is removed, and the curd is cut into slices and placed in a sieve to drain. After draining is completed, the curd is kneaded to a paste. More cream may be added, then seasoning, and the curd is placed in wicker molds. The cheese is meant to be eaten while it is fresh; however, it will keep for several days under refrigeration.

Fromage Fort

Fromage Fort, which is one of several French cooked cheeses, is made in the Department of Ain. Well drained, skim-milk curd is melted, and the melted mass is put into a cloth and pressed. It is then buried in dry ashes to remove as much whey as possible. Then the mass is grated fine and, after ripening for 8 to 10 days, milk, butter, salt, pepper, wine, etc., are added, and the mixture is ripened further.

Cooked cheeses are made by similar but slightly different methods in other parts of France, and they are known by any one of several names. Canquillote, sometimes spelled Cancoillotte and also called Fromagère, is a cheese of this kind that is made in eastern France, as is also Fondue, made in Lorraine. (See Canquillote.)

Frühstück

Frühstück is a small, Limburger-type cheese made in Germany from whole or partly skimmed cow's milk. It usually is cylindrical in shape and from 2½ to 3 inches in diameter. It may be eaten without much curing, or it may be cured. During the curing process (which is similar to Romadur), yeasts and molds grow first on the surface of the cheese, followed by the so-called red cheese bacteria and formation of a surface smear. The cheese is wrapped in tinfoil or parchment. It may be wrapped when it is partly cured, in which case curing is completed at a temperature of 42° to 45° F. This type of cheese is referred to by various names, such as breakfast, dessert, appetite, and delicate cheese.

Analysis: Moisture, 40 to 60 percent; fat, 17 to 34 percent; and protein, 15 to 25 percent.

Gaiskäsli

Gaiskäsli is a soft cheese made from goat's milk in Germany and Switzerland. The milk is set with enough rennet to coagulate it in about 40 minutes. The curd is then broken up, stirred, and dipped into cylindrical molds about 3 inches in diameter. Each mold is filled with enough curd to make a cheese 1½ or 2 inches thick that weighs about half a pound. The molds are set on mats which allow the whey to drain freely, and salt is sprinkled on the surface of the cheeses. After 2 days the cheeses are turned and salted on the other surface. The cheese ripens in about 3 weeks and is said to have a very pleasing flavor.

Gammelost

Gammelost, made from sour skim milk in Norway (principally in the counties of Hardanger and Sogn), is a semisoft, blue-mold, ripened table cheese, with a rather sharp, aromatic flavor. The principal ripening molds are species of *Mucor, Rhizopus,* and *Penicillium.* The rind is brownish and the interior is brownish-yellow with a blue-green tint; the color darkens with age. The cheese is round and flat, usually about 6 inches in diameter, and from 5 to 6 inches thick. It weighs usually between 6 and 9 pounds, although some cheeses may weigh more than 25 pounds. The cheese is made by one method in Hardanger and by a slightly different method in Sogn.

In the Hardanger method, about 0.5 percent of lactic starter is added to skim milk and, after souring for a day or two at 66° F., it is put into a vat and warmed slowly to 145°. After about 30 minutes at that temperature, the curd is dipped into cloth bags and pressed heavily. After pressing, the curd is removed from the bags, broken up, and packed in cloth-lined forms which then are covered and placed in boiling whey for 3½ hours. This practically sterilizes the cheese and changes its texture. The next day the cheese is removed from the forms and put in a warm place for a day or two to dry, after which it is pierced with metal needles that have been inoculated with a mold—*Penicillium roqueforti,* or a related species—that develops a greenish-blue mold throughout the cheese. It is then placed on shelves in a curing room which is maintained at a temperature of 50° to 55° and a relative humidity of 90 percent. A *Mucor,* which is propagated by handrubbing the surface with mycelium from older cheeses, develops on the surface of the cheese. The cheese is inverted daily or at least every other day, and rubbed or cleaned if necessary. The curing period is about 4 weeks or somewhat longer.

In the Sogn method, 1½ to 2 percent of starter is added to the skim milk, and it is soured at a temperature of 72° to 75° F.; on the second day, the milk may be transferred to the cheese vat where souring is completed at a temperature of 77°. When the milk has reached the desired stage of souring (a later stage than in the Hardanger method), it is heated slowly to the boiling point. The whey is removed, and the curd is heated to about 195°, then placed in forms to drain. The forms are covered with cloths and kept in a warm place. After the whey has drained off, the curd is removed from the forms, crumbled fine, inoculated with mold, and repressed. The next day the cheeses are removed from the forms, dried in a warm place for 4 or 5 days, and then taken to the curing room. The curing process is the same as in the Hardanger method.

In both methods, after the cheese is partly cured, it may be put in chests lined with straw that has been treated with heated juniper extract. The yield of cured cheese is between 4 and 5½ pounds per 100 pounds of skim milk.

Analysis: Moisture, not more than 52 percent (usually 46 to 52 percent); fat, 0.5 to 1.0 percent; protein, 45 to 50 percent; ash, 2.5 percent; and salt (in the ash), 1 percent.

Gautrias

Gautrias cheese, which resembles Port du Salut, is made in the Department of Mayenne, France. The cheese is cylindrical in shape, and each cheese weighs about 5 pounds. (See Port du Salut.)

Gavot

Gavot cheese is made from cow's, ewe's, or goat's milk in the Department of Hautes-Alpes, France.

Geheimrath

Geheimrath, which is made in small quantities in the Netherlands, is a deep yellow cheese that resembles a small Gouda and is made by a similar method. (See Gouda.)

Géromé

Géromé, also known as Gérardmer, is a soft cheese made in the Vosges mountain region of France, and in Switzerland. It derives its name from Gérardmer, a village in the region where it has been made for a century or more.

Cow's milk is used in making Géromé, but at times a little goat's milk is added. Fresh milk is set with rennet at a temperature between 80° and 90° F. About half an hour later, the curd is cut into rather large cubes; an hour after cutting, the whey is dipped off. Sometimes anise is added to the curd at this time, then the curd is put into cylindrical hoops of wood or tin. The hoops vary in size but usually are 6 or 7 inches in diameter, and they are piled one on another to a height of 14 or 15 inches. The cheeses are turned after 6 hours and again after 12 hours, then twice daily for the next 2 or 3 days, the hoops being changed each time. The temperature of the room should be between 60° and 70° during this process. After hooping, the cheeses are salted. The quantity of salt used is from 3 to 3.5 percent of the weight of the cheese.

Then the cheeses are dried in a well ventilated room for several days. When dry, they are transferred to the curing cellar, where they are turned frequently and washed with warm salty water to keep the surface free of mold. They are cured for 6 weeks to 4 months, depending on their size; they range in weight from 8 ounces to 5 pounds or more. The cured cheese often has a greenish tint.

Gex

Gex, a hard, cow's-milk cheese, is named for the town of Gex in the Department of Ain, France, where it was first made more than a hundred years ago. Production has been confined largely to this region, but some Gex is made in the Departments of Jura and Isère, in southeastern France. It is one of the group of blue-mold cheeses known in France as Bleu cheeses or Fromage Persillé; the group includes Sassenage, Septmoncel, and several others resembling Roquefort.

Rennet is added to the fresh milk as soon as possible after milking. After a coagulation period of 1½ to 2 hours, the curd is broken up and stirred until it is in a semiliquid condition. After about 10 minutes, during which time the curd settles to the bottom of the vat, the whey is drained off. Then the curd is worked by hand, salted slightly, and put into hoops about 12 inches in diameter and 5 inches deep. In about an hour the cheeses are turned, and a disk and weight are placed on them. Turning is repeated 3 or 4 times a day; the hoops are removed at the end of the first day. The cheeses are salted and then taken to the curing room where a penicillium mold, which soon develops on them, gives them a bluish appearance. (The mold is not introduced into the interior of the cheese while it is being made, as is done with Roquefort.) The curing process requires from 3 to 4 months and is completed in cellars or natural caves. A cured cheese weighs between 14 and 15 pounds.

Analysis: Moisture, 32 percent; fat, 30 percent; and protein, 30 percent.

Gislev

Gislev is a hard cheese made in Denmark from cow's milk.

Analysis: Moisture, 49.2 percent; fat, 3 percent; and protein, 41.5 precent.

Gjetost

Gjetost is a Norwegian boiled-whey cheese. The "Gje-" indicates that it is a goat's-milk product. However, it is commonly made from the whey obtained when cheese is made from a mixture of cow's milk and not less than 10 percent of goat's milk. When cheese is made from goat's milk only and the whey so obtained is made into boiled-whey cheese, it is called ekte (genuine) Gjetost, or Geitmysost.

The whey is stirred and condensed by heating to about one-fourth its original volume, when it will have the consistency of heavy cream. The cheese is golden brown; its principal constituent is lactose. Usually a cheese weighs about 9 pounds, but cheeses weighing 1 pound and ½ pound are also made. (See Mysost.)

Analysis: Moisture, 13 percent; fat in the solids, 33 percent.

Gloucester

Gloucester is a hard cheese made in England in the county of Gloucester, for which it is named. Gloucester and Derby are said to be almost identical and are made in practically the same way. Single Gloucesters, made originally in farm dairies, are 16 inches in diameter, between 2 and 3 inches thick, and weigh about 15 pounds. Double Gloucesters, which have become relatively uncommon, are also 16 inches in diameter, but they are between 4 and 5 inches thick and weigh about 24 pounds. When the cheese is about a month old it may be colored with red or brown dye.

The surface of an uncolored cheese is clear yellow and is said to have well-developed blue mold on the sides. The cheese is very firm, the texture is smooth, close, and waxy, and the flavor is mild and rich. (See Derby.)

Analysis: Moisture, 32.3 to 36 percent; fat, 29 to 33 percent; protein, 27.6 to 28.1 percent; and salt, 2 to 2.5 percent.

Glumse

Glumse, which resembles Cottage cheese, is made in western Prussia. Skim milk, curdled by souring, is heated until firm either by heating slowly to about 105° F., which causes the curd to contract and expel whey, or by pouring hot water into the sour, coagulated milk. A perforated ladle or dipper is used to remove the curd, which is drained in a sieve. Milk or cream is mixed with the curd before it is eaten.

Goat's- Milk

Goat's-milk cheeses of many kinds are made by using goat's milk instead of cow's milk and making the cheese in the usual way. Also, cheese often is made from a mixture of goat's milk and either cow's milk, or ewe's milk, or both. In many instances, goat's-milk cheese is not identified by any particular name to distinguish it from cow's milk cheese. However, in France, Chevret or Chevrotin designate goat's-milk cheese, and Gratairon, Lamothe, and Poitiers are local names for cheeses made from goat's milk. In Italy, Formaggio di Capra designates goat's-milk cheese, and the adjective "caprino" is used to indicate a product made from goat's milk. In German-speaking countries, Ziegenkäse or Gaiskäsli designate goat's-milk cheese. However, in certain parts of Germany and in Switzerland, Gaiskäsli is the name of a particular soft cheese made from goat's milk. (See Gaiskäsli.)

Gomost

Gomost is a whole-milk Norwegian cheese, made usually from cow's milk but also at times from goat's milk. The milk is curdled with a small quantity of rennet and is condensed by heating until it has a butter-like consistency. The method for making Gomost is very much like the method for making Mysost. (See Mysost.)

Gorgonzola

Gorgonzola, known also as Stracchino di Gorgonzola, is the principal blue-green veined cheese of Italy. It is said to have been made in the Po Valley since 879 A. D. It is named for the village of Gorgonzola, near Milan, but very little is made there now. It is made chiefly in Lombardy—where its manufacture is an important industry—and in Piedmont. It formerly was made during September and October, because winter conditions favor curing. However, curing caves have been built in cliffs in the Alps, especially near Lecco, and it is now made throughout the year. It is made also in numerous other countries; in the United States it is made mostly in Wisconsin and Michigan.

The interior of the cheese is mottled with blue-green veins like those in Roquefort. In Italy the mold is called *Penicillium glaucum* rather than *P. roqueforti*—the name used in the United States—but it is the same mold, at least in some instances. The surface of the cheese formerly was protected by covering it with a reddish coat resembling clay, which is prepared from barite or brick dust, lard or tallow, and coloring matter. Now, however, tinfoil and stout containers are used. The cheeses, which are cylindrical and flat, are from 8½ to 11 inches in diameter and from 6½ to 8 inches thick, and weigh between 14 and 17 pounds.

Evening milk is warmed to 86° F., or sometimes 90°, and enough rennet added to coagulate it in 15 to 20 minutes. The curd is cut slowly, allowed to settle, collected in a cloth, and hung up to drain overnight in a room in which the temperature is between 60° and 68°. Curd is prepared similarly from morning milk and is drained but not cooled. Expandable wooden hoops, 8 to 12 inches in diameter and 10½ to 12 inches deep, are lined with cloth and placed on rye straw or drain mats on a drain table. The two lots of curd are cut into rather large slices or portions, and mold powder is sprinkled in as the portions are placed alternately in the hoops. The warm (morning) curd is placed mainly in the bottom and at the periphery and piled up on top, with the cool (evening) curd between. This distribution of the curd is considered a critical part of the making process. It aids in developing mechanical openings in the interior of the cheese and in binding the surface and making it smooth. The piled-up curd is covered with the edges of the cloth lining, and the cheese is turned. It is repressed and turned every 2 hours at first and less frequently thereafter for a day. Then the cloth is removed and the cheese is replaced in the hoops, left on the straw or drain mat, and turned twice daily for several days. It is salted with dry salt, heavily at first and lightly later, a total of 8 to 12 times in from 1 to 3 weeks. The temperature of the room is held at 50° or a little higher.

The cheese is dried and initial curing takes place in a room in which the temperature is between 52° and 60° F., and the relative humidity is 75 to 80 percent. During this period—20 to 30 days—the cheese is turned and rubbed by hand every other day and kept clean. It is scraped with a knife occasionally.

The cheese then is moved to a room in which the temperature is from 48° to 50° F., and the relative humidity 85 to 90 percent, where the second stage of curing takes place. This period lasts 2 months. If the cheese was not punched earlier, it is punched at this stage (see Roquefort).

Final curing takes place in a room in which the temperature is from 40° to 43° F., and the relative humidity is even higher than in the other curing rooms. The entire curing period is at least 90 days, frequently is 6 months, and may be a year.

The yield is 13 to 15 pounds of fresh cheese, or 10 to 12 pounds of cured cheese, per 100 pounds of milk.

Analysis: Moisture, not more than 42 percent (usually 35 to 38 percent); fat, 31 to 33 percent (not less than 50 percent of the solids); protein, 24 to 26 percent; and salt, 3 to 4 percent.

Gouda

Gouda, first made in the vicinity of Gouda in the Province of South Holland, Netherlands, is a semisoft to hard, sweet-curd cheese similar to Edam except that it contains more fat. It is made from whole or partly skimmed cow's milk, but skimmed less than milk used in making Edam. Gouda usually is shaped like a flattened sphere and pressed in molds with rounded ends. The molds vary in size but usually are nearly 14 inches in diameter and 4½ to 5 inches deep. The cheeses usually weigh between 10 and 25 pounds but may weigh as little as 6 or as much as 50 pounds. Gouda is made also in a loaf weighing about 8 pounds. A so-called "baby Gouda" is oval, weighs a pound or slightly less, may be coated with red wax, and wrapped in a cellophane-type wrapper. The red surface is not necessarily an identifying characteristic, however, as it is of domestic and imported Edam.

Gouda is made in much the same way as Edam. (See Edam.) Some slight modifications in the details of manufacture are mentioned here. Although the milk may be set at any temperature between 84° and 90° F., it usually is set at 90°. After the curd is cut, the whey is drained off, heated, and poured back into the vat. This procedure is repeated once or twice, in order to increase the temperature of the curd to between 100° and 106°. Other factors being equal, cheese made from curd heated to the higher temperatures (within this range) will have a firmer body, will cure more slowly, and will have better keeping quality. Some salt is added to the curd before it is put into the hoops (molds) for pressing. Salting is usually completed by immersing the cheese in a salt solution; however, it may be completed in the curing room by rubbing dry salt on the cheese daily for 7 to 10 days. The cheese cures in 2 to 3 months, but it improves in flavor if it is cured for 5 to 6 months.

About 12½ pounds of uncured cheese can be made from 100 pounds of whole milk, and about 8 pounds of cured cheese from 100 pounds of milk containing from 3 to 3.5 percent of fat.

Analysis: Moisture, not more than 45 percent (usually 36 to 43.5 percent); fat, 29 to 30.5 percent (not less than 46 percent in the solids); protein, 25 to 26 percent; and salt, 1.5 to 2 percent.

Gournay

Gournay, a soft cheese of the fresh Neufchâtel type, is named for the village of Gournay in the Department of Seine-Inférieure, France, where it is made. It is similar to the Cream cheese made in the United States. It usually is round and flat, about 3 inches in diameter and ¾ inch thick, and weighs about 4 ounces. However, it is made also in 2⅓ inch squares that are ¾ inch thick. Gournay contains between 1 and 2 percent of salt, and usually is wrapped in tinfoil. A similar cheese, Gournay fleuri, is ripened to some extent with a surface mold—*Penicillium candidum*—which gives it the flavor of Camembert.

Goya

Goya cheese, manufactured in the Province of Corrientes in Argentina, resembles medium-cured Asiago. Either whole or partly skimmed milk is heated to a temperature between 75° and 85° F., and enough rennet is added to coagulate it in 15 to 30 minutes. The curd is cut and put in sacks to drain, after which it is pressed in molds and then salted.

Grana

Grana refers to a group of Italian cheeses with the following special characteristics: Granular body and texture (hence the name Grana); sharp flavor (they are widely known for intensity and exquisiteness of flavor); hardness (they are among the most suitable for grating); very small eyes; good keeping quality, even in hot climates; and excellent shipping properties (they require no careful packaging).

Grana-type cheeses are said to have been made in the Po Valley as long ago as 1200 A. D., at which time that was the most important cheese-making center in Europe. According to Italian authorities, there are two main types of Grana cheeses: (1) Grana Lombardo, which is made largely in the Province of Lombardy (north of the Po); and (2) Grana Reggiano, which is made largely in Reggio, in the Province of Emilia (south of the Po). There are numerous subvarieties of each type, named usually for the place of manufacture. Lodigiano (named for Lodi) is similar to Lombardo; Emiliano (for Emilia) and Parmigiano (for Parma) are similar to Reggiano, and there are others. The subvarieties differ principally in details of manufacture (acidity of the milk, cutting the curd, cooking temperature, curing period, etc.), and in shape and size.

Considerable quantities of both types of Grana cheeses are exported from Italy, usually under the name Parmesan (the common name outside of Italy, and sometimes in Italy, for these cheeses). Both types are imported into the United States as Parmesan, and Grana Reggiano is also imported as Reggiano Parmesan. Both types are made in the United States and may be known by either name (Parmesan or Reggiano).

A more complete description of each of these cheeses is given under its specific name.

Granular or Stirred-Curd

Granular or Stirred-curd cheese, which is made in considerable quantities in the United States, is similar to Cheddar and Colby. It may be made from either raw or pasteurized milk. The raw-milk cheese must be cured for at least 60 days unless it is to be used in manufacturing.

This cheese is made in the same way as Cheddar, except that (as in making Colby) the curd is not matted and milled. However, water is not added to the curd while it is being stirred to cool it, as is done in making Colby.

After the curd has been cut, stirred, and heated (as in the Cheddar process), some of the whey is drained off and the curd is stirred and drained alternately, or stirred continually, until it is dry enough to salt.

After salting, with continual stirring, the curd finally is placed in hoops and pressed like Cheddar. (See Cheddar.)

Analysis: Moisture, not more than 39 percent (usually 37 percent); fat in the solids, not less than 50 percent; and salt, 1.5 to 1.8 percent.

Grated

Grated cheese is prepared by grinding hard, dry, low-fat, well-aged natural cheese to a powder. Italian cheeses of the Parmesan type are usually used; also such cheeses as Asiago old, dry Jack, Romano, Sapsago (Schabziger), and Sbrinz. The cheese should be cured for at least 6 months before it is grated. After it is grated, it may be dried further on trays in a current of hot, dry air; then it is packed in moisture-and-air-proof containers.

Some manufacturers prepare a so-called "grated" cheese by adding nonfat dry milk solids and cheese color to dry (usually low-fat) American-type cheese, grinding the mixture, and then drying it. This product, however, usually lacks full flavor.

The U.S. Department of Agriculture developed a method for dehydrating natural American Cheddar cheese of normal fat content without loss of fat. The cheese is first grated and partly dried immediately in moving air at room temperature. This seals up the fat in numerous casehardened particles of curd; then the cheese is dried in a tunnel or chamber drier with a gradual increase in temperature and circulation of air. The dried cheese can be powdered for use as grated cheese.

Gray

Gray cheese, which is so named because the interior of the cured cheese is grayish in color, is made in the Tyrol from sour skim milk. When the milk has curdled, the curd is firmed by moderate heating. It is then dipped into cheesecloth; the flocculent material at the bottom of the kettle is mixed carefully and thoroughly with the rest of the curd, in order to insure a uniform product. The curd is then put under pressure for about 10 minutes, after which it is broken up by hand or in a mill, and salt and pepper are added. To insure proper ripening, a little grated well-ripened gray cheese or bread crumbs with the characteristic mold growth are mixed with the curd, and it is put into forms of various shapes and sizes which are perforated to facilitate drainage. The cheese is pressed in the forms for about 24 hours, and then taken to the drying room where the temperature is maintained at 70° F. The length of the drying period is determined by the appearance of the cheese. As soon as it has dried sufficiently, it is taken to the curing cellar. The cured cheese has a pleasant taste.

Gruyère

Gruyère cheese (Greyèrzerkäse), also known as Groyer and in some localities as Vachelin, has been made for more than 200 years. It is named for the village of Gruyère, in the Canton of Fribourg, Switzerland, which is near the French border. The manufacture of Gruyère cheese is an important industry in France (especially in the Departments of Daubs and Jura) and in nearby areas in Switzerland.

Gruyère cheeses are about 20 inches in diameter, from 4 to 4¾ inches thick, and weigh between 55 and 110 pounds. Gruyère is made from cow's whole milk in much the same way as Swiss; however, Gruyère is smaller, has smaller eyes and a sharper flavor, and usually is cured in a more humid curing room. There often is an aroma of ammonia in the curing room, indicating some surface ripening. The cheese is cured for not less than 90 days.

Analysis: Moisture, 33 to not more than 39 percent; fat, 29 to 33 percent (usually 50 but not less than 45 percent in the solids); protein, 26 to 29 percent; and salt, 2 percent.

Güssing

Güssing is an Austrian cheese that resembles very much the Brick cheese made in the United States; it is made in practically the same way, except that skim milk is used. The cheeses weigh between 4 and 8 pounds. (See Brick.)

Hand

Hand cheese, a small, sour-milk, surface-ripened cheese, is so named because originally is was molded in final shape by hand, and still is in some parts of Europe. It is very popular among Germanic peoples and is made in several countries. There are many local names for Hand cheese, among which are the following: In Germany—Mainzer Handkäse or Harzkäse, Alte Kuhkäse, or Berliner Kuhkäse, Ihlefeld, Satz, and Thuringia Caraway cheese; in Austria—Olmützer Quargeln and Olmützer Bierkäse; and in Russia—Livlander. Some of these are described under their particular names.

The method of making Hand cheese differs in different localities. Following is a general description: Buttermilk or lactic starter is added to skim milk, which is then coagulated at room temperature. The curd is broken up or cut, stirred, and heated slowly to a temperature of about 120° F. It is held at this temperature for about 3 hours, and stirred for the first hour. At the end of the heating period, the curd is put in cloths or in forms, while the whey drains either with or without pressure. Then the curd is either mixed thoroughly or ground in a curd mill, and salted. Sometimes caraway seed is added. The cheeses then are molded by hand, or pressed in small forms, into the desired shape. They are dried in a warm room and then placed on shelves in a cool, moist cellar to cure. The cheeses are kept clean while curing. When surface ripening has begun, they are wrapped and packed in boxes. They are cured for 6 to 8 weeks at a temperature no higher than 50°. At higher temperatures they cure too rapidly. Well-ripened Hand cheese has a very sharp, pungent flavor and aroma; the consumer sometimes must become accustomed to it before he finds it agreeable.

In the United States, cheese of this type is made by farm families of German descent in Pennsylvania and in a few factories in New York, Wisconsin, and northern Illinois. The curd is prepared in much the same way as Cottage-cheese curd, either with or without rennet. The drained curd is salted and either molded by hand or pressed in forms into cakes 2 to 3 inches in diameter and less than an inch thick. The cheeses then are cured in a cool, moist room. Action of bacteria, yeasts, and molds causes surface ripening, and a smear usually appears. Regulation of the temperature and humidity in the curing room is essential to control surface ripening; it is controlled also by frequent rubbing or washing of the cheese.

Queso de mano (Hand cheese) is a sour-milk, cooked-curd, small, round cheese made in small quantities in Venezuela and some other Latin-American countries for local consumption. Usually it is made from cow's milk, but it is said to be made also from goat's milk. The cheeses are 6 or 7 inches in diameter.

Harzkäse

Harzkäse is a type of Hand cheese made in Germany. It usually is about 2 inches in diameter, from ½ to ¾ inch thick, and weighs about 4 ounces. (See Hand cheese.)

Analysis: Moisture, 50 to 56 percent; fat, 1 to 2 percent; protein, 22 to 37 percent; and salt, 4 percent.

Hauskäse

Hauskäse is the German name for a Limburger-type cheese made in the shape of a disk with a diameter of about 10 inches.

Hay

Hay cheese, also called Fromage de Foin, is a skim-milk cheese made in the Department of Seine-Inférieure, France. It derives its name from the fact that it is ripened on freshly cut hay, which imparts a characteristic aroma to the cheese. In some respects it resembles a poor grade of Livarot. It is about 10 inches in diameter and 2 or 3 inches thick.

The milk is set with rennet at a temperature of 80° to 85° F. In about an hour the curd is cut and the whey is removed. The curd is pressed to remove more whey after which it is pressed by hand into molds. After draining for about 2 days, it is put in the drying room for about 3 weeks. Then it is taken to the curing cellar and buried in hay, where it remains for 6 weeks to 3 months. The cheese is then ready for sale. Most of it is consumed locally.

Herkimer

Herkimer, which is a Cheddar-type cheese, was made in rather large quantities in Herkimer County, N. Y., at one time but now is made only to a limited extent, if at all. There is considerable acid development and the cheese is cured for a long time. As no color is added to the milk the cheese may be nearly white. It has a fairly dry and crumbly texture and a sharp flavor.

Herrgårdsost

Herrgårdsost (Manor cheese) is very popular in Sweden, where it has been made since the 1890's. It has a medium firm, pliable body, a mild, sweet, nutty flavor, and a pleasing aroma. The cured cheese contains eyes similar to those in Gruyère, that is, they are smaller than those in Swiss cheese. The cheeses usually are about 15 inches in diameter, 4 to 6 inches thick, and weigh from 26 to 33 pounds.

Herrgårdsost is made from partly skimmed cow's milk, usually pasteurized. Lactic starter is added to the milk, and propionic bacteria are added if the milk does not contain enough to cause normal eye formation. The curd is heated to a temperature of not more than 111° F. At some factories, the curd is removed from the whey and pressed in hoops in the conventional manner. At other factories, the milk is set in a long vat with rounded ends, and after the curd is heated some of the whey is drawn off. Perforated metal gates are inserted at each end of the vat and pulled toward the center, thus enclosing the curd in a rectangular area. A press lid is lowered onto the curd, and the curd is pressed under the remaining whey with a hydraulic press. Strong pressure is applied for 20 to 30 minutes. Then the whey is drained off, and the flat, rectangular block of curd is cut vertically into smaller blocks, one for each cheese. The curd for each cheese is placed in a round, metal, cloth-lined hoop, and the hoops are placed one above another in tiers and pressed in a hydraulic press.

The cheeses are salted in brine; from 10 to 14 days later they are dipped in paraffin or cheese wax. They are cured for 3 to 4 months—the first month at a temperature of 63° to 68° F. and then at 50° to 59°. Between 8½ and 9 pounds of cheese is obtained from 100 pounds of partly skimmed milk.

Analysis: Moisture, 39.5 percent; fat, 29 percent (45 percent or slightly more in the solids); protein, 27 percent; and salt, 1.5 percent.

Hervé

Hervé is a Limburger-type cheese made in Belgium. The cheeses are about 6 inches square and 3 inches thick.

Analysis: Moisture, 37.5 percent; fat, 23.9 percent; and protein, 20.9 percent.

Holstein Health

Holstein Health cheese, known locally as Holstein Gesundheitskäse, is a German cooked cheese made from sour, skim milk. The curdled milk is heated, the whey drained off, and the curd pressed heavily. It is then mixed well and put into a kettle. Cream and salt are added, and it is stirred while being heated over a fire to a melting temperature, after which it is put into molds which hold about half a pound.

Holstein Skim-milk

Holstein Skim-milk cheese (German, Holsteiner Magerkäse), or so-called Buttenkäse, is made principally in the Prussian Province of Schleswig-Holstein and nearby areas. Usually the skim milk contains about 0.75 percent of fat, and the cheese contains not more than 15 percent of fat in the solids. When practically all the fat is removed from the milk, the cheese is called Leather cheese (see p. 66). In some instances as much as 6 percent of fresh buttermilk is added to the skim milk.

The milk may be pasteurized, lactic starter and cheese color are added, and rennet is added at a temperature of 80° to 86° F. About 30 minutes later the curd is cut into rather large pieces and then left for about 5 minutes to become firmer. Stirring and cutting then are continued for another 30 minutes, until the pieces of curd are about ¼ inch in diameter, and, if considerable fat was left in the milk, the curd is warmed to 96°. Then the whey is dipped or drained off, and the curd is collected, stirred, and pressed somewhat to remove more whey. It is kneaded carefully, and 2½ to 3 pounds of salt is added per 1,000 pounds of milk. Caraway seed may be added also. The curd is placed in cylindrical cloth-lined forms, 10½ to 12 inches in diameter and depth. The cheeses are pressed for about 12 hours, with gradually increasing pressure until the final pressure is 10 to 12 times the weight of the cheese. They are turned and redressed once or twice. Then they are removed from the press and are placed in a rather dry room for 2 or 3 weeks, after which they are cured in a moist room at a temperature of 50° to 57°. They are cleaned and turned daily while drying and about twice a week while curing. The cheese is fully cured in 5 to 6 months. Between 7 and 10 pounds of cheese (depending on the fat content of the milk) is obtained per 100 pounds of milk. Cheeses weigh from 12 to 14 pounds.

Hop

Hop (or Hopfen) is a German cheese that is cured between layers of hops, which accounts for its name. It is very much like Nieheimer, which is also packed with hops for curing. In fact, although they are not identical, Nieheimer is known as Hop cheese in some localities. Likewise, in some localities Hop cheese is called Krauterkäse, although elsewhere Krauterkäse is a local name for Sapsago (Schabziger) cheese. (See Nieheimer and Sapsago.)

After the curd is prepared and salted, spices such as caraway seed usually are mixed in, and it is ripened for 3 or 4 days. Then the ripened curd is mixed with fresh curd, and the mixture is molded into small cheeses. These are placed in a well-ventilated room to dry, and when they are quite dry they are packed in casks to ripen between layers of hops. Cheeses are about 2½ inches in diameter and an inch thick, and weigh 3 to 4 ounces.

Hvid Gjetost

Hvid Gjetost is a goat's-milk cheese made in Norway, for local consumption. The milk is set at 70° F. or higher. The curd is broken up and cooked in the usual manner, after which it is pressed in forms 9 or 10 inches long, 6 inches wide, and 4 inches deep.

Ilha

Ilha, a Portuguese word meaning island, is the name of a rather firm, cow's milk cheese made in the Azores and exported to Portugal. The cheese is 10 to 12 inches in diameter and about 4 inches thick.

Analysis: Moisture, 28 to 37 percent; fat, 27 to 32 percent; protein, 24 to 31 percent; and salt, 1.5 percent.

Incanestrato

Incanestrato (basketed) cheese is so named because the curd often is pressed in wicker molds (baskets). The imprint of the wicker remains on the cheese.

As made in Sicily, it is a plastic-curd (pasta filata) cheese made from ewe's milk or a mixture of ewe's and cow's milk. When made from ewe's milk only, it is called Pecorino Incanestrato. The milk is curdled, preferably with kid rennet, in about 45 minutes. The curd is stirred thoroughly, and sometimes water is added. After the curd settles, it is separated from the whey; it may be pressed by hand and may be allowed to ferment for 2 or 3 days. Then it is heated in whey, pressed and salted. Various spices may be added. Pepper may be added, and then it is called Pepato. The cheese is cured for about a year.

Majocchino, a similar cheese, is made from cow's, goat's, or ewe's milk in the Province of Messina, Sicily. It contains olive oil.

In the United States, Incanestrato and also Pepato are made from cow's milk, usually by the Romano process. (See Romano.)

Isigny

Isigny cheese, which is said to be of American origin, is named for a town in France. It is the same shape as Camembert—about 5 inches in diameter and 1 to 2 inches thick—and is made like Camembert except that the cheese is washed and rubbed occasionally while it is curing to check the growth of molds on the surface. The ripened cheese has a firmer body than Camembert and has a flavor and aroma like mild Limburger. The composition varies considerably. (See Camembert.)

Island of Orléans

Island of Orléans cheese (Le Fromage Raffiné de l'Ile d'Orléans) is a soft cheese with a strong, characteristic flavor. It has been made since 1679 by farmers on the Island of Orléans, which is in the St. Lawrence

River a few miles below Quebec. Undoubtedly the method was introduced by early settlers from France, and the cheese resembles other soft, piquant French cheeses.

Whole milk is set with rennet directly after the cows are milked. After the milk coagulates, the curd is cut; then the whey is drained off and the curd is transferred to forms on rush mats. The forms of curd are turned frequently. When firm, the cheeses are removed from the forms, and they are wrapped in cloth for curing. They are ripened partly by molds and yeasts that grow on the surface. They are fully cured in about 3 weeks and deteriorate rapidly after curing is completed. They are round and flat, and each cheese weighs about 5 ounces. About 12 pounds of cheese is obtained from 100 pounds of milk.

Analysis: Moisture, 50 percent or slightly more; and fat, 25 percent.

Italian

Italian cheese refers not only to varieties now made in Italy, but also to those that originated in Italy and that now are made in other countries as well. Parmesan, Romano, and Provolone are among the best known, and they are made in considerble quantities in the United States. Parmesan, one of the group known in Italy as Grana, includes Lodigiano or Lombardo, Reggiano-Parmigiano or Emiliano, and the less-known varieties, Veneto or Venezza and Bresciano or Bagozzo.

The plastic-curd (pasta filata) cheeses include the hard Caciocavallo, Provolone, Provoletti, Panedda, Pera di vacca, Casigiolu, and Moliterno, and the soft Provole or Provatura, Scamorze, Mozzarella, Manteca, and Trecce.

Swiss-type cheeses made in Italy include Sbrinz or Spalen, Fribourg, Battelmatt, Montasio, Fontina, Bitto, and Urseren. Other hard cheeses are Romano, Sardo, Incanestrato, Asiago, Pepato, Bra, and Cotronese.

The Italian blue-green veined cheeses are Gorgonzola and similar cheeses, including Gex, Pannarone, Sassenage, Septmoncel, and Moncenisio.

The principal soft cheeses are Bel Paese, Crescenza, Cacio fiore, Raviggiolo, Robbiole, Robbiolini, Reblochon, Mascarpone, Formagelle, Formaggio crema, Mont d'Or, Montpellier, Milano or Quartirolo, and Bernarde. Fresh Ricotta, which is made from coagulated whey protein, usually with 5 to 10 percent of whole or skim milk added, is another soft cheese.

Formaggio and cacio mean cheese. Stracchino, which refers to a condition of milk for making cheese, has come to mean soft, rich, ripened cheese in northern Italy.

Pecorino, used with the name of a cheese, indicates that it was made from ewe's milk (as Pecorino Romano); Caprino, that it was made from goat's milk; and Vacchino, that it was made from cow's milk.

The names of some Italian cheeses indicate the season in which they are made. Maggengo refers to cheese made between April and September, chiefly Milano and Grana; Quartirolo, to Milano (or Milano-type) cheese made from September to November; Terzolo, to cheese made in winter, chiefly Milano and Grana; and Invernengo, to cheese made in winter, chiefly Grana.

Jochberg

Jochberg cheese is made in the Tyrol from a mixture of cow's and goat's milk. The cheese is about 20 inches in diameter, 4 inches thick, and weighs about 45 pounds.

Josephine

Josephine cheese, which is made in Silesia from cow's whole milk, is a soft cheese that is cured in small cylindrical packages.

Kajmak

Kajmak (a Turkish word meaning "cream") is a cream cheese made from ewe's milk in Serbia, where it is a very popular food. It is also known as Serbian butter. The making process is primitive. Milk is boiled and then poured into large shallow pans, which are usually made of wood. About 12 hours later the cream is collected, usually salted, and it is put into wooden containers. It is usually sold while fresh when the flavor is mild; however, as it ages it develops more flavor and it may develop as much flavor as Roquefort. Different lots vary greatly in composition.

Analysis (average of 10 samples): Moisture, 31.55 percent; fat, 55.79 percent; protein, 6.25 percent; ash, 4.50 percent; and salt (in the ash), 3.07 percent.

Kareish

Kareish is one of the so-called pickled cheeses made in Egypt. Skim milk is coagulated by souring, the whey is drained, dry salt is added, and the curd is packed in earthenware vessels in a salt-brine solution. It is made like Domiati, except that salt is added to the curd, not to the milk. (See Domiati.)

Karut

Karut is a very dry, hard, skim-milk cheese made in Afghanistan and northwestern India.

Kaskaval

Kaskaval is made from partly-skimmed ewe's milk in Siebenbürgen, Rumania, by a method that is very similar to that used in making Katschkawalj. (See Katschkawalj.) The ripened curd is placed in a tub and worked until it is elastic, as in making Provolone, and then it is put into oval forms 5 to 8 inches in diameter and about 3 inches deep. Holes are punched in the cheese to let whey out and to admit salt. The cheese is salted in brine for a few hours and later rubbed with salt. It may be marketed within a month. It is cured for 2 to 3 months. The cheeses weigh 4½ to 6½ pounds.

Analysis: Moisture, 50.5 percent; fat, 14.1 percent; protein, 28.1 percent; and ash, 4.8 percent.

Peneteleu (Cascaval de Peneteleu) is a drier cheese made in Rumania from ewe's milk by a similar method.

Analysis: Moisture, 27.41 percent; fat, 20.13 percent; protein, 45.63 percent; ash, 5.11 percent; and salt (in the ash), 1.91 percent.

A variation, containing more moisture and less fat, is called Peneteleu-Burduf cheese.

Kasseri

Kasseri is a hard cheese made in Greece, usually from ewe's milk.

Katschkawalj

Katschkawalj is a plastic-curd, Caciocavallo-type cheese made from ewe's milk in Serbia, Rumania, Bulgaria, and Macedonia. The milk is curdled with lab (a rennet-starter preparation), and the curd is drained, spread out on a table, enclosed in cloth, and ripened until it becomes elastic when heated. Then it is placed in metal canisters, cooked in water, and worked like bread dough until it is very elastic. It is cut into pieces weighing about 6 pounds, and each is worked to a spherical shape, placed in a metal or wood form, cooled, washed with whey, dried, salted by repeatedly rubbing in salt, and cured.

A similar cheese called Zomma, which is said to contain at least 30 percent of fat, is made in Turkey.

Analysis (average of 10 samples): Moisture, 35.72 percent; fat, 31.00 percent; protein, 24.24 percent; ash, 6.28 percent; and salt (in the ash), 4.01 percent.

Kefalotyi

Kefalotyi is a hard, grating-type cheese made in Greece and Syria from either goat's or ewe's milk. It is about 10 inches thick and is said to resemble a Greek hat, or Kefalo, which undoubtedly accounts for its name.

Cheese of this type is made also from goat's milk in the Ozark region in Arkansas.

Kjarsgaard

Kjarsgaard is a hard, skim-milk cheese made in Denmark from cow's milk.

Kloster

Kloster cheese (or Klosterkäse) is a soft, ripened, Romadur-type cheese made in Germany from cow's whole milk. It is about 3½ inches long, 1¼ inches square and weighs about ¼ pound.

Kopanisti

Kopanisti, which is made in Greece, is a blue-mold cheese with a sharp, peppery flavor. Fresh, whole milk is coagulated with rennet as in making Feta, except that the coagulation period is longer and therefore the curd is firmer. The curd is cut, then dipped into cheesecloth, and the whey is drained off. Then the curd is kneaded by hand and formed into round balls about the size of a small orange. These are placed on a grating in a trough or an earthenware container to dry. They soon are covered with a blue-green mold. The balls of curd are salted, then kneaded until the mold and salt are mixed thoroughly in the mass of curd, which is then packed tightly in earthenware containers, and covered with a dry cloth. The cloth is changed daily. The cheese is ready to eat after ripening for 1 to 2 months.

Koppen

Koppen, also called Bauden, is a sour-milk cheese that is made by herders in their huts in the Sudetic Mountains between Bohemia and Silesia. The cheese, which is said to be made from goat's milk, has a sharp, pungent flavor. It is made in 2 shapes—1 conical, 3½ inches in diameter and height and about a pound in weight; the other cylindrical, about 5 inches in diameter and 2½ inches thick, and about 2 pounds in weight. The milk is coagulated at a temperature of 80° to 85° F., the whey is removed, and the curd is placed in forms. The cheeses are salted, and they are cured.

Analysis: Moisture, 54 to 56 percent; fat, 24 to 25 percent; and protein, 16 to 18 percent.

Kosher

Kosher cheese is made especially for Jewish consumers, to conform with Jewish dietary custom. Typically, it is made without animal rennet. Sometimes the milk is curdled by natural souring; sometimes a starter is added to the milk. Among the Kosher cheeses are soft cheeses, like Cream and Cottage cheese; Kosher Gouda; and a cheese that is made by the Limburger process but, unlike Limburger, is eaten fresh. Kosher cheese bears a label by which it can be identified.

Krutt

Krutt, or Kirgischerkäse, is made by the nomadic tribes of the middle Asiatic Steppes from the skim milk of cows, goats, ewes, or camels. The milk is coagulated by souring, salt is added, and the curd is hung up in a sack to drain, after which it is pressed moderately. The curd is then made into small balls, which are placed in the sun to dry.

Analysis: Moisture, 8 to 10 percent; fat, 1 to 1.5 percent; protein, 70 to 80 percent; and salt, 8 to 13 percent.

Kühbacher

Kühbacher is a soft, ripened cheese made in upper Bavaria, Germany, from whole or partly skimmed cow's milk. It is cylindrical in shape—about 6 inches in diameter and 3 inches thick—and weighs about 2 pounds.

Kuminost

Kuminost, also called Kommenost, is a spiced cheese made in the Scandinavian countries from whole or partly skimmed cow's milk. There are several types, of which the best known is a skim-milk cheese made in numerous dairies in Denmark. Cumin and caraway seed are mixed with the curd before it is pressed. Except for its spiced flavor, it resembles Colby and Granular cheese. Kuminost is commonly made in loaves that weigh from 5 to 7 pounds. (See Spiced cheese.)

Small quantities are imported into the United States from Norway and Sweden. Unless designated otherwise, and in all instances in the United States, the cheese contains at least 50 percent of fat in the solids. The cheese made from partly-skimmed milk contains at least 20 percent of fat in the solids.

Labneh

Labneh is a sour-milk cheese made in Syria. It is said that about one-third of the cheese made in Syria is Labneh cheese.

Laguiole

Laguiole, also called Guiole, is a hard cheese named for the village of Laguiole, in the Department of Aveyron, France. It resembles Cantal but is considered to be a better cheese. Whole or partly skimmed milk is set with rennet and about 30 minutes later the curd is cut. After ripening for about 24 hours it is put into hoops and pressed. It is cured for at least a month.

Analysis: Moisture, 34.5 percent; fat, 25.2 percent; protein, 28.7 percent; and ash, 5.4 percent.

Lancashire

Lancashire cheese is named for the county in England where it is made and where much of it is consumed. It is said to be the most popular cheese in some sections of England. It is similar in shape to Cheshire and Cheddar, but white in color, softer (the body is more salvy), moister, and has a stronger flavor. A single cheese may weigh between 40 and 50 pounds; however, a smaller size—about 7 inches in diameter and 10 inches thick, weighing about 12 pounds—is also made. The fully cured cheese is said to be especially suitable for toasting and for use in making Welsh rarebit.

Evening milk, which may be partly skimmed, is mixed with morning milk, and the mixture warmed to a temperature in the range of 82° to 88° F., depending on the season. Starter is added, and the milk may be ripened to an acidity of not more than 0.19 or 0.20 percent. Rennet is added and in about an hour, when the curd is firm, it is cut with ½-inch curd knives. After some further development of acidity, the whey is drained slowly. The curd is placed on a drainer or in a cloth and pressed lightly. When the curd has reached a certain stage of acid development, it is cut into 4-inch cubes, repressed lightly, and then recut into smaller cubes. This operation is repeated until the curd is sufficiently acid and firm and the cubes of curd are the size of kernels of corn. At this stage it is customary to put some of the curd aside for later use; curds of different ages, up to 3 days, and different stages of acidity may be mixed together to produce curd with a loose, friable body and texture. Salt is mixed in at the rate of 2 pounds per 100 pounds of curd, and the curd is placed in forms. Pressing is begun the next day; the cheese is pressed usually for 3 days, with a pressure of about 1,000 pounds, and it is dressed in cloth daily. Because the curd undergoes considerable soaking in the whey, the cheese is rather soft and lacks elasticity, and the flavor develops rapidly. The cheese is turned daily while it is in the curing room. Sometimes it is marketed after it has cured for a month at 60° F.; sometimes it is cured for several months at a lower temperature.

Analysis: Moisture, 43 to 45 percent; fat, 23 to 26 percent; and salt, 1.5 percent.

Langres

Langres is a soft cheese, similar to Livarot, that is made in northeastern France, mostly for local consumption. It is named for the village of Langres in the Department of Haute-Marne, where it is said to have been made since the time of the Merovingian kings. Fresh milk is set with rennet at a temperature of 90° to 95° F. After a coagulation period of several hours, the curd is put into cylindrical forms, 5 inches in diameter and 8 inches deep. When the cheeses are firm enough to hold their shape, they are removed from the forms, salted, and cured for 2 to 3 months. When ripe, the cheeses weigh between 1½ and 2 pounds.

Lapland

Lapland cheese, which is like a very hard Swiss, is made by the Laplanders from reindeer milk. The cheese has a very unusual shape; it is round and flat and is so formed that a cross-section resembles a dumbbell with angular rather than round ends.

Leather

Leather cheese, also known as Leder and as Holstein Dairy cheese, is made in the Province of Schleswig-Holstein, Germany, from cow's skim milk, with 5 to 10 percent of buttermilk added. It is very similar to Holstein skim-milk cheese.

The milk is warmed to a temperature of 95° to 100° F., and set with enough rennet to coagulate it in from 25 to 35 minutes. The curd is cut with a harp and stirred with a so-called Danish stirrer until the particles are the size of peas. It is then piled on one side of the vat or kettle for about 10 minutes, after which the whey is dipped off. The matted curd is cut with a knife into pieces the size of the hand, put into a wooden or tin bowl, pressed for half an hour, and then put through a curd mill. It is salted, put into a cloth, and again pressed for 12 hours. During this period the pressure is increased gradually, and the cheese is turned occasionally and put into a fresh, dry cloth. The cheese is then put into a salt bath, for 40 to 48 hours, after which it is transferred to the curing cellar where it is cured for about 4 months. During the curing period it is wiped with a dry cloth every day for about a week and thereafter twice a week. The cured cheese has small eyes. It is cylindrical, from 10 to 12 inches in diameter and from 4 to 6 inches thick, and weighs from 15 to 25 pounds.

Leicester

Leicester cheese, first made in Leicester County in the midlands of England, is a hard, mild cheese made from cow's whole milk. It is said that at one time Leicester was the finest cheese made in England, with the possible exception of Stilton. It resembles Cheddar, but has more color and a higher moisture content and ripens more rapidly; it is also similar to Derby and Cheshire. The cheeses are about 18 inches in diameter and 6 inches thick, and weigh about 40 pounds.

A mixture of evening and morning milk is colored with annatto. Lactic starter and rennet are added at a temperature of 80° to 84° F. in winter and 76° to 78° in summer. About 75 minutes later, when the curd is very firm, it is cut with a curd breaker or ⅜-inch curd knives. It is stirred carefully for a few minutes, then heated to a temperature of 92° in 45 minutes, stirred about 10 minutes longer, and then the whey is drained off. A curd rack is laid on the curd and weighted, to expel whey. The lightly pressed, matted curd then is cut into 6-inch blocks. The blocks of curd are piled on a rack in a vat and covered with a cloth to keep them from cooling. The curd is cut into smaller pieces and inverted at 20-minute intervals, until it acquires the desired acidity and firmness, when it is milled. Salt is added at the rate of about 2 pounds per 100 pounds of curd, and the curd is then transferred to forms and pressed. A few hours later, the cheese is removed from the forms, dressed in cloth, and repressed with gradually increasing pressure until a final pressure of about a ton is used. After the cheese has been in press a day or more, it is salted again with dry salt and then is transferred to the curing room where it is cured on shelves at a temperature of approximately 60°. It may be marketed after curing for about 2 months, but usually it is cured for 6 to 8 months and it may be cured for as long as a year.

Analysis: Moisture, 33 to 37 percent; fat, 29 to 30 percent; and salt, 1.5 to 2 percent.

Lescin

Lescin cheese is made in the Caucasus. Ewes are milked directly into a skin sack; rennet is added to the milk, the curd is broken up, and the whey is drained. The curd is put into forms and pressed lightly. When the cheese is removed from the press, it is wrapped in leaves and bound with grass ropes. After a week or two, it is unwrapped and salted with dry salt, and again wrapped in leaves for curing.

Leyden

Leyden, which is also known as Komijne Kaas, is a spiced cheese made in the Netherlands from partly skimmed cow's milk to which color is added. It is made both in factories and on farms.

The factory cheese is round and flat like Gouda, but sometimes it is made with sharp edges on one side. It is imported into the United States in different sizes, some cheeses weighing about 8 pounds and others as much as 16 to 20 pounds.

On the farms about 5 percent of buttermilk may be added to the milk, and it is set with rennet at a temperature of 82° to 86° F. About 30 minutes later the curd is cut with a harp, stirred, and warmed to about 92° by pouring in hot whey. The curd is dipped with a cloth and kneaded. Caraway and cumin seeds, and sometimes cloves, are added to a portion of the curd, and the curd is then put into cloth-lined hoops in three layers with the spiced curd as the middle layer. The cheese is pressed for about 3 hours, then it is redressed, inverted, and again pressed overnight. It may be salted with dry salt, or it may be immersed in a salting bath. It is cured in a cool, moist cellar. If the rind becomes too hard, it is washed with whey or salty water. It is said that milk may be rubbed on the surface occasionally, and that an alkaline solution containing litmus may be used to tint the surface blue.

Analysis: Moisture, 40.6 percent; fat, 13.5 percent; and protein, 37.8 percent.

Liederkranz

Liederkranz is the trade name of a soft, surface-ripened cheese that is made in Ohio from cow's whole milk. It is similar to a very mild Limburger in body, flavor, aroma, and type of ripening.

The milk is pasteurized, starter is added, and the milk is set with rennet at a temperature of about 86° F. The curd is cut with ½-inch curd knives, and when it has firmed sufficiently it is dipped into perforated metal forms. After the whey has drained off, the cheeses are removed from the forms, salted with dry salt, and then cured at a temperature of about 45° for 3 or 4 weeks. Surface-growing micro-organisms produce progressive ripening from the surface inward. The cheeses, which are rather perishable, are wrapped in tinfoil for marketing. They may be wrapped and shipped after curing for 12 to 15 days. They are about 2½ inches long, 1½ inches wide, and an inch thick, and they weigh 5 to 6 ounces.

Analysis: Moisture, 54 percent; fat, 24.2 percent (fat in the solids, more than 50 percent); protein, 16.8 percent; and ash, 3.9 percent.

Limburger

Limburger is a semisoft, surface-ripened cheese with a characteristic strong flavor and aroma. Usually it contains small irregular openings. The cheeses vary in size from a 3-inch cube that weighs less than a pound to a cheese 6 inches square and 3 inches thick that weighs about 2½ pounds.

Limburger was first made in the Province of Lüttich, Belgium, and is named for the town of Limburg, where originally much of it was marketed. It is made also in other parts of Europe, especially in Germany and Austria, and in the United States, especially in Wisconsin and New York. Other similar European cheeses are: Allgäuer Limburger and Stangen, made in Bavaria; Romadur and Hervé, made in Belgium; Schloss, made in Germany and Austria; Marienhofer and Tanzenberger, made in Carinthia, Austria; Backsteiner, made in Germany; and Void, made in France.

The method of making Limburger differs in different factories, but in general is as follows: Fresh milk, preferably whole milk, may be pasteurized, and it is warmed in a vat or kettle to a temperature usually between 86° and 92° F., but in some factories to as high as 96°. Lactic starter and rennet are added. Usually about 30 minutes after setting, but in some factories an hour later, the curd is cut into cubes about ½ inch in diameter. If the milk was set at the lower temperatures, the curd is stirred slowly as it is warmed to about 96°, and it is stirred gently at intervals as it acquires firmness. When the curd is sufficiently firm, most of the whey is drained off. In some factories, the curd is washed with weak salt brine to lower its acidity.

The curd is dipped into large rectangular metal or wooden forms that rest on a drain table. Sometimes the forms are divided into sections the size of the individual cheeses; sometimes the forms are not divided, and after the block of curd is removed from the forms, it is divided to make the individual cheeses. In some factories, a light-weight board is placed on the curd to furnish light pressure. The forms of curd are turned frequently.

When the cheeses are firm enough to retain their shape, they are removed from the forms and salted. In some factories, they are packed close together in dry salt on a salting table for at least a day, and they are turned frequently until they have absorbed salt on all surfaces; in other factories, they are rubbed with salt daily for about 3 days; and in still other factories, they are immersed in salt brine for a day at a temperature of 55° to 60° F.

After the cheeses are salted, they are cured on shelves at a temperature of 50° to 60° F. and a relative humidity of about 90 percent. According to some authorities, surface-ripening micro-organisms are responsible for the characteristic flavor and aroma. Yeasts, which reduce the acidity, predominate at first, and these are followed by *Bacterium linens,* which produces a characteristic reddish-yellow pigment.

The cheeses are placed close together on the shelves at first, and separated later. As the cheese cures, slime forms on the surface and the rind acquires a reddish-yellow color. In some factories, the cheeses are rubbed and turned every 2 or 3 days; in other factories, they are washed with salty water. The older cheeses are rubbed or washed before the younger ones; in this way, the younger ones are inoculated with the surface-ripening micro-organisms. After they have cured for 2 or 3 weeks, they are wrapped in parchment or waxed paper and an outer layer of metal foil, and curing is continued at a lower temperature. If the cheese was made from raw milk, it is cured for at least 60 days. From 11 to 13 pounds of cured cheese is obtained per 100 pounds of whole milk.

Analysis: Moisture, not more than 50 percent (usually 43 to 48 percent); fat, 26.5 to 29.5 percent (not less than 50 percent of the solids); protein, 20 to 24 percent; ash, 4.8 percent; and salt, 1.6 to 3.2 percent.

Liptauer

Liptauer (or Liptoi) is a soft, so-called pickled cheese that is named for the Province of Liptow in northern Hungary, where it is made. Cheese of this type, either identical or very similar, is made in numerous villages in the Carpathian mountain region of Czechoslovakia and Hungary. It is known in the different villages by different local names, among which are Landoch, Zips, Siebenburger, Neusohl, Altsohl, Klencz, and Bryndza (or Brynza). The German for Bryndza is Brinsen. Similar cheese made in Macedonia is called Ftinoporino.

Liptauer usually is made from ewe's milk, although in some localities as much as 10 percent of cow's milk is added. An unusual feature is that herdsmen prepare the curd daily, and the raw cheeses (Gomolya) are collected weekly and taken to centralized factories (brynziar) where the cheese is made and cured.

The milk is warmed in a copper kettle over a fire to a temperature of 75° to 85° F. Rennet, prepared locally from the stomachs of suckling calves, lambs, or pigs, is added. After a coagulation period of 15 to 20 minutes, the curd is broken up, collected, and pressed into large lumps which are hung up in cloths to drain for a day or two. These lumps of drained curd, which are about 6 inches in diameter, are the Gomolya. They are collected weekly and taken to the factory where they are placed on boards or in large wooden casks and cured until they reach the desired stage of ripening, about 10 days. Then the rinds are removed, and the curd is cut into small pieces and salted. It is packed in a tub and ripened for several days. When it is soft and buttery, it is run through a roller mill and then packed in casks or packages of various sizes, for shipment. About 9½ pounds of Gomolya is obtained per 100 pounds of milk.

Analysis: Moisture, 46 to 49.2 percent; fat, 17.0 to 24.6 percent; protein, 21.0 to 28.2 percent; and salt, 1.9 percent.

Livarot

Livarot, which is a soft, cow's-milk cheese, is named for the village of Livarot, in the Department of Calvados, France, where the industry is centralized. The cheeses are about 6 inches in diameter and 1¾ inches thick. Livarot is very much like Camembert, which is made in the same region.

The milk, which is more or less skimmed, is set with rennet at a temperature of from 95° to 104° F. About 1½ or 2 hours later the curd is cut and placed on a rush mat or a cloth to drain for about 15 minutes, during which time it is crumbled fine. It is then put into tinned hoops about 6 inches in diameter and 6 inches deep. The cheeses are turned very frequently until they become firm, after which they are salted and then left on the draining board for 4 or 5 days. At this stage they sometimes are sold as white cheese.

More often the cheeses are placed in a well-ventilated room for 15 or 20 days, after which they are taken to the curing cellar where they are cured for 3 to 5 months. The curing cellar is not ventilated, in order to keep from dissipating the aromas that help to give the cheese a strong, piquant flavor. While curing, the cheeses are turned two or three times a week and occasionally they are wiped with a cloth that has been moistened with salty water. About 10 or 12 days after they are placed in the curing cellar they are wrapped in laiche leaves (*Typha latifolia*). After they are cured, they are colored with annatto and marketed.

Analysis: Moisture, 52 percent; fat, 15 percent; protein, 26 percent; and salt, 2.9 percent.

Loaf

Loaf cheese refers to the rectangular, loaf-like shape in which several cheeses are packaged and marketed, rather than to a specific variety. Before 1940, loaf cheese usually referred to process cheese. However, since about 1940, natural cheeses of various kinds, such as Brick, Cheddar, Cream, and Swiss, have also been packaged and marketed in loaf shape.

Lodigiano

Lodigiano, a Grana- or Parmesan-type cheese, is made in the vicinity of Lodi, Italy, from which it derives its name. It is similar to Lombardo; in fact, according to some authorities they are the same. The cheeses are 15 to 20 inches or more in diameter, 6½ to 9 inches thick, and weigh between 65 and 110 pounds. They are cylindrical, with convex faces. The surface of the cheese is colored dark and is oiled; and the interior is yellow. The cheese is sharp, fragrant, and sometimes slightly bitter. It is larger, contains less fat, has larger eyes, and ripens more slowly than Reggiano. It may be cured for as long as 3 or 4 years, and it is used for grating. (See Grana and Parmesan.)

Analysis: Moisture, 25 to 32 percent; fat in the solids, 25 to 33 percent (in the United States, not less than 32 percent); and salt, 2.6 to 3.5 percent.

Lombardo

Lombardo, an Italian Grana- or Parmesan-type cheese, is similar to Lodigiano; according to some authorities they are the same. The cheeses are 12 to 16 inches in diameter, 6 to 8 inches thick, and weigh between 40 and 60 pounds. They are cylindrical and flat; in the spring and summer they are made with convex sides. The surface of the cheese may be colored, and it is oiled. The cheese has a sharp and aromatic flavor and granular texture. It contains a few small eyes, frequently unevenly distributed. It is cured for at least a year and usually for 1½ to 2 years, and the aged cheese is used for grating. (See Grana and Parmesan.)

Analysis: Moisture, 27 to 32 percent at 1 year of age; 20 to 30 percent at 2 years; fat in the solids, 27 to 35 percent (in the United States, not less than 32 percent).

Lorraine

Lorraine, a small, sour-milk, hard cheese, is named for Lorraine, Germany, where it is made and where it is regarded as a delicacy. It is seasoned with pepper, salt, and pistachio nuts and is eaten while comparatively fresh. Each cheese weighs about 2 ounces.

Lüneberg

Lüneberg cheese is made in the small valleys between the mountains in the Province of Vorarlberg in western Austria. Cheesemaking was introduced into this region from Switzerland, and copper kettles and Swiss-type presses are used. The milk, which is colored with saffron, is warmed to a temperature of 87° to 90° F., and enough rennet is added to coagulate it in from 20 to 30 minutes. The curd is cut into pieces the size of hazelnuts and is heated, with stirring, to a temperature of 122°. It is then dipped into cloths which are put into wooden forms and pressed lightly. After 24 hours in the press, during which time the cheeses are turned and the cloths are changed occasionally, they are taken to the curing cellar. The cheeses are salted on the surface, and they are rubbed and washed occasionally while curing. When ripe, the cheese is said to be about midway in characteristics between Swiss and Limburger.

Maconnais

Maconnais is a goat's-milk cheese made in France. It is about 2 inches square and 1½ inches thick.

Macqueline

Macqueline is a soft cheese which is similar to Camembert but is said to be inferior. It is made from whole or partly skimmed milk in the Department of Oise, France, where Camembert is also made.

The milk is set with rennet at a temperature of about 80° F. After a coagulation period of about 5 hours, the curd is put into hoops. The hoops are removed 24 hours later, and the cheese is salted and then taken to the curing room for a period of 20 days or more. Each cheese is about 4 inches in diameter and 1¼ inches thick, and weighs about 4 ounces. One cheese can be made from 4½ pounds of milk.

Maile

Maile is a ewe's-milk cheese that is made in the Crimea. The curd is cooked and then drained in a cloth for 2 hours, after which it is salted, molded in forms, and put into salt brine in which it may be kept for as long as a year.

Maile Pener

Maile Pener (fat cheese) is made from ewe's milk in the Crimea. The milk is set at 100° F. with enough rennet to coagulate it in from 15 to 30 minutes. The curd is broken up and the whey is dipped off. Then the curd is put in a linen cloth to drain for from 2 to 6 hours. It is pressed with a board and salted in brine. It may be kept for as long as a year. When cured, the cheese has a crumbly, open texture and an agreeable flavor.

Mainauer

Mainauer cheese is named for an island in Lake Constance, a lake bordered by Germany, Switzerland, and Austria. The cheese is similar to Radolfzeller Cream cheese (made in this area, also) and to Münster (although it is somewhat firmer and cures more slowly than Münster). A single cheese weighs about 3 pounds.

Usually fresh whole milk, but sometimes partly skimmed milk, is heated in a kettle to a temperature of 86° to 90° F., and rennet is added. After a coagulation period of 40 to 45 minutes, the curd is cut into pieces about an inch in diameter, stirred, and then heated slowly to a temperature as high as 104°. After the curd settles, the whey is removed, and the curd is transferred to perforated forms to drain for about 12 hours during which time the forms of curd are inverted occasionally. Then the cheeses are removed from the forms and salted on the surface. They are cured for 4 to 5 months in much the same way as Münster. (See Münster.) Between 11 and 12 pounds of cured cheese can be made from 100 pounds of whole milk.

Analysis: Fat in the solids, 40 percent.

Mainzer Hand

Mainzer Hand cheese (Mainzer Handkäse) is a sour-milk, small, round, cured cheese made in Germany. Curd from partly skimmed, naturally soured milk is kneaded by hand, pressed in small portions, dried, and then cured in a cool cellar (sometimes in kegs or jars) for as long as 6 to 8 weeks. (See Hand cheese.)

Analysis: Moisture, 53.74 percent; fat, 5.55 percent; and protein, 37.33 percent.

Malakoff

Malakoff is a soft, Neufchâtel-type cheese made in France. It is about 2 inches in diameter and ½ inch thick. It may be eaten either fresh or after curing.

Manteca

Manteca or Manteche "cheese," which is made in Italy, is in reality butter (usually whey butter) enclosed in a bag of plastic cheese curd. It is also known as butirro, burriello, burrino, and even burro (the Italian word for butter). The plastic-curd bag preserves the butter by protecting it from the air, thus preventing its deterioration even in a warm climate. The whey butter used in making Manteca usually is produced as a byproduct in the manufacture of Caciocavallo and Provolone.

Heated, plastic curd—which is prepared like curd for making Scamorze—is formed into a bag with walls about a half-inch thick. From ¼ to ½ pound of butter is put into the bag, the edges are closed, and the whole is immersed in cold water to solidify the butter which was melted by contact with the heated curd. The "cheese" is shaped like a small, rounded Caciocavallo. The outer surface of the bag usually is smoked, which gives it a yellow-brown color, but the butter within remains straw-colored.

Manur

Manur cheese is made in Serbia from either cow's or ewe's milk. The milk is heated to boiling and then cooled until the fingers can be held in it. A mixture of buttermilk, fresh whey, and rennet is added. The curd is lifted from the whey in a cloth and drained, and then is kneaded, salted lightly, and dried.

Maquée

Maquée, known also as Fromage Mou, is a soft, brick-shaped cheese made from cow's milk in Belgium.

Marches

Marches is a hard, Pecorino (ewe's-milk) cheese made in Tuscany, Italy. The Province of Tuscany borders on the Province of Marche, for which this cheese is named.

Marienhofer

Marienhofer is a Limburger-type cheese made in Marienhof-Pichlern, Carinthia (Kärnten), Austria. Enough fat is removed from the evening milk so that when it is mixed with the whole morning milk the mixture will have about 75 percent of the normal fat content. The cheeses are about 4⅓ inches square and about 1½ inches thick, and they weigh a pound or slightly more. They are wrapped in tinfoil.

Märkisch Hand

Märkisch Hand cheese is made by the usual Hand-cheese process, except that after the curd is salted it is put into a linen sack and is pressed heavily. It is then removed from the press and cut into oblong pieces, and these are dried and cured in the same way as the usual Hand cheese. (See Hand cheese.)

Marolles

Marolles (or Maroilles) is a soft, cow's-milk cheese similar to Pont l'Évêque and Livarot. It is made in numerous villages in the Departments of Aisne and Nord, France. The details of manufacture differ in the different villages, the cheeses are various shapes and sizes, and they are known by different local names. For example, Marolles (made at Marolles) is 6 inches square and 2 inches thick; Marolles (made at St. Aubin) is 5 inches square and 3 inches thick; Larron is about 2¼ inches square and 1½ inches thick; Tuile de Flandre is about twice as large as Larron; Dauphin is shaped like a half moon and contains herbs; and Boulette is pear-shaped and sometimes contains some buttermilk.

Fresh, whole milk is recommended, although skim milk or partly skimmed milk is often used. The milk is set with rennet at a temperature of about 75° F., and the coagulation period varies from 1 to 4 hours. The curd is put into boxes with perforated bottoms, and the whey drains from the curd for 1 to 2 hours. Then the curd is transferred to forms, 5 or 6 inches square and 3 or 4 inches deep. The cheeses in the forms are turned frequently. When they are firm, they are removed from the forms, salted on the surface, and taken to the curing cellar. They are cured for 3 to 5 months, and they are washed frequently with salty water while curing, to prevent the growth of molds.

Analysis (whole-milk Marolles): Moisture, 40 percent; fat, 30 percent; and protein, 20 percent.

Mascarpone

Mascarpone is a soft, cream cheese that is made in Lombardy, Italy, during the winter. It is like fresh Ricotta in consistency and has a mildly acid, buttery flavor. It is cylindrical, from 2 to 2½ inches in diameter and about 2⅓ inches thick, and weighs about 4 ounces. Cream is heated to about 195° F., and dilute acetic acid, vinegar, tartaric acid, or lemon juice is stirred in. The curd is drained in a bag and then is placed in muslin-lined forms. After additional draining for a day, the cheese is removed from the forms. It may be salted, and it is packaged. It is eaten while fresh. The yield is 40 to 55 pounds of cheese per 100 pounds of cream.

Mecklenburg Skim

Mecklenburg Skim, a hard, skim-milk cheese, was first made in northern Germany in the Province of Mecklenburg, for which it is named. The milk is placed in a copper kettle and is warmed with steam. It is colored with saffron, and enough rennet is added to coagulate the milk in 30 minutes. The curd is broken into particles about the size of peas and is stirred while being heated slowly to about 92° F. Then the curd is dipped with a cloth and placed in hoops. It is pressed for a day with gradually increasing pressure, until the final pressure is about 15 times the weight of the cheese. The cheese is placed in a drying room at a temperature of about 70°, where it is held until the rind has formed. Salt is sprinkled and rubbed on the surface. The cheese is cured at a temperature of approximately 60° and a relative humidity of 85 to 90 percent.

Melun

Melun, or Brie de Melun, is a French cheese of the Brie type, but Melun usually has a somewhat firmer curd and a sharper flavor than Brie. It is the size of a small Brie. (See Brie.)

Mesitra

Mesitra is a soft, ewe's-milk cheese made in the Crimea. Fresh milk is set with rennet in a copper kettle. The curd is cut, then is heated over a slow fire. The curd is dipped when it is comparatively soft, and it is pressed lightly. The cheese often is not salted, and it is eaten while fresh.

Mignot

Mignot, which has been made in the Department of Calvados, France, for more than 120 years, is a soft cheese that resembles Pont l'Évêque and Livarot. It may be either cylindrical or cubical in shape. There are two types of Mignot: (1) White, which is a fresh cheese and is made from April to September; and (2) passé, which is a ripened cheese and is made the rest of the year.

Milano

Milano or Stracchino di Milano, which is known also as Fresco and Quardo and, when made in the fall, as Stracchino Quartirolo, is a soft, sweet, fast-ripening table cheese made in Lombardy, Italy. It is classed in the group with Crescenza, and is similar to Bel Paese. It is square, from 1½ to 2¾ inches thick, and weighs between 3 and 6½ pounds. It is colored yellow, has a thin rind, and may be enclosed in muslin.

The milk is curdled with rennet extract at a temperature of 86° to 91° F. in 35 to 45 minutes. The curd is cut into pieces the size of almonds. After the curd settles, it is gathered in a cloth and hung up to drain; then it is put into forms, pressed lightly, and salted after 2 or 3 days. It is cured at a temperature of 60° to 65°. It is ready to eat after curing for about 20 days and will not keep much longer than 60 days.

Analysis: Moisture, 40 to 50 percent; casein, about 20 percent; fat, 30 percent or more.

Mintzitra

Mintzitra is a soft cheese made in Macedonia from ewe's milk.

Mitzithra

Mitzithra cheese, which also is called "Pot" cheese, is made by shepherds in the vicinity of Athens, Greece, from the whey which is a byproduct of Feta cheese. It is made under primitive conditions, and the method of making is simple. The whey and fresh milk, usually ewe's milk, are mixed in a vat, and curdled. After a curdling period of 4 or 5 days, the whey is removed and the residual curd is collected, drained, and pressed. The fresh cheese is sold by the shepherds to merchants, for resale in Greece and for export, chiefly to Greek colonies.

Modena

Modena and Monte are the names of some Parmesan-type cheeses (that contain less fat than Parmesan) which were made in the United States during World War II.

Moliterno

Moliterno, a plastic-curd (pasta filata) cheese, was made originally in the Departments of Calabria and Lucania and now is made also in the Province of Basilicata, Italy. It is said to be similar to Cotronese. When made from ewe's milk only, it is called Pecorino Moliterno. It is made by much the same process as Caciocavallo and other plastic-curd cheeses. (See Caciocavallo.)

Moncenisio

Moncenisio is a blue-mold, Gorgonzola-type cheese made in Italy.

Mondseer Schachtelkäse

Mondseer Schachtelkäse, a Münster-type cheese that is popular in Austria, is made from either whole or partly skimmed milk. It has a somewhat sharp, acid flavor, similar to mild Limburger. The cheeses are about 6 inches in diameter and 2 inches thick, and weigh about 2¼ pounds. One whole-milk cheese of this type is called Mondseer Schlosskäse.

The milk is set with rennet at a temperature of about 86° F. The curd is cut coarsely an hour later or, if firmer curd is desired, the coagulation period may be as long as 3 hours. When the curd has settled, the whey is drained off and the curd is transferred to cylindrical, perforated, cloth-lined forms; it is turned frequently for a period of several hours. Then the cheeses are removed from the forms and dried for 3 or 4 days. When dry, they are salted on the surface and transferred to a cool, moist cellar where they are cured for 3 to 6 weeks. While curing, they are washed every few days with warm water or warm, salty water; and a reddish-yellow smear develops on the surface. The cheeses are wrapped separately, and they are shipped in wooden containers called schachteln.

Monostorer

Monostorer is a ewe's-milk cheese that is made in Transylvania, Rumania. Fresh milk is set with rennet at a temperature of 86° to 88° F. The curd is broken by hand, the whey is drained and pressed out, and the curd is crumbled into pieces and salted. Then it is sprinkled with warm water, subdivided, and mixed, after which it is pressed strongly by hand and again crumbled. The curd is placed in cloth-lined forms, about 8 inches long, 4 inches wide, and 2 inches deep, and pressed for 8 to 10 hours. The cheeses are removed from the forms, salted in brine for 2 days, and cured for 8 to 10 weeks. They are washed regularly with salty water while curing. About 15 pounds of cheese is obtained from 100 pounds of milk.

Montasio

Montasio, a hard cheese similar to Fontina and Bitto, was first made in Friuli, Italy (formerly Friaul, Austria). The annual output in Friuli is large, and production has spread to nearby areas. Montasio is made usually of a mixture of cow's and goat's milk, but in some places only ewe's milk is used.

Either whole or partly skimmed milk is heated in a kettle to 95° F., and enough rennet is added to coagulate the milk in 30 to 40 minutes. The curd is cut very carefully to the size of peas and is heated gradually (in about 30 minutes) to a temperature of 120°. Then heating is stopped, but the curd is stirred for another 30 to 40 minutes. Some of the whey is dipped from the kettle, and a cloth is used to remove the curd. The cheese is pressed for 24 hours, during which time it is turned frequently. From 2½ to 3 percent of salt is added over a period of about a month. After salting is completed, the cheese is taken to a well-ventilated room to dry. While drying, it is turned frequently and rubbed to keep the surface free of mold. When dry it is scraped carefully and is then taken to the curing cellar, where it is rubbed frequently with a coarse cloth. When the rind has become firm, olive oil usually is applied. Sometimes the rind is blackened with soot.

The fresh cheese is almost white. The cured cheese is yellow and granular and has a sharp taste and characteristic aroma. It is usually cured for 3 to 12 months, but may be cured longer. It is eaten as a table cheese when made from whole milk and not fully cured; it is grated for use as a condiment when made from partly skimmed milk and fully matured.

Montavoner

Montavoner is a sour-milk cheese made in Austria. Dried herbs (*Achillea moschata* and *A. atrata*) are added to the curd during the making process.

Mont Cenis

Mont Cenis, a hard, blue-mold cheese that resembles Gex and Septmoncel, is made in the region of Mont Cenis in southeastern France, usually from a mixture of cow's, ewe's, and goat's milk. It is about 18 inches in diameter, 6 or 8 inches thick, and weighs about 25 pounds.

Primitive methods of cheesemaking are used in making Mont Cenis. Evening milk usually is skimmed and added to morning milk. The mixture is set with rennet at a temperature of about 85° F. When the milk has coagulated, the curd is cut and the whey is drained from the curd overnight. The next morning, fresh curd is made and mixed with that prepared the previous day, and a penicillium mold is sometimes incorporated. The mixture is put into molds and pressed with moderate pressure for several days, during which time it is turned frequently and salted. Then it is transferred to the curing cellar, and it is cured for 3 or 4 months. While curing, it is turned frequently and washed with salty water to check the growth of mold on the surface of the cheese.

Mont d'Or

Mont d'Or, a soft cheese similar to Pont l'Évêque, is named for Mont d'Or, near Lyon, in the Department of Rhône, France, where it is said to have been made for more than 300 years. It is made also in other parts of France, especially in the Departments of Eure and Oise.

It formerly was made from goat's milk, but now usually is made from cow's milk to which a small quantity of goat's milk may be added. Whole or partly skimmed milk is set with rennet at a temperature of 90° to 100° F. The coagulation period varies from 30 minutes to 2 hours. Sometimes the curd is cut before it is put in the hoops and sometimes it is put in the hoops without being cut. It is put into circular hoops, about 4½ inches in diameter and 3 inches deep, that have been placed on a draining board covered with straw. About an hour later the cheeses are turned, and they are turned frequently thereafter until they are firm. A disk with a light weight is sometimes placed on each cheese to hasten drainage of the whey. The cheese is salted on the surface. Mont d'Or is often sold without curing; however, it may be cured for about a week in summer and from 2 to 3 weeks in winter, during which time it is turned frequently and washed with salty water to retard the growth of molds on the surface of the cheese.

Analysis: Moisture, 42 percent; fat, 30 percent; protein, 20 percent; and salt, 2 percent.

Monterey

Monterey (or Jack) cheese was first made on farms in Monterey County, Calif., about 1892, and manufacture on a factory scale was begun about 1916. The name Monterey has largely replaced Jack, except for the type known as High-moisture Jack.

The cheese is made from pasteurized whole, partly skimmed, or skim milk. Whole-milk Monterey is semisoft; Monterey made from partly skimmed or skim milk (called grating-type Monterey, dry Monterey, or dry Jack) is hard and is used for grating. High-moisture Jack is made from whole milk by a slightly different process.

Monterey is made by a method similar to Colby, but the making process takes less time. The curd is cooled to a temperature of about 86° F. by running water either into the vat jacket or directly into the curd. (Colby is cooled to about 80° by running water directly into the curd.) The curd is salted after the whey has drained. Enough curd to make each cheese is placed in a square of muslin; as the four corners of the cloth are pulled together, the curd is formed as nearly round as possible; the cloth is tied tightly with a string, and the excess cloth is spread evenly over the top of the curd. Then the cheese is pressed either between boards or in a hoop. The pressed cheeses are round and flat and may have indentations on one surface where the cloth was tied before pressing. The sides are straight if the cheese was pressed in a hoop and round if it was pressed between boards. The cheeses are about 9½ inches in diameter and usually weigh between 6 and 9 pounds and never more than 12.

Whole-milk Monterey contains more moisture and is softer than either Granular or Colby. It is cured for 3 to 6 weeks at a temperature of about 60° F. and a relative humidity or 70 percent.

Grating-type Monterey is cured for at least 6 months. The cheeses may be coated with oil containing pepper.

In making High-moisture Jack, the curd is heated to a temperature no higher than 96° F. (which is 6 to 8 degrees lower than in making Monterey); part of the whey is drained off, and the curd is cooled quickly to 72° by running water directly into the vat. It is cured at a temperature between 40° and 50°, rather than 60°. It contains more moisture and is softer than whole-milk Monterey.

Analysis: Moisture, not more than 44 percent for whole-milk Monterey; not more than 34 percent for grating-type Monterey; and not less than 44 but less than 50 percent for High-moisture Jack; fat in the solids, not less than 50 percent for whole-milk Monterey and High-moisture Jack; not less than 32 percent for grating-type Monterey; and salt, about 1.5 percent.

Monthéry

Monthéry, which is very much like Brie, is a soft, surface-ripened, cow's-milk cheese made in Seine-et-Oise, France. It is made in two sizes. The larger is about 14 inches in diameter and 2 inches thick, and weighs about 5½ pounds; the smaller weighs about 3 pounds. Monthéry is made from either whole or partly skimmed milk. Rennet is added and, when the curd is sufficiently firm, it is broken up, put into molds, and pressed. The cheese is salted and is placed in a drying room for 8 to 15 days, where curing begins. Then it is transferred to a cellar where curing is completed at a temperature of about 55° F. As it ripens, a whitish mold grows on the surface of the cheese, and this is followed by a blue mold in which red spots appear. The cheese is ready for sale after curing for about a month.

Mozarinelli

Mozarinelli is a cheese made in Italy from cow's or buffalo's milk.

Mozzarella

Mozzarella is a soft, plastic-curd cheese that is made in some parts of Latium and Campania in southern Italy. It originally was made only from buffalo's milk, but now it is made also from cow's milk. It is made in much the same way as Caciocavallo and Scamorze; however, it more nearly resembles Scamorze, as both Mozzarella and Scamorze are eaten while fresh, with little or no ripening. It is irregularly spherical in shape and weighs 8 ounces to a pound. It is used for the most part in cooking. The yield is 13 to 15 pounds per 100 pounds of cow's milk. Ricotta is often made from the whey. (See Caciocavallo and Scamorze.)

Considerable Mozzarella is made in the United States, especially in New York. The milk is set with rennet at a temperature of 86° to 88° F. (if pasteurized milk is used the setting temperature should be 96°); the curd is cut and it is put into bags to drain. It is common practice to ship the curd to a dealer at this stage, as is done with cottage-cheese curd. The dealer stores the curd until he is ready to market the cheese. Then he completes the manufacturing process (heating and kneading the curd in the same way as in making Scamorze), and markets the fresh cheese.

Münster

Münster (or Muenster) is a semisoft, whole-milk cheese that was first made in the vicinity of Münster in the Vosges Mountains near the western border of Germany. It is similar to Brick cheese but has less surface smear and undergoes less surface ripening while curing. It contains numerous small mechanical openings. Géromé (or Gérardmer), which is made in nearby France, is similar.

The cheeses usually are cylindrical and flat, about 7 inches in diameter and from 2 to 7 inches thick. Those 2 inches thick weigh about 2 pounds; those 7 inches thick weigh as much as 10 pounds. Usually they are 4 to 5 inches thick and weigh between 4 and 6 pounds. In some factories the cheeses are made in loaf shape.

Good-quality milk is essential in making Münster. In the United States, the milk is pasteurized. Lactic starter is added, and annatto color may be added. The milk is warmed to a temperature of 86° to 90° F., and rennet is added. From 30 to 40 minutes later the curd is cut into pieces about ½ inch in diameter; then it is stirred and heated. (In Europe, the time from setting to cutting may be as long as 2 hours; the curd is left undisturbed in the whey for 30 to 45 minutes after it is cut, and it is not heated.)

When the curd is sufficiently firm, the whey is drained off, sometimes caraway seed is mixed with the curd, and it is dipped into perforated cloth-lined metal forms. The forms are in two parts, which fit together.

The forms of curd are turned and the cloths are changed several times the first day; usually at the end of the first day, the upper half of each form and the cloth lining are removed. The curd remains in the lower half of the forms for 3 or 4 days and is turned twice daily. Then the cheeses are removed from the forms and salted. Usually they are rubbed with salt daily for 2 or 3 days; if necessary, they are replaced in the forms between saltings until they are firm enough to retain their shape. In some factories, they are salted in brine.

The cheeses are dried, then cured at a temperature of 50° to 55° F. and a relative humidity of about 75 percent. They are turned and cleaned at least twice a week. In some factories they are washed with salty water; in others, they are washed with water and rubbed lightly with salt. Sometimes they are rubbed with vegetable oil. In the United States they usually are cured for 6 to 8 weeks, but frequently are sold after ripening only a week or two; in Europe they are cured for as long as 3 months. The cheeses are wrapped in parchment or waxed paper and packed in boxes. From 10 to 12 pounds of cheese is obtained from 100 pounds of whole milk.

Analysis: Moisture, not more than 46 percent (usually 42 to 44 percent); fat, 28 to 29.6 percent (not less than 50 percent in the solids); and salt, 1.8 to 2 percent.

Mysost

Mysost cheese is made in the Scandinavian countries (Norway, Sweden, and Denmark) and in a few factories in the United States, principally in northern Illinois, Michigan, New York, and Wisconsin, from the whey obtained in the manufacture of other cheeses. There is considerable variation in the composition of the whey used in different factories and in different localities, and in the manufacturing procedure and the composition of the cheese; and it is known by different local names. Mysost is made from cow's-milk whey. Similar cheese made from goat's-milk whey is called Gjetost. In some instances a small proportion, usually not more than 10 percent, of buttermilk or whole milk, or even cream is added to the whey. Cheese made from such whey contains more fat and is softer and sometimes is called Primost or Fløtost. Cheese made by the same method from whole milk rather than whey is called Gomost.

The cheese consists principally of caramelized lactose (milk sugar) but contains also the fat, protein, and minerals present in the whey. It is light brown in color, has a buttery consistency and a mild, sweetish flavor. It does not undergo appreciable ripening but keeps well when packaged properly.

Sometimes, if the whey contains considerable acid, neutralizer is added to prevent a sour or bitter flavor in the cheese. If sweet whey is used, lactic starter usually is added. The whey is strained into a kettle and boiled (condensed) until it is a viscous mass, which may take 5 hours or longer. It is stirred while boiling. The albuminous material that rises to the surface is skimmed off. When the whey is reduced to about one-fourth its original volume and has the consistency of heavy cream, the albumin skimmed off earlier is stirred in thoroughly. Some manufacturers also stir in as much as 10 percent of brown sugar and some add spices, such as cloves or cumin seed. Then, while hot, it is poured or dipped into a round tank or vat equipped with a stirrer, and, while cooling, it is stirred constantly to prevent the formation of lactose crystals. When cool, it is poured into greased round or rectangular forms. When hard (firm), the cheeses usually but not always are cut into pie-shaped or small rectangular segments. Then, the whole cheese or, if cut, the individual segments may be dipped in wax or paraffin, and they are wrapped tightly, preferably in metal foil, to prevent contamination, and packed in cartons. The flat, cylindrical cheeses frequently weigh about 18 pounds.

Analysis: Moisture, frequently about 13 percent and preferably not more than 18 percent; fat in the solids, frequently 10 to 20 percent but preferably not less than 33 percent.

Nägeles

Nägeles (Fresh) cheese is made in the Netherlands from cow's skim milk. Cloves and cumin seed are mixed with the curd. It is shaped like Derby, that is, it is round, about 16 inches in diameter and 5 inches thick. (See Spiced cheese.)

Natural Rindless Loaf

Natural Rindless Loaf cheese is natural (not process) cheese that is packaged and marketed in a transparent, flexible wrapper by one of several variations of a method that was developed about 1940. Large quantities of various kinds of cheese, including Brick, Cheddar, and Swiss, are now marketed in this way. There is no rind formation on such cheese, and drying losses are minimized or eliminated. The cheese may be packaged by the manufacturer, by the warehouse operator, or by the retailer, and either before or after it is cured. The type of wrapper and the method used depend on the kind of cheese packaged and the place of packaging.

A brief description of the method of making rindless Cheddar cheese follows:

Cheddar cheese for packaging should be made from pasteurized milk because pasteurized-milk cheese produces gas at a relatively low rate while curing and therefore will not cause the wrapper to "bulge." The curd is pressed in rectangular forms, to make blocks of cheese weighing 20, 40, 60, or 80 pounds.

The blocks of cheese are wrapped in various types of films, boxed to maintain shape and stored at curing temperatures. When the desired flavor has developed the blocks are cut into consumer-size prints, wedges, sticks, or slices. These are wrapped in film to prevent rind formation. To prolong keeping quality the packages may be evacuated or gas flushed with nitrogen. Packages may contain a mold-inhibiting ingredient if so stated. All natural cheese should be kept under refrigeration until consumed.

Nessel

Nessel is a soft, cured cheese made in England from cow's whole milk. The cheeses are round and thin.

Neufchâtel

Neufchâtel cheese (Fromage de Neufchâtel), as made originally in France—especially in the Department of Seine Inférieure—is a soft, mild cheese made from whole or skim milk or a mixture of milk and cream. It may be eaten fresh or it may be cured. Bondon, Malakoff, Petit Carré, and Petit Suisse are other French cheeses that differ from Neufchâtel mainly in fat content and in size and shape.

Lactic starter is added to fresh milk at a temperature of 82° to 86° F., and enough rennet is added to coagulate the curd in 16 to 18 hours, or overnight. The coagulated curd is poured into a cloth, and it is either hung up to drain or placed in a drainer for 2 to 4 hours or longer. When the whey has practically stopped dripping, the curd is gathered up in the cloth, as in a bag, and chilled with ice. Then it is pressed between boards with a weight on top for 6 to 8 hours. The pressed curd is removed from the cloth bag, salted, either run through a curd mill or kneaded by hand, and then pressed in molds about 2½ inches in diameter and 2 or 3 inches deep. Salt may be rubbed on the surface of the cheeses when they are removed from the molds. Next, they are dried on a draining board for about 24 hours. Then they are transferred to a cool, damp curing room or cellar where they are kept clean and are inverted frequently. While curing, microorganisms—including *Mycoderma casei, Penicillium candidum,* and *P. camemberti,* as well as the so-called red cheese bacteria—grow on the surface of the cheese; a thin coating of white mold develops, followed by a yellow or reddish growth. The cheese, which is ready to market in 3 to 4 weeks, is wrapped in parchment or tinfoil. About 15 pounds of cured Neufchâtel cheese can be made from 100 pounds of rich, whole milk.

Neufchâtel frais (fresh) refers to Neufchâtel cheese made in France that is eaten without curing. It is cylindrical and flat, about 2 inches in diameter and 2½ inches thick, and weighs less than 8 ounces. It is made usually from whole milk and contains at least 45 percent of fat in the solids.

In the United States, Neufchâtel is made from pasteurized milk or a pasteurized milk-and-cream mixture in much the same way as Cream cheese, but it contains less fat and more moisture. (See Cream cheese.)

Analysis (fresh, domestic Neufchâtel): Moisture, 55 to 60 percent (not more than 65 percent); fat, not less than 20 percent but less than 33 percent; protein, 18 percent; and salt, 0.8 to 1.2 percent.

Nieheimer

Nieheimer, a sour-milk cheese, is named for the city of Nieheim in the Province of Westphalia, Prussia, where it is made. Like Hop cheese, which it resembles, it is packed with hops for curing. Although the two cheeses are not identical, Nieheimer is known as Hop cheese in some localities. (See Hop cheese.)

The sour milk is heated to a temperature between 100° and 120° F. The curd is collected in a cloth, and the whey is drained from it for a 24-hour period. Then the curd is worked until it is mellow, after which it is shaped into cakes. The cakes of curd are ripened in a cellar for 5 to 8 days, during which time they are turned frequently. When they have ripened sufficiently, they are broken up, and salt, caraway seed, and sometimes beer or milk, are added. The mixture is molded into small cheeses, shaped like flattened spheres, that weigh about 4 ounces. The cheeses are covered lightly with straw, and when they are sufficiently dry they are packed in casks with hops to ripen.

Noekkelost

Noekkelost (or Nögelost), which is a Norwegian spiced cheese, is similar to other spiced cheeses such as Kuminost and Dutch Leyden. Cumin seed, cloves, and sometimes caraway seed are the spices used. In Norway, Noekkelost usually is made from partly skimmed milk; in the United States, it may be made from either whole or partly skimmed milk. In the United States, Noekkelost usually is made in a loaf that weighs between 5 and 7 pounds, and it may be coated with paraffin or wax. Imported Noekkelost may be this shape and size, but the cheeses usually are cylindrical and weigh about 18 pounds although some cheeses weigh as much as 32 pounds. (See Spiced cheese.)

Analysis: Imported—Moisture, usually not more than 45 percent; fat in the solids, usually about 30 percent and not less than 20 percent. Domestic, whole-milk—Fat in the solids, not less than 50 percent. Domestic, part-skim—Fat in the solids, not less than 20 percent.

Nostrale

Nostrale is the local name for two kinds of cheese made from cow's milk in the mountainous region of northwestern Italy. One kind is a hard cheese (Formaggio Duro) that is made in the spring while the herds are still in the valleys; the other is a soft cheese (Formaggio Tenero) that is made in the summer when the herds are pastured in the mountains. The cheese is said to be a very old variety, and the methods of manufacture have remained primitive. A cheese called Raschera, which is made in the region of Mondovi, Italy, is probably the same as Nostrale.

Oka

Oka cheese, made in the Trappist monastery at Oka, Canada, is a type of Trappist or Port du Salut cheese. (See Trappist and Port du Salut.)

Old Heidelberg

Old Heidelberg, a soft, surface-ripened cheese, is made in Illinois. It is said to be very much like Liederkranz.

Olivet

Olivet, a soft, cow's-milk cheese, undoubtedly is named for Olivet, in the Department of Loiret, France, the center of manufacture.

There are three types of Olivet: (1) Unripened, made from whole milk, sometimes with cream added. This is consumed as fresh, summer, white, or cream cheese. (2) Half-ripened or blue, made from whole or partly skimmed milk. This is the most common type. (3) Ripened, also made from whole or partly skimmed milk.

The curd is made by a process similar to that used in making Camembert. Rennet is added to the milk, and after a coagulation period of about 2 hours the curd is transferred to a container that is perforated on the sides and bottom to facilitate drainage of the whey. About 24 hours later, the curd is put into forms, and pressed. The cheeses are turned and salted the next day, and they are then ready for consumption as unripened (fresh) cheese.

If half-ripened (blue) Olivet is being made, on the day following salting, the cheeses are placed on straw-covered shelves in the first curing room, which is maintained at a temperature of about 65° F. A reddish tint appears on the surface in a few days, and this is soon followed by a bluish tint. The blue color appears in from 10 to 15 days in summer and in about a month in winter. It is a sign of maturity, and the cheeses then are ready for consumption as half-ripened (blue) cheese. When cared for properly, this type keeps for several months.

If ripened Olivet is being made, when the blue color appears the cheeses are transferred to a second curing room where ripening is continued for an additional 15 to 30 days. Sometimes they are covered with ashes, which is believed to hasten the ripening process.

Analysis (cheese made from milk with cream added): Moisture, 28.4 percent; fat, 48.2 percent; and protein, 14.0 percent.

Olmützer Quargel

Olmützer Quargel, a sour-milk spiced Hand cheese made in western Austria and Bohemia, is similar to Mainzer Hand cheese (Mainzer Handkäse). It contains caraway seed. The cheeses are about 1½ inches in diameter and ⅓ of an inch thick. They are formed, dried, then soaked for a short time in salty whey. Then they are packed in kegs and cured for 8 to 10 weeks. (See Hand cheese and Spiced cheese.)

Analysis: Moisture, 44 to 52 percent; fat, 3.5 to 8 percent; protein, 38 to 41 percent; and salt, 5 percent.

Oschtjepek

Oschtjepek (or Oschtjepka) is a plastic-curd cheese made from ewe's milk in Slovakia. It is said to be made in the same way as the Italian Caciocavallo. (See Caciocavallo.)

Ossetin

Ossetin cheese, also called Tuschinsk and Kasach, is made in the Caucasus from either ewe's or cow's milk. However, Ossetin made from ewe's milk is considered to be better cheese than that made from cow's milk. Enough rennet is added to fresh, warm milk to coagulate it quickly. The curd is broken up by hand and cooked until it is firm; then it is kneaded while the whey drains off. It is put into round forms and sprinkled with salt. After 2 days, it is placed in brine for 2 months to a year or more. The cheese will be softer and milder if it is left in the brine for only 2 months.

Ovcji Sir

Ovcji Sir cheese is made in the Slovenian Alps from ewe's milk. Evening and morning milk are mixed in a kettle that holds about 110 pounds, and warmed to a temperature between 86° and 95° F. over an open fire. Enough rennet is added to coagulate the milk in about 30 minutes. The curd is broken up, heated to 122°, drained for an hour in a rack, and then placed in a wooden hoop. Salt is rubbed on the surface of the cheese daily for a week. It is cured for about 3 months in a cool, moist cellar. When cured, a cheese weighs between 6 and 10 pounds.

Paglia

Paglia is a Gorgonzola-type cheese made in the Canton of Ticino, Switzerland. It is circular, about 8 inches in diameter and 2 inches thick. Enough rennet is added to the milk at a temperature of 100° F. to curdle it in 15 minutes. The curd is cut or broken up, stirred, drained, and put in hoops. When it is sufficiently dry, the cheese is taken to a cool, moist cellar and placed on straw to ripen. The fermentation (ripening) usually is rapid and intense. It is controlled to some extent by salting the cheese; salting is continued for about a month. The cheese has a rather soft, mellow body and a pleasing aromatic flavor.

Pago

Pago cheese is made from ewe's milk on the Island of Pag (Italian, Pago), in Yugoslavia. It weighs between ½ and 8 pounds.

Pannarone

Pannarone cheese, also known as Stracchino di Gorgonzola bianco and Gorgonzola dolce, is a fast-ripening Gorgonzola-type cheese with white curd but without blue veining. It is made in much the same way as Gorgonzola except that Pannarone undergoes rapid fermentation for 7 or 8 days at a temperature of 77° to 82° F. before it is placed in the cold room. It is said to be unsalted, and the curing period is only 15 to 30 days. Each cheese weighs between 17 and 22 pounds. (See Gorgonzola.)

Parenica

Parenica, or Parenitza, is a ewe's-milk, Caciocavallo-type cheese made in Hungary and Slovakia.

Parmesan

Parmesan is the name in common use outside of Italy, and sometimes in Italy, for a group of very hard cheeses that have been made and known in that country for centuries as Grana. Included in the group are Parmigiano, Reggiano, Lodigiano, Lombardy, Emiliano, Veneto or Venezza, and Bagozzo or Bresciano. They differ in size and shape and in the extent to which the milk is skimmed, and there are slight differences in the methods of manufacture. This type of cheese was first made in the vicinity of Parma, in Emilia, hence the name; its manufacture has spread to other parts of Italy and to other countries. It is made mostly from April to November. Following is a general description of the process of making Parmesan-type cheese:

Cow's milk, which is skimmed more or less in different localities and in different seasons, is warmed to a temperature between 90° and 98° F., in copper kettles that hold as much as 1,600 pounds, and a starter containing heat-resistant lactobacilli and *Streptococcus thermophilus* is added. Cheese color may be added. Enough rennet extract, diluted in water, is added to produce curd firm enough to cut in 20 to 30 minutes. Then the curd is cut with a so-called cheese harp; cutting and stirring are continued until the particles of curd are ⅛ to 3/16 inch in diameter and are uniform in size. The curd is heated in 35 to 50 minutes, with stirring, to a temperature of 115° to 125°, or as high as 130° if necessary to firm the curd sufficiently.

When the curd is sufficiently firm, stirring is discontinued and the curd is allowed to settle for about 10 minutes. It may be pressed in the bottom of the kettle with a curd presser, then lifted with a scoop as a cloth is placed under it; or it may be dipped into a cloth like that used in dipping Swiss. The curd in the cloth is lifted and hung up to drain for 20 to 40 minutes; then it is placed in a hoop on a drain table. The hoop is 18 or more inches in diameter and up to 10 inches deep. The cloth is folded over the curd; a circular board is placed on top, and pressure is applied. The cloth is changed and the cheese is turned four or five times, frequently at first and then at longer intervals; then the cloth is removed and the pressure is increased. The cheese remains under pressure in the hoop for 18 to 20 hours. It is then taken to the salting room, which is maintained at a temperature of 60° to 65° F., where it may be left in the hoop for about 3 days. Then it is removed from the hoop and salted in brine for 12 or 15 days, or as long as 20 days, depending on the size of the cheese. It is dried for 8 to 10 days, usually on shelves but sometimes in the sun.

It is cured on shelves for about a year (the first stage of curing) in a room which usually is a few degrees cooler than the salting room and which has a relative humidity of 80 to 85 percent. The cheese is turned frequently and is kept clean by washing and scraping; it is rubbed with oil from time to time, and dark coloring may be rubbed on the surface. In the second stage of curing, it usually is held by dealers in large curing rooms, at a temperature of 54° to 60° F. and a relative humidity as high as 90 percent. It may be coated with a mixture of burnt umber, lamp black, and dextrin, dispersed in wine or grapeseed oil.

The yield of cheese cured for 4 months is 5 to 6 pounds per 100 pounds of partly skimmed milk.

Fully cured Parmesan is very hard but keeps almost indefinitely. It can be grated easily, and is used as grated cheese on salads and soups, and with macaroni. Considerable quantities are imported into the United States for use as grated cheese. However, successful domestic production, largely in Wisconsin and Michigan, is displacing the imported product to some extent. In the United States, Parmesan is cured for at least 14 months.

Analysis: Moisture, 30 percent (not more than 32 percent); fat, 28 percent (not less than 32 percent in the solids).

Parmigiano

Parmigiano, which is about the same as Reggiano, is one of the subvarieties of Grana (commonly called Parmesan), the hard Italian cheeses used for grating. It is made in Parma (hence the name Parmigiano), Reggio Emilia, Modena, Mantua, and Bologna, usually between April and November. The cheeses usually are from 12½ to 18 inches in diameter, from 7 to 9 inches thick, and they weigh between 48 and 80 pounds. The surface of the cheese is colored dark and coated with oil; the interior is the color of straw. The cheese may have no eyes or it may contain a few small eyes. It is cured for 1 to 2 years or longer. (See Grana, Parmesan, and Reggiano.)

Analysis: Moisture, 27 to 32 percent at 2 years; 18 to 27 percent at 3 years; fat in the solids, 32 to 38 percent; salt, 2.4 to 3 percent.

Pasta Filata

Pasta Filata (plastic curd) are Italian cheeses characterized by the fact that, after the whey is drained off, the curd is immersed in hot water or hot whey and is worked, stretched, and molded while it is in a plastic condition. The principal varieties of pasta filata cheeses are: Hard cheeses—Caciocavallo, Provolone, and Provolette; soft, moist cheeses—Mozzarella, Provole, Scamorze, and Provatura. There are numerous others. A description of each is given under its specific name.

Patagras

Patagras is a hard cheese made in Cuba from pasteurized, whole or slightly skimmed cow's milk. Gouda and Patagras are almost identical and are made by a similar process. Patagras is shaped like Gouda, weighs from 7 to 9 pounds, is coated with red wax, and usually is wrapped in a cellophane-type wrapper. It is considered one of the best Cuban cheeses. (See Gouda.)

Analysis: Moisture, 40.3 percent; fat, 26.0 percent; and salt, 3.0 percent.

Pecorino

Pecorino (Formaggio Pecorino) are Italian cheeses that are made from ewe's milk. There are numerous more or less clearly defined kinds. The most common is Pecorino Romano. (Romano made from cow's milk is called Vacchino Romano; and from goat's milk, Caprino Romano.)

Although Pecorino Romano was first made in Italy, it has been made in Sardinia since 1920, where it is known as Sardo, Sardo Romano, and Pecorino Sardo. More than 60 percent of the total output is now made in Sardinia. (See Romano and Sardo.)

A type known as Pecorino Dolce is colored artificially with annatto, and the curd is subjected to considerable pressure after it is placed in the forms. Pecorino Tuscano is a smaller cheese than Romano; it usually is about 6 inches in diameter and 2 to 4 inches thick, and weighs between 2 and 5 pounds. Some local names for other Pecorino cheeses are: Ancona, Cotrone, Iglesias, Leonessa, Puglia, and Viterbo. The milk used in making Viterbo is curdled with rennet obtained from the wild artichoke, *Cynara scolymus.*

Pecorino Urbina and Pecorino Grosseto, which are very much alike, are other Italian ewe's-milk cheeses. They are small, soft, mild cheeses.

Peneteleu

Peneteleu cheese is made in Rumania by the general process used in making Italian Caciocavallo and Rumanian Kaskaval.

Analysis: Moisture, 27.4 percent; fat, 20.1 percent; protein, 45.6 percent; and salt, 1.9 percent.

Pepato

Pepato or Siciliano Pepato is a Romano-type, spiced cheese made in Sicily and southern Italy. Sometimes the curd is packed and cured in layers, with pepper between the layers, and sometimes the pepper is mixed with the curd in the vat. Some cheese of this type is made also in northern Michigan. (See Romano and Spiced cheeses.)

Petit Suisse

Petit Suisse is a small, rich, unripened cheese made in France. It is similar to Carré, but contains more fat. It is made from fresh milk with cream added, and is not salted. It is cylindrical and flat and is made in two sizes: one about 1⅔ inches in diameter and 2 inches thick, the other 1¼ inches in diameter and 1⅔ inches thick.

Analysis: Moisture, 54.6 percent; fat, 35.0 percent (77.1 percent in the solids); and protein, 7.3 percent.

Pfister

Pfister cheese is named for Pfister Huber, a Swiss who is supposed to have originated it. It is classed in the same group as Swiss cheese although the method of making differs considerably.

Cow's fresh, skim milk is set with rennet at a temperature of 85° F., and this temperature is maintained until the curd is hooped. After a coagulation period of 30 minutes the curd is cut coarsely, and when the curd settles some of the whey is removed. Then the curd is stirred for 5 minutes, after which it is left undisturbed for another 5 minutes, while it settles again, before it is collected in a cloth and pressed in hoops for a day. The hoops of curd are redressed and turned occasionally. The next day the cheeses are removed from the hoops, salted in a brine tank for about 3 days, and then transferred to a moist room to cure for about 6 weeks. They are cleaned and salted frequently while curing. The cheeses, which weigh about 50 pounds, are shaped like small wheels of Swiss cheese.

Pickled

Pickled cheese is the term used to describe a group of cheeses to which considerable salt is added in order to prolong their keeping quality. They usually are soft cheeses with a white curd and are made in warm climates, principally in the countries bordering the Mediterranean Sea. The salt may be added either to the milk or to the curd, or the cheese may be packed in either salt brine or dry salt. Included in the group are: Domiatí and Kareish, which are made in Egypt; Feta, made in Greece; and Teleme, made in Bulgaria, Greece, Rumania (where it is called Brândza de Braila), and Turkey. A description of each of these is included under its specific name.

Pie

Pie cheese is any cheese, such as Bakers' or Cottage cheese, which is used in making cheese pie, cheese cake, or other bakery goods. Usually Bakers' cheese is used; however, in making cheese rolls, some bakers use well-aged American cheese or a mixture of American and Bakers' cheese.

Pimento

Pimento cheese is any cheese to which ground pimentos have been added. Pimentos are added most often to cheese spreads and to Neufchâtel cheese and Cream cheese; sometimes to Club cheese and Cottage cheese; and occasionally to hard cheese of the Cheddar type. (See Process.)

Pineapple

Pineapple cheese is supposed to have been first made about 1845 in Litchfield County, Conn. It derives its name from its shape and the diagonal corrugations on its surface that resemble the scales of a pineapple.

The curd is prepared as in making Cheddar or Granular or Stirred-curd cheese except that it is heated until it is firmer. The curd is pressed in pineapple-shaped forms of various sizes, to make cheeses weighing up to 6 pounds. After the cheeses are pressed, they are immersed in hot water (120° F.) for a few minutes; then each is hung up in a small, loose-meshed net to dry and cure. (See Cheddar and Granular or Stirred-curd.)

The cheeses are cured for several months. While curing, they are kept clean and are rubbed with oil several times; they may be shellacked to give the surface a hard, shiny, varnish-like finish.

Analysis: Moisture, 12 to 30 percent; fat, 33 to 45 percent; protein, 27 to 35 percent; and salt, 2 to 3 percent.

Piora

Piora, made in the Canton of Tessin in the Swiss Alps, is a hard cheese with small eyes, similar to Tilsiter. It is made from whole milk, either cow's milk or a mixture of cow's and goat's milk. It is round and flat, usually 12 to 16 inches in diameter, 3 to 4½ inches thick, and 18 to 35 pounds in weight.

A mixture of evening and morning milk is warmed to a temperature of about 92° F. in round kettles, and a starter usually is added. Rennet is added, and about 40 minutes later the curd is cut. The curd is stirred slowly with a harp or curd breaker, steadily for 10 to 15 minutes; then at intervals for about 20 minutes; then steadily for 35 to 45 minutes while it is being warmed gradually to a temperature of 118° to 125°, and stirring is continued for another 30 to 40 minutes or until the curd is firm enough to dip.

The curd is transferred to wooden hoops and pressed in Swiss-type presses for about 12 hours, after which the cheeses are removed from the presses and salted in a salt tank for a day. They are cured on shelves in a curing room at a temperature usually between 50° and 55° F. and a relative humidity of 85 to 90 percent, for 3 to 6 months. They are washed, rubbed with dry cloths, and turned frequently while curing. About 10½ pounds of unripened cheese is obtained per 100 pounds of whole milk.

Analysis: Moisture, 43.2 percent; fat, 29.0 percent; and salt, 1.5 percent.

Pont l'Évêque

Pont l'Évêque, a soft cheese similar to Romadur, is manufactured in the vicinity of Pont l'Évêque, in the Department of Calvados (Normandy), France. It is mold-ripened like Camembert, but there are differences in the making process and also in the finished cheese. In making Pont l'Évêque, the milk is set at a higher temperature; the coagulation, draining, and curing periods are shorter; the cheeses are washed while curing; and there is less development of surface mold. When cured, Pont l'Évêque has a firmer body and is a yellower color.

St. Rémy cheese, which is made in the Department of Haute-Saône, France, is very much like Pont l'Évêque; and Brioler, Steinbuscher, and Woriener are German cheeses that are similar to Pont l'Évêque but milder.

Pont l'Évêque is made usually from cow's milk, either whole or slightly skimmed; preferably the milk should contain at least 3.7 percent of fat. Usually cheese color and lactic starter are added to the milk, which is warmed to a temperature of 90° to 95° F. Enough rennet is added so the curd will be ready to cut in 35 to 40 minutes. After the curd is cut and has settled, it is transferred to a cloth, which is spread on a drain rack, and it is covered to retard cooling. When the whey has drained off and the curd is sufficiently firm, it is put into square, perforated, metal forms, which rest on straw mats on a drain board. The forms of curd are turned and the mats are changed every 5 minutes for the first half hour, and 5 or 6 times more during the first day, and then less frequently. At the end of the second or third day, the cheeses are removed from the forms and salted on the surface with fine, dry salt. Then they are placed in a well-ventilated room to dry.

After several days in the drying room, the cheeses will be sufficiently dry to transfer to shelves in the curing room. However, in some factories the cheeses are packed close together in a large wooden box and covered with a damp cloth before drying is completed, and they are kept in the box in the curing room for a few days to favor the development of surface mold. Then they are placed on the shelves. The curing room is maintained at a temperature of 55° F. and a relative humidity of 80 to 85 percent. Successful manufacture of Pont l'Évêque depends largely on careful regulation of the temperature and humidity in the curing room. The cheeses are cured for 3 to 6 weeks. They are turned daily while curing and are washed occasionally with salty water. A normal growth of grayish-white mold soon covers the surface, but it is not permitted to develop as much as on Camembert.

The cheeses are about 4¼ inches square and 1¼ to 1½ inches thick and weigh about 12 ounces. When cured, they are wrapped in wax paper or parchment. Between 11½ and 12 pounds of cured cheese is obtained from 100 pounds of cow's milk.

Analysis: Moisture, 45 to 50 percent; fat, 25.3 to 28 percent; protein, 18.2 to 22 percent; and salt, 2 percent.

Poona

Poona, a whole-milk, surface-ripened, soft cheese, was first publicized widely in 1949. It is said to have been made originally in New York State. The connotation of the name is unknown. Poona is round and flat, about 4 inches in diameter and 1¾ inches thick, and weighs about a pound. It has an aroma like that of mild Limburger and has a reddish smear on the surface. It is cured for 6 weeks. During the curing period, it is rubbed daily to control surface ripening and to produce some firmness of the rind.

Port du Salut

Port du Salut (or Port Salut) cheese was first made about 1865 by Trappist Monks at the Abbey at Port du Salut, which is near Laval in the Department of Mayenne, France. Its manufacture has spread to abbeys in various parts of Europe, especially Austria, Czechoslovakia, and southern Germany, and also to Canada and to the United States, where it is made in at least one monastery in Kentucky. The Trappists have kept the exact process secret, but similar cheese is made outside the monasteries in central and southern Europe. In France, cheese of this type made outside the monasteries is called St. Paulin.

The curd of Port du Salut cheese is compact and elastic, similar to Pont l'Évêque; the flavor is similar to Gouda; and in some instances the aroma is like very mild Limburger. The cheeses are cylindrical and flat. In France, they usually are 10 inches in diameter, nearly 2 inches thick, and weigh about 5 pounds; in Austria (and Kentucky), they are about 7 inches in diameter, 2 inches thick, and weigh nearly 3 pounds.

The details of the making process differ in different localities, but in general are as follows:

Usually the cheese is made from cow's milk. Although the milk may be partly skimmed, it is recommended that it contain not less than 3.5 percent of fat. The milk is ripened slightly; or, if fresh milk is used, lactic starter is added. Cheese color may be added. Rennet is added to the milk at a temperature between 82° and 95° F. The coagulation period varies from 35 or 40 minutes to 60 or 80 minutes; it is longer if fresh milk rather than ripened milk is used, if rennet is added at a relatively low setting temperature, or if the curd is to be heated later.

The curd is cut carefully and stirred in much the same way as Swiss-cheese curd. Cutting and stirring is continued for 20 to 30 minutes. When the curd particles are cut to ⅛ to ¼ inch in diameter, part of the whey is removed, and sometimes the curd is heated, with stirring, to a temperature between 96° and 105° F., the final temperature depending on the acidity of the milk. Then, after the curd settles, much of the whey is removed.

The curd is stirred vigorously and then transferred rapidly to perforated, cloth-lined metal forms, which are either 7 or 10 inches in diameter and about 3 inches deep, and which rest on small drain boards. The curd is heaped high in the forms and weighted with a disk. The curd remains in the forms for 10 to 12 hours. The cheeses are turned and the cloths are changed every 20 minutes the first hour and less frequently thereafter. Then the cheeses are removed from the forms, dried for about 20 hours, and salted. Usually they are rubbed with dry salt and then placed in a salt bath for a day. They are cured in a cellar on clean shelves for 6 to 8 weeks. Some authorities recommend curing at a temperature of 55° F.; others recommend as high as 65°. Some recommend a relative humidity of 85 or 90 percent, others suggest a relatively dry room. At regular intervals during the curing period, the cheeses are washed with salty water, wiped nearly dry, and turned. They are wrapped in parchment and packed in boxes for marketing. These cheeses may be marketed before they are fully cured. Usually between 7 and 8 pounds of cured cheese is obtained from 100 pounds of cow's milk, but the yield may be as high as 9.5 pounds.

Analysis: Moisture, 40 to 46 percent; fat, 25 to 30 percent; and salt, 1.3 to 2.5 percent.

Potato

Potato cheese is made in Thuringia, central Germany, usually from cow's milk but also at times from ewe's or goat's milk. The curd is made either from sour milk or from milk to which rennet is added. Potatoes are peeled, boiled, and either mashed or put through a sieve. The curd and potatoes are mixed in various proportions, such as 3 parts of potatoes to 2 parts of curd, or 1 part of potatoes to 2 or 3 parts of curd. Salt is added, and sometimes caraway seed is added also. The mixture is ripened for 2 to 4 days. Then it is mixed thoroughly again and placed in forms for a day. The cheeses are removed from the forms and dried, sometimes covered with beer or cream, and then placed in tubs and ripened for about 2 weeks.

Prato

Prato cheese (Queijo Prato), which is made in Brazil, is a pasteurized-milk, semicooked, pressed, small-eyed, Gouda-type cheese. It is similar to the Cuban cheese, Patagras.

Prattigau

Prattigau is a cow's skim-milk cheese that is named for the Prattigau Valley in Switzerland, where it was first made. It is made also in France. It is made in much the same way as Limburger. The cheeses weigh between 20 and 25 pounds. (See Limburger.)

Prestost

Prestost, also called Saaland Pfarr, is a cow's-milk cheese that has been made in Sweden since the 18th century. The cheeses usually are cylindrical in shape and weigh from 5 to 30 pounds. Fresh, whole milk is set with rennet at a temperature of 90° F. When the curd is very firm, it is cut coarsely, then put in a sieve to allow the whey to drain off. The curd is collected in a cloth and kneaded to expel more whey. Whisky is mixed with the curd, then the curd is packed in a basket and salt is sprinkled on the surface. Curing is done in a cool, moist cellar. The cloth covering is changed daily for 3 days, and the cheese is washed with whisky after the third day.

Process

Process (or Pasteurized Process) cheese is made by grinding fine, and mixing together by heating and stirring, one or more cheeses of the same or two or more varieties. An emulsifying agent is then added to the mixture and the whole worked into a homogeneous, plastic mass. However, Cream, Neufchâtel, Cottage, Creamed Cottage, Cooked, hard grating, semisoft part-skim, part-skim spiced, and skim-milk cheeses are not used. Lactic, citric, acetic, or phosphoric acid or vinegar, a small amount of cream, water, salt, color, and spices or flavoring materials may be added. The cheese may be smoked, or it may be made from smoked cheese, or so-called liquid smoke or smoke "flavor" may be added.

Cheese was heated and preserved in cans in Germany and Switzerland as early as 1895. Hard, ripened Process cheese was made in Switzerland in 1911. Canned Camembert cheese from Germany was marketed in the United States as early as 1914, and the first United States patent for processing cheese was issued in 1916. It is estimated that at least one-third of all cheese made in the United States, excepting the soft, unripened cheeses, is marketed as Process cheese. American Cheddar cheese is processed in greatest quantities, but considerable quantities of other American-type cheeses, such as Washed-curd, Colby, and Granular, and also Swiss, Gruyère, Brick, Limburger, and others are processed. Most of this is manufactured in a few large plants, as small-scale production is not practical.

Considerable skill is required in selecting the cheese to be used. It is selected on the basis of flavor, texture, body, age, acidity, and composition. Desirable cheese flavor is obtained by using sharp, fully-cured cheese, but cheese with minor defects such as imperfect rind, pinholes, gassiness, and open texture—as well as some mild flavor defects—can be used because these defects are either eliminated or minimized in processing.

Uniform composition, body, flavor and texture in the finished cheese are obtained by using cheese from two or more vat lots (in some instances as many as 20 or 30 vat lots) in each batch or blend. A vat lot is the cheese made from the milk in one vat.

The cheese for each batch is cleaned, cut if the cheeses are large, and run through a grinder into a steam-jacketed kettle or a horizontal cooker. The other ingredients are added either as the cheese is run through the grinder or while it is being heated.

Steam-jacketed kettles, equipped with mechanical agitators to stir the cheese, are available in various sizes but frequently hold from 200 to 400 pounds of cheese. As much as 30 minutes is required to heat the cheese in a large kettle.

In most large factories, horizontal cookers that hold 500 pounds or more of cheese are used. The cookers are equipped with screw-type propellers to stir the cheese, and live steam injected directly into the cheese heats it in from 3 to 5 minutes.

The cheese is heated to a temperature of at least 150° F., and usually 155° to 160°, and it is held at that temperature for at least 30 seconds but usually for about 5 minutes, the time depending on the physical characteristics of the cheese. When long, thin strings of hot cheese can be drawn from the batch with a spatula and the cheese is smooth, homogeneous, glossy, and creamy, it is ready to be packaged. In most factories, it is packaged automatically by machine in cartons that hold from 8 ounces to 5 pounds. The cartons usually are lined with transparent film, and they are sealed to exclude air. The packaged cheese is cooled to room temperature; then it is placed under refrigeration. The high temperature attained in heating, together with the heat retained during the several hours required to cool the cheese to room temperature, makes the cheese practically sterile; it keeps well and does not ripen further.

Analysis: Moisture, not more than 1 percent more than the maximum legal limit for the kind of natural cheese from which it is made, or 1 percent more than the average of the maximum legal limits if it is made from more than one kind; but in no case more than 43 percent (except 40 percent for Process Washed-curd or Colby; 44 percent for Process Swiss or Gruyère; and 51 percent for Process Limburger). Fat in the solids, not less than the minimum legal limit for the kind of natural cheese from which it is made, or the average of the minimum legal limits if it is made from more than one kind; but in no case less than 47 percent (except 43 percent for Process Swiss and 45 percent for Process Gruyère).

Fruits, vegetables, or meats, or mixtures of these, may be added to Process cheese, in which case the moisture content may be 1 percent more, and the fat in the solids 1 percent less, than in the corresponding Process cheese.

Process Pimento cheese is made by adding at least 0.2 percent of pimentos by weight to Process Cheddar or Cheddar-type cheese.

Analysis: Moisture, not more than 41 percent; fat in the solids, not less than 49 percent.

Process Blended

Process Blended (or Pasteurized Process Blended) cheese is made in the same way as Process cheese, except that Cream cheese or Neufchâtel cheese can be used in mixtures of two or more kinds and neither emulsifier nor acid is added. The moisture content must not be more than the average of the maximum limits of the cheeses blended.

Fruits, vegetables, or meats are sometimes added, in which case the moisture content may be 1 percent more and the fat in the solids 1 percent less than in the corresponding Process Blended cheese.

Process Cheese Food

Process Cheese Food (or Pasteurized Process Cheese Food) is made in the same way as Process cheese, except that certain dairy products (cream, milk, skim milk, cheese whey, or whey albumin) or concentrates or mixtures of any of these may be added, but at least 51 percent of the weight of the finished cheese food must be cheese.

Analysis: Moisture, not more than 44 percent; fat, not less than 23 percent.

Fruits, vegetables, or meats are sometimes added, in which case the fat content must be at least 22 percent.

Process Cheese Spread

Process Cheese Spread (or Pasteurized Process Cheese Spread) is made in the same way as Process Cheese Food, except that it contains more moisture (44 to 60 percent) and less fat (but not less than 20 percent) and must be spreadable at a temperature of 70° F. Fruits, vegetables, or meats may be added.

Provatura

Provatura is a soft cheese of the plastic-curd (pasta filata) type that originated in southern Italy. It was first made from buffalo's milk but is now made also from cow's milk. It is made in much the same way as Caciocavallo. Like Mozzarella, it is eaten while fresh. (See Caciocavallo.)

Analysis: Moisture, 51 to 57 percent; fat, 12 to 18 percent; and protein, 20 to 22 percent.

Providence

Providence cheese, which is very similar to Port du Salut, is made in the monastery of Bricquebec in the Department of Manche, France. It is about 8 inches in diameter and 1½ inches thick.

Provole

Provole, a round, plastic-curd (pasta filata) cheese, is made from buffalo's milk in southern Italy. It is made in the same general way as Caciocavallo, and is similar to Provatura and Scamorze. It is eaten when only a few days old. Each cheese weighs about 2 pounds.

Provolone

Provolone, an Italian plastic-curd (pasta filata) cheese, was first made in southern Italy but is now also made in other parts of Italy and in the United States, principally in Wisconsin and Michigan. It is light in color, mellow, smooth, cuts without crumbling, and has an agreeable flavor.

Provolone is made in various shapes and sizes, each of which is identified by a more or less distinguishing name. Typically, the style called Provolone is pear-shaped and in the United States weighs about 14 pounds; in Italy, it weighs between 6 and 9 pounds and is called Provolone affetale if it weighs between 9 and 14 pounds. Larger styles, weighing as much as 50, 100, or 200 pounds, are called Provolone giganti. Smaller styles, weighing from 1 to 5 pounds, usually are spherical and are called by various names such as Provoletti, Provolotini, and Provoloncini. Another style is sausage-shaped and is called Salame (Italian, sausage) if it weighs about 10 to 12 pounds, Salamini if it is smaller, and Salame giganti if it is larger (up to 200 pounds or more).

The Italian method for making Provolone and Caciocavallo are almost identical. (See Caciocavallo.) However, Provolone contains more fat and the cheeses usually are smoked after they are salted and dried. After the cheeses are smoked, they may be dipped in paraffin; if they are not paraffined, they are oiled. Although Caciocavallo may be used as a table cheese after it has cured for 2 to 4 months, usually it is cured for longer periods and is especially suitable for grating. On the other hand, Provolone is an excellent table cheese after it has cured for 6 to 9 months, and the larger styles are still suitable for use as table cheese after curing as long as 14 months. Sometimes the surface of the cheese is grooved, because it was hung in strings or ropes or because it was molded in a grooved form. The cheeses are kept clean while curing. The yield is 9½ to 10½ pounds of uncured cheese, or 7½ to 8¾ pounds of cured cheese per 100 pounds of milk.

The method for making Provolone in the United States differs in some respects from the Italian method. The milk, which may be either raw or pasteurized, is put in a Cheddar-type vat and starter is added. The milk is set with rennet paste or rennet extract plus an enzyme preparation. After the curd is cut and the whey is removed, as in the Italian method, the curd is matted, like Cheddar curd, and then cut into slabs about 2 by 8 by 24 inches which are worked and stretched in hot water. In some factories, the curd is worked in a mixing machine. The machine, which holds about 500 pounds of curd, is a metal container equipped with an irregular-shaped metal-rod stirrer, with paddle-like elbows, that revolves on a horizontal axis. The water is added at a temperature of about 180° F. and usually is changed at least once during the mixing process. The curd is worked for about 15 minutes and reaches a temperature of about 135°. Then the mass of curd—now shiny, elastic, and stringy—is removed from the machine and cut into pieces for the individual cheeses. These are treated further as described under Caciocavallo. The yield of uncured cheese is from 9 to 9½ pounds per 100 pounds of cow's milk from which very little of the fat has been removed. If the cheese is made from raw milk, it must be cured at least 60 days.

Analysis (domestic Provolone): Moisture, not more than 45 percent (usually 37 to 43.5 percent); fat, 25 to 33 percent (fat in the solids, at least 45 percent and usually 47 percent); and salt, 2 to 4 percent.

Pultost

Pultost cheese, called Knaost or Ramost in some localities, is a sour-milk cheese made in small quantities in the thinly-settled mountainous region of Norway. Sour skim milk is put in a kettle, 2 percent of starter and usually about 10 percent of whole milk is added, and the mixture is cultured for several days; if the milk is not sour enough to curdle on warming, sour buttermilk is added to increase the acidity. When sufficient acid has developed, the mixture of curd and whey is heated slowly, with stirring, to a temperature of 130° to 140° F. It is kept warm for several hours and is stirred frequently to keep the curd from matting. Then the whey is drained off, and the curd is mixed thoroughly. About 4 percent of salt and a small amount of caraway seed are mixed in, and sometimes thick cream is added. The curd is placed in boxes or troughs and stirred occasionally. It is ready to eat in a few days as fresh cheese. However, it is held in storage if it is to be consumed as aged or ripened cheese. About 16 pounds of fresh cheese or 13 pounds of ripened cheese is obtained from 100 pounds of skim milk containing 10 percent of whole milk.

Quacheq

Quacheq is a ewe's-milk cheese made in Macedonia. Sour whey is added to the milk, and when the curd has coagulated it is removed and pressed. The cheese may be eaten while fresh or after it has ripened.

Quartirolo

Quartirolo is a soft, cow's-milk, Italian cheese made originally in Lombardy, in autumn. According to some authorities, it is the name given to Milano cheese that is made from September through November. (See Milano.)

Analysis: Moisture, 52.8 percent; fat, 23.7 percent.

Queso Anejo

Queso Anejo (aged cheese) is a white, rather dry, skim-milk Mexican cheese, with a crumbly texture. The cheeses are made in round forms, and are cured for 6 to 8 months. They weigh from 11 to 22 pounds; they are packed in jute bags, each of which holds 6 or 8 cheeses, for shipment.

Considerable cheese of this type is marketed in Mexico City. It is served with enchiladas and other native dishes. Some wholesalers cover it with red chile powder, and it is then marketed as Queso Enchilado.

Queso Blanco

Queso Blanco (white cheese) is the principal Latin-American cheese. It is made in a few small factories, but for the most part it is made on farms where it provides an important means of using surplus milk. The cheese is made from whole, partly skimmed, or skim milk; or from whole milk with cream or skim milk added. Much of the cheese is eaten fresh, within a day or two after it is made, either without being pressed or after pressing. Some of the pressed cheese is held for periods ranging from 2 weeks to 2 months or more.

The method of making varies in the different countries and on different farms in the same country, but in general is as follows:

Fresh, warm cow's milk is put into a wooden vat or tub, or in some instances a hollowed-out log, and it is curdled with rennet, sometimes after considerable acid has developed in the milk. After a coagulation period of 30 to 45 minutes, the curd is broken up by hand and gently squeezed in the whey until it is rather firm—usually for 15 to 30 minutes. When the curd is sufficiently firm, it is removed from the whey, broken up, kneaded, and salted. Usually the salt is mixed with the curd, but it may be sprinkled on the curd after it has been put in the forms. At this stage the curd is fairly dry, soft, and granular, and has a salty flavor.

If the curd is pressed, it often is worked with the hands before it is put into the forms, to make it more pliable and plastic, and the cheese will be more compact. The forms or cheese boxes are various sizes—usually square or round, cloth-lined wooden frames with perforated bottoms. The cloth liner is drawn up over the cheese and topped with a wooden cover, which is weighted down with a heavy rock or lever press.

The pressed cheese is really hard, crumbly, matted rennet curd with a salty flavor and rather open texture. The high salt content, usually 5 percent or more, retards or prevents curing; however, when the cheese is held it develops a strong flavor and odor and it dries and may be used as a grating cheese. Some of the skim-milk cheese is smoked for 2 or 3 days, which darkens the surface of the cheese and dries it somewhat in addition to giving it a smoked flavor.

The cheese is known by many different local names. For example, fresh, skim-milk, cottage-type cheese is called Queso de Puna in Puerto Rico; and Queso Fresco (fresh cheese) in El Salvador and Venezuela; also, in Venezuela, Queso de Llanero, Queso de Maracay, and Queso de Perija, and other names to denote the place of manufacture.

Fresh cheese made from whole or partly skimmed milk in Mexico is called Panela.

Cheese made from whole or partly skimmed milk and pressed is called Queso de Prensa (pressed cheese) in El Salvador, Mexico, Venezuela, and Puerto Rico; in Puerto Rico, Queso del País or Queso de la Tierra (cheese of the country, native cheese); and in Colombia, Queso Estera (matted cheese).

In Costa Rica, cheese made from skim milk and pressed but not cured is called Queso Descremado (skim-milk cheese) or Queso Huloso (rubber cheese); cheese made from whole milk, heavily salted, pressed, cured for 1 or 2 months, and used as a grating cheese is called Queso de Bagaces; and cheese made from whole milk, salted and pressed lightly, and cured for 2 weeks to 2 months is called Queso de Crema (cream cheese).

The cheeses differ in size. For example, in Panama, Queso Blanco is pressed in 1-pound molds; in Colombia, Queso Estera ranges in weight from 5 to 50 pounds; in Costa Rica, Queso Descremado and Queso de Bagaces are pressed in 100-pound square blocks while Queso de Crema is pressed in 1- to 1½-pound molds; and in making Panela in Mexico, the curd is placed in square molds to make cheeses weighing ½ pound.

More complete descriptions of some of these cheeses are given under their specific names.

Queso de Bola

Queso de Bola, which is a whole-milk cheese similar to Edam, is made on a small scale in Mexico, for local consumption. It is spherical and is cured for about 3 months.

Queso de Cavallo

Queso de Cavallo is a pear-shaped cheese made in Venezuela.

Queso de Cincho

Queso de Cincho, which is also called Queso de Palma Metida, is a sour-milk cheese made in Venezuela. It is spherical, 8 to 16 inches in diameter, and is wrapped in palm leaves.

Queso de Crema

Queso de Crema, which resembles soft Brick cheese, is one of the principal cheeses made in Costa Rica. Whole milk is coagulated with rennet, the curd is broken up, put into forms, and pressed into prints that weigh from 1 to 1½ pounds. It is salted with dry salt for about 3 days and is cured for 2 weeks to 2 months. The yield is about 11 pounds per 100 pounds of rich, whole milk.

Queso de Crema, as made in Cuba, El Salvador, Venezuela, and other Latin-American countries, is a rich, unripened, perishable cheese made from cow's milk heavily enriched with cream. It frequently is used as a substitute for butter. It is especially popular in Cuba. (See Cream cheese.)

Queso de Hoja

Queso de Hoja is a cow's-milk cheese made in Puerto Rico. Fresh milk is coagulated, the curd is cut into blocks about 6 inches square and 2 inches thick, and part of the whey is drained off, which may take several hours. Then the blocks of curd are immersed in water or whey at a temperature of 150° F., which forms a tough layer of curd on the outside of the blocks. They are placed on a table and pressed (flattened) with a broad wooden paddle. Salt is sprinkled on the surface, and each piece of curd is folded in layers, wrapped in cloth, and squeezed to force out the whey. The finished cheese is about 6 inches in diameter and 1 or 2 inches thick, and has slightly rounded top and bottom surfaces. When cut, the thin layers of curd are distinct and look like leaves resting one on another, hence the name Queso de Hoja (leaf cheese).

Queso del País

Queso del País (cheese of the country, native cheese), also known as Queso de la Tierra, is a white, pressed, semisoft, perishable cheese made in Puerto Rico for local consumption. It is made on farms from surplus milk and also in several factories.

It is a cylindrical, flat cheese and is made in three general sizes: (1) Small, which usually is made in farm homes and is 3 or 4 inches in diameter and 2 to 3½ inches thick and weighs 1 to 2 pounds; (2) medium, which is 5 to 6 inches in diameter and 4 to 5 inches thick and weighs 3 to 5 pounds; and (3) large, which usually is made in factories and is 7 to 10 inches in diameter and 6 to 8 inches thick and weighs more than 5 pounds.

Queso del País usually is eaten fresh, in which case it is soft like Cottage cheese; but sometimes it is cured, in which case it is hard and somewhat bitter.

The method of making differs in different localities. In one method, which is like that used in making Queso de Prensa, neither starter nor rennet is used, and the curd is coagulated with heat and acid and is neutralized with sodium bicarbonate. (See Queso de Prensa.)

In another method, which is used in many farm homes where there is a surplus of milk, the fresh warm milk is put into a vat and coagulated either with rennet extract or with a homemade extract prepared by adding calf stomach to warm whey.

The coagulated curd is worked by hand and salted and then is put into metal hoops to drain and acquire the desired shape. About a pound of cheese is obtained per gallon of milk.

Queso de Prensa

Queso de Prensa is a hard cheese made in Puerto Rico from cow's whole milk. The making process differs in different localities. In one method, whole milk is put into a vat to ripen at room temperature for about 6 hours, and rennet is added to coagulate the milk. The curd is broken by hand or with a curd breaker, part of the whey is removed, and the curd is transferred to a drain table and cut into small pieces. Then it is put into wooden forms and salt is added, either by mixing it with the curd or by sprinkling it on top. The curd is covered and pressed lightly. The pressed cheese is removed from the forms and placed on a rack. It is eaten either while fresh or after curing for 2 or 3 months. The cheeses are about 11 inches long, 5½ inches wide, and 3 inches thick, and they weigh about 5 pounds.

In another method, whole or slightly-skimmed milk is put into a vat and heated to a temperature of 180° F. Acetic acid (diluted with water) is added, the mixture is stirred until the curd is coagulated, and sodium bicarbonate is stirred in to neutralize the acid. The curd is transferred to another container, cut into small pieces, and salted. Then it is placed in a circular, tinned metal form, covered with a circular board that fits over the form, and pressed for a day. It is turned a few times during the day. The cheeses, which may be eaten either while fresh or after ripening, weigh from 2½ to 10 pounds.

The firm, white cheese known as Queso Blanco in other Latin American countries, is called Queso de Prensa in El Salvador and Venezuela, and in some rural sections in Mexico. (See Queso Blanco.)

Queso de Puna

Queso de Puna, which is made in Puerto Rico, is like Cottage cheese except that it is molded in forms. The milk is coagulated with rennet, the whey is drained off, and salt is mixed with the curd as it is worked thoroughly or kneaded by hand. Then the curd is put into hoops about 5 inches in diameter, and it is held in the hoops without pressure for 2 or 3 days, until it is about 1½ inches thick and firm enough to retain its shape. It is eaten fresh.

Queso Fresco

Queso Fresco (fresh cheese) is a rather dry cheese of the Cottage-cheese type that is made in El Salvador and some other Latin-American countries from skim milk.

Rabacal

Rabacal is a cylindrical, flat, rather firm cheese made in the vicinity of Coimbra, Portugal, from ewe's or goat's milk. It is 4 or 5 inches in diameter and an inch thick.

Analysis: Moisture, 16.5 percent; fat, 37.4 percent; protein, 35 percent; and salt, 2.4 percent.

Radener

Radener, known also as Skim-milk Rundkäse, is a hard cheese made in Mecklenburg, northern Germany, from cow's skim milk. It is about 16 inches in diameter and 4 inches thick, and weighs between 30 and 35 pounds. It is made in much the same way as Swiss except that the curd is pressed less in making Radener. Radener is cured for 6 to 8 months at a temperature of approximately 58° F. Between 7.6 and 8.5 pounds of cured cheese is obtained from 100 pounds of skim milk. (See Swiss.)

Similar cheese made in Switzerland is known as Magere Schweizerkäse.

Analysis: Fat in the solids, 6 to 10 percent.

Radolfzeller Cream

Radolfzeller Cream cheese, like Mainauer, is made in the vicinity of Lake Constance, which is bordered by Germany, Switzerland, and Austria. It is very much like Mainauer and is similar also to Münster. Fresh, whole milk is coagulated with rennet at a temperature of 86° F. After 3 or 4 hours, the curd is transferred carefully to a cloth, and the whey is drained off. Then the curd is ladled into square or round perforated forms, about 6½ inches in diameter and 4 inches deep. The forms are placed on straw mats and the whey continues to drain. Some time later the forms are turned. The following day, the cheeses are removed from the forms and salted. They are placed on straw mats to cure and are cured for about a month at a temperature of about 60° and a relative humidity of 85 to 90 percent. While curing they are turned daily at first and later every 2 or 3 days; surface ripening is controlled by washing the cheese. About 15 pounds of cured cheese is obtained from 100 pounds of whole milk.

Rangiport

Rangiport cheese, which is practically the same as Port du Salut, is made in the Department of Seine-et-Oise, France. It is about 6 inches in diameter and 2½ inches thick, and weighs about 2½ pounds. (See Port du Salut.)

Raviggiolo

Raviggiolo, which is an uncooked, soft, sweet, creamy, fast-curing cheese very much like Crescenza, is made in Tuscany, Italy, from ewe's milk. (See Crescenza.)

Rayon

Rayon cheese is a special type of Swiss, made in the Canton of Fribourg, Switzerland, largely for export to Italy; some is made also in Italy. It is made of partly skimmed milk; the curd is cooked to a stage that insures a very dry, hard cheese in which there are no eyes. When cured, it usually is shipped to Turin where it is placed on edge on shelves in dry, warm caves; some fat drains out, and the cheese becomes exceedingly dry and hard. When it has reached this stage it is called Raper. It is used for grating.

Reblochon

Reblochon is a soft, French cheese that weighs between 1 and 2 pounds. Enough rennet is added to fresh, whole milk at a temperature of about 80° F. to curdle it in 30 minutes. The curd is cut to the size of peas and cooked to about 95° After the whey is removed, the curd is put into molds about 6 inches in diameter and 2 inches deep, and a 5-pound weight is put on each. The cheeses are turned frequently, and they are salted after they have been in the molds 12 hours. They are cured for 4 or 5 weeks in a moist room at a temperature of about 60°.

Brizecon cheese, which is made in Savoy, France, is similar to Reblochon.

Analysis: Moisture, 53.2 percent; fat, 20.5 percent; protein, 19.3 percent; and salt, 1.8 percent.

Reggiano

Reggiano, which is nearly the same as Parmigiano and Emiliano, is one of the sub-varieties of Grana, the hard Italian cheeses used for grating. It was first made in Reggio Emilia, Italy, from April through November. It is now also made in other countries, including the United States. In the United States, and sometimes in Italy, it is commonly called Parmesan, or Reggiano Parmesan.

Reggiano is made by much the same method as is used in making the other Grana-type cheeses. (See Parmesan.) Reggiano is cylindrical, with plane faces; the cheeses weigh from 55 to 66 pounds. It is softer and finer-textured than Lodigiano, contains more fat, is pressed, and is faster curing. It is cured not less than 14 months and usually not more than 2 years. (See Grana, Parmigiano, and Lodigiano.)

Analysis: Moisture, 25 to not more than 32 percent; fat, 22 to 26 percent (not less than 32 percent in the solids).

Uso Reggiano-Parmigiano cheese, which is made outside the usual source area, is similar to Reggiano.

A Reggiano-type cheese made in Uruguay is called Colonia Hard cheese, and a similar cheese made in Argentina is called Trebolgiano.

Reindeer-milk

Reindeer-milk cheese is made to a very limited extent in Norway and Sweden. Rennet is added to the milk at a temperature of 100° F., and the curd is cut, dipped into forms, and pressed lightly. Then the curd is cut into pieces about 5 by 4 by 2½ inches in size, which are salted on the surface and ripened in a dry curing room.

Requeijão

Requeijão cheese is made in northern Brazil. Skim milk, with or without lactic starter, is held until it coagulates. The coagulated milk is heated, with stirring, to a temperature as high as 175° F., the whey is drained off, and the curd is gathered in bags and pressed. Then it is placed in flat pans, broken up, and washed with warm skim milk in the proportion of 2 parts of skim milk to 1 part of curd. The skim milk-curd mixture is then heated, with stirring, as before. When the curd sticks together and the casein in the skim milk curdles and adheres to the mass of curd, the whey is drained off again, and the curd is pressed and washed with warm skim milk as was done earlier. Heating and stirring of the mixture and draining of the whey are repeated once more. Then the curd is mixed, from 2 to 2.5 percent of salt is added, and it is kneaded on a table for about 15 minutes. Hot butterfat or rich cream is added at the rate of 1 part of butterfat to 5 parts of curd, and the mixture is heated with stirring. The cheese is then molded in parchment-lined boxes. About 11 pounds of cheese is obtained from 100 pounds of skim milk and 3.4 pounds of rich cream.

Analysis: Moisture, 55 to 70 percent; fat, 8 to 20 percent; and protein, 16 to 20.5 percent.

Ricotta

Ricotta cheese is made from the coagulable material (principally albumin) in the whey obtained in the manufacture of other cheeses, such as Cheddar, Swiss, and Provolone. It was first made in Italy and, therefore, is classed as an Italian cheese. However, it is now made in all the countries of central Europe and in some parts of southern Europe. It is made also in the United States, principally in Wisconsin and New York. It is sometimes called whey cheese or albumin cheese; other names for it are Ziger or Schottenziger, Recuit, Broccio, Brocotte, Sérac, Ceracee, and Mejette.

Cheddar-cheese whey usually contains between 0.2 and 0.35 percent of fat, and Swiss-cheese whey contains at least twice as much. In making Ricotta, usually all of the fat is left in the whey, and in the United States from 5 to 10 percent of either whole milk or skim milk is added. Usually whole milk is added if fresh Ricotta is being made, and skim milk if dry Ricotta is being made. The fat is incorporated in the cheese with the coagulated albumin, and it improves the body, flavor, and food value of the cheese.

The manufacturing process should begin soon after the whey is removed from the original cheese, before it has developed excessive acidity; the acidity should not be more than 0.20 percent. The sweet whey is heated in a kettle with a steam jacket to a temperature of 200° F. (near the boiling point). Sometimes live steam is injected into the whey. Sour whey or other coagulant is stirred in. Much of the coagulated albumin rises to the surface, and is dipped out with a perforated ladle or removed with a dipping cloth. The curd may be hung in the dipping cloth to cool and drain, or it may be dipped into perforated forms or spread on a screen platform in a vat. To improve the flavor and promote ripening, lactic starter may be mixed in after the curd has cooled to about 100°. From 1 to 1.5 percent or more of salt may be added at this time.

At this stage the curd is moist, grainy, and lacks cohesiveness; it resembles cottage-cheese curd in consistency. If it is to be marketed as fresh or moist Ricotta, draining is continued or the curd may be pressed for several hours in cheesecloth-lined hoops; then it is packed in paper cartons that usually hold 5 pounds. If it is to be marketed as dry Ricotta, the curd is placed in perforated forms about 6 inches in diameter and 9 inches deep, and it is pressed heavily for a longer period. Then it is salted on the surface, if it was not salted earlier, and it is dried in a curing room at a temperature of 100° F., or slightly higher. Dry Ricotta is suitable for grating.

Approximately 5 pounds of fresh, moist curd is obtained from 100 pounds of unskimmed cheese whey with 5 pounds of added whole milk.

Analysis: Fresh, moist Ricotta—Moisture, 68 to 73 percent; fat, 4 to 10 percent; protein, 16 percent; carbohydrate, 3 percent; and salt, 1.2 percent. Cured, dry Ricotta—Moisture, 60 percent; fat, 5.2 percent; protein, 18.7 percent; carbohydrate, 4 percent; ash, 3.6 percent; and salt (in the ash), 1.5 percent.

Riesengebirge

Riesengebirge is a soft cheese that is made from goat's milk in the mountains of northern Bohemia. The milk is coagulated with rennet at about 90° F. The curd is broken up, the whey is dipped off, and the curd is put into forms and kept in a warm place for 24 hours. Then the cheeses are removed from the forms, salted on the surface, dried for 3 or 4 days, and then placed in a cool, moist cellar to cure. About 18 pounds of cheese can be made from 100 pounds of milk.

Rinnen

Rinnen, a sour-milk, spiced cheese, has been made in the Province of Pomerania, Poland, since the 18th century. It derives its name from the wooden trough in which the whey is drained from the curd and the curd is kneaded. It is made from milk that is sufficiently acid to coagulate when it is heated to about 90° F. The curd is broken up and heated to expel the whey. Then the curd is put in the wooden trough, the whey is drained off, the curd is kneaded by hand, and caraway seed is added. The curd is shaped in forms and pressed; salt is rubbed on the surface of the cheeses, they are dried, and put in wooden boxes in which they ripen.

Riola

Riola, a soft cheese with a strong flavor, usually is made from ewe's or goat's milk. It is made like Mont d'Or, except that it is ripened for 2 to 3 months instead of a week. (See Mont d'Or.)

Robbiole

Robbiole, which is similar to Crescenza, is a soft, rich, fast-ripening cheese made in the Italian Alps, especially in Lombardy. It is circular and flat and weighs between 8 ounces and 2 pounds. Usually it is made from milk that is skimmed after creaming for about 12 hours, but sometimes it is made from whole milk. The method of making Robbiole is very simple. Rennet is added to the milk at a temperature of 90° F., and about 30 minutes later the curd is cut fine and is put into forms with perforated bottoms. The forms are about 8 inches in diameter and 6 inches deep. The cheeses are removed from the forms about 5 hours later and are placed on straw mats on a drain board; they are turned frequently. After they have been on the drain board for 2 or 3 days, they are salted on the surface and are then placed in a cool, moist cellar for 12 to 15 days to ripen.

Analysis: Moisture, 46 percent; fat, 28 percent; protein, 20 percent; and salt, 3 percent.

Robbiolini

Robbiolini, which is very similar to Crescenza, is a soft cheese made mostly in Lombardy, Italy, in winter. It is made from cow's milk or from a mixture of cow's milk and either ewe's or goat's milk. Each cheese weighs about 3½ ounces. About 10 percent of acid whey is added to the milk, which then is coagulated with rennet at a temperature of 60° F. After 24 hours the curd is cut into slices, it is drained for 3 or 4 hours, then kneaded by hand into small rolls. About 3 percent of salt is mixed with the curd while it is being kneaded. The cheese ripens in a few days; it should be held at a temperature of not more than 50° until consumed.

Rocamadur

Rocamadur is a soft cheese made from ewe's milk in southern France. Rennet is added to the milk at a temperature of about 77° F.; when the curd has coagulated, it is dipped into terra cotta forms and the whey is drained off and salt is sifted into the forms. The cheese remains in the forms for a day. Each cheese weighs about 2 ounces.

Roll

Roll cheese is a hard cheese made in England from cow's whole milk. It is cylindrical, about 9 inches in diameter and 8 inches thick, and weighs about 20 pounds.

Rollot

Rollot, a soft, ripened cheese similar to Camembert, is made in the Departments of Somme and Oise, France. It is about 2½ inches in diameter and 2 inches thick, and weighs about 6 ounces.

Romadur

Romadur is a soft, ripened cheese made in southern Germany, especially in Bavaria, from either whole or partly skimmed cow's milk. It is similar to Limburger and has the same origin, but is smaller, has a milder aroma, and contains less salt. There is less smear on the surface during ripening and, according to some authorities, its quality is better. Whole-milk Romadur is similar to Liederkranz. The cheeses usually are about 2 inches square and 4½ inches long, and weigh about a pound. However, there are smaller sizes also that weigh ¼ to ⅓ pound.

The milk, sometimes with color added, is set and the curd is prepared as in making Limburger. The forms often are like those used in making Weisslacker, that is, they are divided into sections for the individual cheeses; otherwise, the curd is cut into rectangular sections for the individual cheeses after the curd is firm. The forms are laid on a screen or mat while the whey drains off and the curd becomes firm. After the cheeses are removed from the forms, they are rubbed with dry salt several times during a 12-hour period. They are cured for a shorter time and less intensively than Limburger and at a slightly lower temperature—in some factories the final curing temperature is as low as 42° to 45° F.—and there is less surface smear. The cheeses are wrapped in parchment and tinfoil and are packed in wooden boxes for shipment. About 12 pounds of cured cheese is obtained from 100 pounds of whole milk. (See Limburger.)

Schützenkäse, which is made in Austria, is similar to Romadur. Schlosskäse, made in Austria and Germany, and Harracher, Hochstrasser, and Kremstaler, made in Hungary, are also similar.

Analysis: Moisture, 48.5 to 55.5 percent; fat in the solids, 47 percent in whole-milk Romadur.

Romanello

Romanello (little Romano) is a very hard, Italian cheese usually made from partly skimmed or skim milk. The cured cheese has a sharp flavor and is suitable for grating and use as a condiment. It is made like Romano. The curd often is drained in wicker baskets, and the imprint of the basket remains on the surface of the cheese. Sometimes, however, it is pressed in hoops. The interior of the cured cheese is white and contains numerous small openings. The cheeses are 8 to 9 inches in diameter, 4 or 5 inches thick, and weigh from 9 to 12 pounds.

Romanello is made from cow's milk in a few factories in New York and Wisconsin. It is also made in Argentina. It is similar to Romano in composition.

Romano

Romano, which is sometimes called Incanestrato, is one of the most popular of the very hard Italian cheeses. It was first made from ewe's milk in the grazing area of Latium, near Rome, but it is now made also from cow's and goat's milk and in other regions in southern Italy and in Sardinia. When made from ewe's milk, it is called Pecorino Romano; from cow's milk, Vacchino Romano; and from goat's milk, Caprino Romano. Romano-type cheese made in Sardinia is called Sardo. Some Romano cheese is made in the United States from cow's milk, and considerable quantities are imported from Italy and Sardinia.

The cheeses are round, with flat ends; they vary in size but frequently are about 10 inches in diameter and 6 inches thick. A single cheese usually weighs between 15 and 20 pounds but may weigh as much as 25 pounds. The interior is somewhat granular and has practically no holes or eyes.

The milk usually is partly skimmed, and it may be pasteurized. It is put into a vat, warmed to a temperature of about 90° F., and rennet is added. If the milk is pasteurized, starter must be added. After a coagulation period of 15 to 20 minutes, the curd is cut, and then heated with stirring to about 118°. In some factories, the curd is dipped from the whey into the hoops, which are circular and lined with cloth; in other factories, the whey is drained off, then the curd is stirred and part of the salt is mixed in before the curd is hooped. The hoops of curd are pressed, and they are turned frequently. Sometimes in Italy the cheeses are punched with holes to aid drainage; this practice, however, may result in growth of mold within the cheese.

When the cheeses are removed from the press, they are immersed in salt brine and later salt is rubbed on the surface. They are cured on shelves at a temperature of 50° to 65° F. They are kept clean (they may be scraped to clean them), and they are turned frequently. They may be colored black on the surface, and may be rubbed with olive oil toward the end of the curing period.

Romano is cured for not less than 5 months. It is used as a table cheese after curing for 5 to 8 months, and after longer curing—usually at least a year—it is hard, very sharply piquant, and suitable for grating. About 8 pounds of Romano is obtained per 100 pounds of milk.

Analysis: Moisture, not more than 34 percent (usually 32 percent); fat in the solids, not less than 38 percent; and salt, 5 to 6 percent.

Roquefort

Roquefort, a blue-veined, semisoft to hard cheese, is named for the village of Roquefort in the Department of Aveyron in southeastern France, where its manufacture has been an important industry for more than two centuries. At one time shepherds prepared the curd, but now the milk is collected and the curd is prepared in centralized dairies.

A French regulation limits use of the word Roquefort to cheese made in the Roquefort area from ewe's milk. Other French cheese of the Roquefort type is called Bleu cheese, and Roquefort-type cheese made in the United States and other countries is known as Blue cheese. In addition, there are the distinctive blue-veined cheeses of England (Stilton) and Italy (Gorgonzola). (See Bleu, Blue, Stilton, and Gorgonzola.)

Roquefort cheese is characterized by its sharp, peppery, piquant flavor, and by the mottled, blue-green veins throughout the curd and the whiteness of the curd between the veins. Powder containing spores of *Penicillium roqueforti* mold is added to the curd as it is being put into the hoops, and the veins result from growth of the mold during the curing period. The powder is prepared by inocculating loaves of fresh bread with a pure culture of mold; when the mold has permeated the bread—in 4 to 6 weeks—the interior is crumbled, dried, ground, sifted, and stored for use in the cheese.

Following is a brief description of the making process: Ewe's whole milk is set with rennet at a temperature between 76° and 82° F. It is customary to heat fresh milk to between 122° and 140° and then to add enough cold milk to adjust the mixture to the setting temperature. After a coagulation period of 1½ to 2 hours, the curd is cut, the free whey is removed, and the curd either is transferred onto a cloth to drain or is mixed and drained in the vat. Then it is transferred to perforated metal hoops, about 7½ inches in diameter and 6 inches deep, which rest on drain mats on drain boards. The curd is put into the hoops in 3 or 4 layers, and blue-mold powder is sprinkled between each layer.

The curd is not pressed, but the hoops are turned several times the first day, and two or three times daily for the next 4 or 5 days. Then the cheeses are removed from the hoops, and they are taken to the caves for salting and curing. There are many natural caves in the Roquefort area and additional excavations have been made. The caves are a network of caverns and grottoes connected with one another and with the outside surface by numerous channels through which a brisk movement of cool, moist air keeps the temperature at not more than 50° F. (often as low as 40°) and the relative humidity at about 95 percent throughout the year, thus providing natural conditions that are favorable to mold growth and ripening of Roquefort cheese.

The cheeses are dry salted, piled in two or three layers for 3 days, then salted again and piled in layers for another 3 or 4 days—making a total salting period of a week. Besides improving the flavor, the rather heavy salting retards growth of slime-forming micro-organisms and foreign molds and is one of the factors that control normal ripening. When salting is completed, each cheese is punched with 60 or more holes, which permit air to reach the interior of the cheese so that the blue mold can grow. The cheeses are then placed on edge on racks, and they are cleaned every 2 or 3 weeks by scraping and brushing. The curing period is 2 to 5 months, depending on the extent of ripening desired. When ripened sufficiently, the cheeses are cleaned, wrapped in tinfoil, and boxed. They may be stored at a temperature of 40° F. The yield of cured cheese is said to be nearly 20 percent of the weight of milk used.

Analysis: Moisture, 38.5 to 41 percent (not more than 45 percent); fat, 32.2 percent; fat in the solids, not less than 50 percent; protein, 21.1 percent; ash, 6.1 percent; and salt (in the ash), 4.1 percent.

Royal Brabant

Royal Brabant is a small, Limburger-type cheese that is made in Belgium from cow's whole milk.

Runesten

Runesten cheese, which was first made in Denmark, is made also in the United States, in Minnesota and Wyoming. It is similar to Swedish Herrgårdsost (Manor cheese). The cured cheese resembles Swiss cheese, but the eyes are smaller and each "wheel" is much smaller, weighing about 5 pounds. The cheeses are cured for about 3 months. They are wrapped in red transparent film.

Saanen

Saanen, which also is called Walliser or Walliskäse, is a hard cheese similar to Swiss and to Spalen or Sbrinza. It is made from cow's milk in the Cantons of Bern and Wallis (Valais) and nearby areas in Switzerland, where its manufacture dates back to the sixteenth century. The cheeses are 12 to 16 inches in diameter, 3 to 3½ inches thick, and weighs usually between 12 and 25 pounds. The curd is very firm, and in aged cheese it is brittle and deep yellow in color.

Saanen is made in much the same way as Swiss except that, like Spalen, the curd is heated to a higher temperature, it is firmer, and it contains less moisture; the eyes are smaller and fewer in number; and the cheeses are smaller and they are cured for a much longer period. They are cured for at least 3 years and not infrequently for 7 years or more. Much of the fully cured (aged) cheese is used for grating.

It is not unusual for a cheese to be accorded great honor in a household and for it to be kept for many decades. It is the custom to make a cheese at the birth of a child and to eat portions of the cheese on feast days during his life and at his burial and also to honor his descendants on similar occasions. It is said that one cheese was kept for such use for 200 years.

Analysis: Moisture, 25 percent.

Sage

Sage cheese is an American-type, spiced (sage-flavored) cheese made by either the Cheddar or Granular or Stirred-curd process; it is pressed in any of the shapes and sizes in which those cheeses are pressed. The curd has a green, mottled appearance throughout. At one time, green sage leaves were added to the curd before it was hooped. Now, sage extract is added for flavor; and the green, mottled appearance is produced as follows: Succulent green corn is cut fine, and the juice is pressed out. This juice is added to a small part of the milk, which is made into curd in the usual way; the rest of the milk is also made into curd, and the two lots of curd are mixed just before hooping. (See Cheddar, Granular or Stirred-curd, and Spiced.)

Analysis: Moisture, 38 to 39 percent; fat in the solids (whole-milk Sage), not less than 50 percent; fat in the solids (partly skimmed-milk Sage), not less than 20 percent.

St. Benoit

St. Benoit, which is a soft cheese similar to Olivet, is made in the Department of Loiret, France. Charcoal is added to the salt which is rubbed on the surface of the cheese. It is cured for 12 to 15 days in summer and 18 to 20 days in winter. The cheeses are about 6 inches in diameter.

St. Claude

St. Claude is a small, square, goat's-milk cheese made in the vicinity of St. Claude, in the Department of Jura, France. The milk is curdled with rennet, and the curd is placed in molds for 6 to 8 hours. The cheeses, which are salted on the surface, may be eaten fresh or may be ripened in a cool, moist cellar. The cheeses weigh between 4 and 8 ounces.

St. Marcellin

St. Marcellin cheese, known in some parts of France as Fromage de Chèvre, is made in the Department of Isère, France, from goat's milk to which either ewe's or cow's milk is sometimes added. The cheeses are about 3 inches in diameter and ¾ of an inch thick, and weigh about 4 ounces. St. Marcellin is made by a method similar to that used in making Brie and Coulommiers. Blue mold is cultivated on the surface of the cheese, but not in the interior, and it is not classed as a blue cheese. (See Brie.)

St. Stephano

St. Stephano cheese, which is similar to Bel Paese, is made in small quantities in Germany. It is made from whole milk and is cured at a temperature slightly below 40° F.

Salamana

Salamana, which is made in southern Europe, is a soft, ewe's-milk cheese. The curd is put into bladders to ripen. When cured, the cheese has a very pronounced flavor. It is used as a spread for bread, and it is also mixed with corn meal and used in cooking.

Salame

Salame (Italian, sausage) usually refers to a large-style Provolone, and this style is made not only in Italy but also in other countries, including the United States. (See Provolone.)

Stracchino Salame and Formaggio Salame refer to soft cheeses of the Bel Paese type.

Saloio

Saloio is a Hand cheese made from cow's skim milk on farms in the region of Lisbon, Portugal. It is a small cylindrical cheese, 1½ to 2 inches in diameter, and it weighs about 4 ounces. (See Hand cheese.)

Analysis: Moisture, 76.3 percent; fat, 1.8 percent; protein, 11.4 percent; and salt, 2.5 percent.

Sandwich Nut

Sandwich Nut cheese is made by mixing chopped nuts with fresh Neufchâtel or Cream cheese.

Sapsago

Sapsago cheese has been made in the Canton of Glarus, Switzerland, for at least 500 years and perhaps more; it is made also in Germany. It is known by various other names, including Schabziger, Glarnerkäse, Grünerkäse, Krauterkäse, and Grünerkrauterkäse. It is a small, very hard cheese that frequently is dried. A powder prepared from clover leaves is added to the curd, which gives it a sharp, pungent flavor, a pleasing aroma, and a light-green or sage-green color. The cured cheeses are cone-shaped, 3 inches thick at the base, 2 inches at the top, and 4 inches tall, and weigh 1 to 2¼ pounds. The fully cured, dry cheese can be used for grating.

Sapsago is made from slightly sour, skim milk. The milk is put into a round kettle and stirred while it is heated to boiling temperature. Cold buttermilk is added slowly as heating and stirring are continued. The coagulum that appears on the surface is removed, set aside, and added to the curd when it is put into the forms. Then enough sour whey is added to precipitate the casein, as in making Ricotta, and stirring is stopped. If too little whey is added, the curd will be too soft and moist; if too much or too sour whey is added, the curd will be too firm and dry. The curd is collected in a cloth or strainer and spread out to cool as the whey is drained off. Then the coagulum that was set aside is mixed with the curd, salt may be added, and it is placed in perforated wooden forms, covered with a press lid, and pressed under heavy pressure at a temperature of 60° F. The curd is ripened (cured) under light pressure at this temperature for at least 5 weeks. At this stage, it is ready for use in making the cheese. In many cases it is sold and transported in large sacks or casks to a distant factory where the cheese is made.

The ripe, dry curd is ground, and about 5 pounds of salt and 2½ pounds of dried, powdered leaves of the aromatic clover, *Melilotus coerulea,* are added to each 100 pounds of curd. The mixture is stirred into a homogeneous paste, then packed in the small cloth-lined, cone-shaped forms.

About 10 or 11 pounds of fresh curd is obtained per 100 pounds of skim milk and about 65 pounds of Sapsago is obtained per 100 pounds of fresh curd.

Analysis: Moisture, as much as 40 to 43 percent but usually much less (cheese imported into the United States, not more than 38 percent); fat, 5 to 9.4 percent; protein, 40 to 42.5 percent; and salt, 4 to 5 percent.

Sardo

Sardo, or Sardo Romano, is a Romano-type cheese made on the Island of Sardinia. Originally it was made from ewe's milk only, but now it is made from a mixture of cow's and ewe's milk. When made from ewe's milk only it is properly called Sardinian Pecorino Romano or, briefly, Pecorino Sardo. Sardo is made also in the United States and in Argentina. The aged cheese is used for grating. (See Pecorino and Romano.)

Sarrazin

Sarrazin, which has been described as a Roquefort-type cheese, is made in the Canton of Vaud in southwestern Switzerland.

Sassenage

Sassenage, a hard, blue-veined cheese about 12 inches in diameter and 3 inches thick, is almost exactly like Gex and Septmoncel. It is named for the village of Sassenage, which is in the Department of Isère, France. It is made from cow's milk to which small quantities of goat's or ewe's milk are usually added. The milk, usually a mixture of skim milk and whole milk, is set with rennet; the curd is cut, drained, and molded; and the cheese is cured in the same way as Gex and Septmoncel. The ripening period is about 2 months. (See Gex and Septmoncel.)

Scamorze

Scamorze (or Scarmorze), which is a small, soft, mild, plastic-curd (pasta filata) cheese, was first made in Abruzzi and Molise in central Italy from buffalo's milk. Production has spread to other parts of Italy, and it is now made also from cow's milk and occasionally from goat's milk. It is made mostly in autumn. Like Mozzarella, it is eaten while fresh. It is said to be very tasty when toasted with bread or fried with an egg. The surface has a yellow tint. It is oval in shape, with an indentation and lappets at the top, for handling. The cheeses usually weigh between ¼ and ½ pound but may weigh as much as 2½ pounds.

Scamorze is made in much the same way as Caciocavallo, except that Scamorze is not cured. Cream from the evening milk is mixed with morning milk in a kettle and warmed to a temperature of 95° to 98° F. Starter is added, color may be added, and sufficient rennet is added to coagulate the milk in from 30 to 35 minutes. The surface is turned under with a scoop; a few minutes later the curd is stirred with a paddle and then it is cut with a harp to pieces the size of a hazelnut. The whey and curd are stirred with a mechanical stirrer. After the curd settles, the whey is removed and the curd is collected in a cloth and transferred to a vat. More whey is squeezed out of the curd; then warm water or whey (at a temperature of 113° to 122°) is poured over the curd, and it is kneaded and stretched in the hot liquid and then collected in a mass. The temperature of the whey or water is increased to between 130° and 140° to keep the curd very warm, and kneading and stretching are continued until the curd is smooth and cohesive and will form long threads when it is stretched.

At this stage, the curd is cut into portions and each portion is cut into slices which are placed in a vat. Water heated almost to the boiling point (or preferably hot fresh whey) is poured over the slices, and they are kneaded and pressed with a paddle while they are immersed. The mass then is stretched by hand and with the paddle until it is very compact and elastic. It is drawn out into a rope, and this is divided into portions the size of a turkey egg or lemon—one for each Scamorze. In making soft Scamorze, each piece is folded several times; in making firm Scamorze, the pieces are drawn out and wound on a reel. Then each piece is immersed in hot water, and as it cools it is shaped by hand and then is placed in a small mold. Later, the cheeses are tied in pairs and immersed in salt brine. They are dried in air and then are ready for shipment. The yield is 10 to 11 pounds per 100 pounds of cow's milk.

Analysis: Moisture, 40 to 45 percent; fat, 25 to 27 percent (fat in the solids, 46.5 to 49 percent); protein, 24 to 26 percent; and ash, 3.5 to 4.5 percent.

Scanno

Scanno cheese is made in Abruzzi, Italy, from ewe's milk. The milk is coagulated with rennet, and the curd is dipped from the whey. It is washed in salty water, then in hot water; then it is collected in a linen cloth and dipped in a 0.25-percent solution of iron oxide in sulfuric acid (in which part of the oxide or rust is undissolved). The curd is left in the solution for 24 hours, during which time it is turned frequently. Then the curd is taken to a dry room, but it is dipped occasionally in a similar but weaker solution. The exterior of the cheese is black and the interior is deep yellow. The cheese has a buttery consistency and a burned flavor. It usually is eaten with fruits.

Schamser

Schamser cheese, which is known also as Rheinwald, is made in the Canton of Graubünden, Switzerland, from cow's skim milk. It is about 18 inches in diameter and 5 inches thick, and weighs from 40 to 45 pounds.

Schlesische Sauermilchkäse

Schlesische Sauermilchkäse is made in Silesia in much the same way as Hand cheese. The cheeses are placed on straw-covered shelves, by the stove in winter and in a latticework house in summer, to dry until they are very hard. Then they are cured for 3 to 8 weeks in a cellar. While curing they are washed with warm water every few days. (See Hand cheese.)

Schloss

Schloss cheese (in German, Schlosskäse), known also as Castle cheese, is a small, soft, ripened cheese made in Germany and northern Austria. It is very much like Romadur, that is, similar to but milder than Limburger.

It is molded in small rectangular blocks, slightly more than 1½ inches square by 4 inches long, which are wrapped in parchment with an outer covering of tinfoil.

Schottengsied

Schottengsied is a whey cheese made for home consumption by peasants in the Alps.

Schützenkäse

Schützenkäse is a Romadur-type cheese made in Austria. It is made in small rectangular blocks, slightly more than an inch square and 4 inches long, that weigh less than 4 ounces each. The cheeses are wrapped in tinfoil.

Schwarzenberger

Schwarzenberger, which is a Limburger-type cheese, is made in southern Bohemia, western Hungary, and Austria; it is popular in Austria as a beer cheese. It is made in cubes that weigh slightly more than a pound. It is made from cow's milk in the proportion of 1 part of skim milk to 2 parts of fresh, whole milk. Enough rennet is added to the milk to coagulate it in an hour, after which the curd is broken and stirred thoroughly. The curd is dipped into wooden forms and pressed slightly for about 12 hours. After 4 or 5 days, the cheese is rubbed with salt and is taken to the curing cellar. It is cured for 2 to 3 months and is washed frequently with salty water as it cures.

Sénecterre

Sénecterre is a soft, whole-milk cheese that was first made in St. Nectaire, in the Department of Puy-de-Dôme, France. It is cylindrical in shape and weighs about 1½ pounds.

Septmoncel

Septmoncel cheese, which is known also as Jura Bleu, is named for the village of Septmoncel, near St. Claude, in the Department of Jura, France, where most of it is made. It is a hard, blue-mold cheese, very much like Gex and Sassenage. It is made by a method similar to that used in making Roquefort, but somewhat more primitive as Septmoncel usually is made on isolated farms rather than in centralized plants.

Septmoncel cheese is made from cow's milk to which a small proportion of goat's milk is sometimes added. The milk, which usually is partly skimmed, is set with rennet at a temperature of about 85° F. About 1½ hours later, the curd is cut and stirred. Then, after the curd settles, the whey is poured off. The curd is stirred and the whey is drained several times to firm the curd. When it is firm enough, it is put into the hoops and moderate pressure is applied for a few hours. After 24 hours in the hoops, the cheeses are salted, and salting is repeated daily for several days. Then the cheeses are placed in the first curing room (which is cool and moist) for 3 or 4 weeks; during this time a blue mold grows on the surface of the cheeses. Then they are transferred to cellars or natural caves, where curing is completed in another 3 or 4 weeks.

Analysis: Moisture, 28.2 percent; fat, 31.3 percent; and protein, 32.1 percent.

Serra da Estrella

Serra da Estrella, which is named for the Serra da Estrella mountain range along which it is made, is the most highly prized of several kinds of cheese made in Portugal. Usually it is made from ewe's milk, but it also is made from a mixture of goat's and ewe's milk, or only goat's milk, and occasionally from cow's milk. It is rather soft and has a pleasing, acid flavor.

The method of making is simple. The milk is warmed in a kettle with little regard to the temperature. In most cases, an extract of the flowers of a kind of thistle is added to coagulate the milk. The coagulating period is from 2 to 6 hours, depending largely on the quantity of extract used. The curd is broken up with a ladle or by hand, squeezed to remove most of the whey, and then put into circular hoops. When firm, the cheeses are removed from the hoops and cured for several weeks, during which time they are washed frequently with whey and are salted on the surface. The cheeses differ in size; the largest is about 10 inches in diameter and 2 inches thick and weighs about 5 pounds.

Another Portuguese cheese known as Castello Branco is similar to Serra da Estrella.

Analysis: Moisture, 24 to 50 percent; fat, 19 to 40 percent; protein, 18 to 32 percent; and salt, 1 to 5 percent.

Silesian

Silesian cheese, known locally as Schlesische Weichquarg, is made from cow's skim milk by a method similar to that used in making Hand cheese. In fact, one style is known as Silesian Hand cheese. The milk is coagulated by souring, and the curd is broken up and cooked at a temperature of 100° F. for a short time. Then the curd is put into a sack and pressed lightly for 24 hours, after which it is kneaded by hand and salted. Either milk or cream and sometimes flavoring substances, such as onions or caraway seed, are added. The cheese is eaten either fresh or after slight ripening.

Siraz

Siraz is a Serbian semisoft cheese made usually from whole milk. The milk is curdled at a temperature of 104° F., and the curd is dipped into a cloth and pressed into round, flat cakes from 4 to 6 inches in diameter and an inch thick. The cakes are placed in the sun to dry until the fat begins to exude; then they are rubbed with salt several times. When a crust has formed on the cheeses, they are placed in wooden containers to ripen. The ripened cheese has a mellow and compact body.

Sir Iz Mjesine

Sir Iz Mjesine cheese is made in Yugoslavia (formerly Austria) from ewe's skim milk. The milk is warmed in a bottle over a fire and coagulated very quickly with rennet made from the dried stomachs of calves or hogs. The curd is broken up with a wooden spoon, then is heated and stirred by hand. When sufficiently firm, it is placed in forms about 8 inches square and pressed into cakes about 2 inches thick. These cakes of cheese are sometimes eaten fresh. However, they usually are dried for a day, then cut into cubes, salted, and cured in the fresh skin of a goat or sheep.

Sir Mastny

Sir Mastny cheese is made in Montenegro, Yugoslavia, from ewe's milk. Fresh milk is coagulated with rennet, and the curd is cut, stirred, and heated to a temperature of 100° F. or somewhat higher. The whey is removed, and the cheeses are molded in forms.

Sir Posny

Sir Posny cheese, known also as Tord and Mrsav, is made in Montenegro, Yugoslavia, from ewe's skim milk. The milk is curdled with rennet, and the curd is heated to a temperature of approximately 100° F., drained, and molded in forms.

Slipcote

Slipcote, known also as Colwick, is a soft cheese that is made from cow's whole milk in Rutlandshire County, England, where it has been well known since the middle of the 18th century. Its peculiarity is that when it is ready to eat (ripe), the surface softens and loosens and has a tendency to slip off. The cheeses are either round or rectangular, from 4 to 6 inches wide and 1 to 2 inches thick.

The milk is coagulated with rennet, and the curd is first drained on a strainer and then is placed in suitable forms to drain until firm. The cheeses are said to be ripened between leaves of cabbage for 3 days to a week, after which they are ready to eat.

Smoked

Smoked cheese, which is characterized by the flavor and aroma of smoke, usually is American-type or Cheddar cheese. Only good-quality cheese should be smoked. The smoked flavor is imparted in 1 of 3 ways:

(1) A chemical or so-called liquid smoke may be added to the milk from which the cheese is made, or to the curd shortly after it is cut.

(2) The cheese may be salted with so-called smoked salt. However, this sometimes gives the cheese a streaked appearance.

(3) The cheese may be smoked in the same way as meat. The smoking facility consists of two rooms. In one room, wood—preferably hickory—is burned slowly, in a smothered condition. An opening or pipe conveys the

smoke to the second room. The temperature in this room should be low enough so the cheese will not melt—preferably not over 100° F. The cheese is cut into small portions, which may be wrapped loosely in parchment, and they are placed on shelves in the second room for a day. Then the cheese is rewrapped for marketing.

Some Italian cheeses, such as Provolone, are also smoked. Some manufacturers make smoked process cheese, cheese foods, and cheese spreads. The principal ingredient in these is smoked American cheese.

Spalen

Spalen, which is named for the wooden containers (spalen) in which the cheeses are shipped, is a very hard cow's-milk cheese that was first made in the Swiss Canton of Unterwalden, where it is known also as Nidwaldner Spalenkäse. It is now made in other parts of Switzerland, and also in the Italian Alps, where it is known as Sbrinza (or Sbrinz) and in some areas as Sbrinz de Raspa. This type of cheese is made also in Argentina and Uruguay, where it is called Sbrinz. Like Fribourg and Battelmatt, Spalen is a cooked-curd cheese of the Swiss type.

Cured Spalen has a grainy texture and a sharp, nutty flavor; if there are eyes, they are small. When fully cured it is used as a grating cheese. The cheeses usually are 18 to 20 inches in diameter, 3 to 4 inches thick, and weigh 30 to 45 pounds. Sbrinz from Argentina is smaller, weighing about 12 pounds.

The method of making is not uniform in the different factories and consequently the cheese is not a uniform product. However, the method is in general as follows:

Usually whole milk is used, but sometimes the milk is partly skimmed. The milk is put in a round kettle and warmed to a temperature of about 85° F. Rennet is added and after a coagulation period of about 30 minutes the curd is cut and stirred with a scoop. Then it is heated gradually to a temperature of 130° to 135° and cutting and stirring are continued until the curd particles are about ¼ inch in diameter and relatively firm. Then the curd is dipped into hoops and pressed with heavy weights for 12 to 24 hours. The cheeses are rubbed liberally with salt several times over a period of 3 to 4 weeks. They are cured in a cool room, sometimes for as long as 3 years, and in winter they are rubbed with oil. About 7 pounds of cheese is obtained from 100 pounds of whole milk.

Analysis: Moisture, 28.1 percent; fat, 33.7 percent (fat in the solids, 47 percent or more); protein, 30.8 percent; and salt, 4.5 percent.

Spiced

Spiced cheese is cheese to which one or more spices are added during the making process in such a way that the spices are distributed evenly throughout the finished cheese. Spices used include caraway seed, cumin or cumin seed, pepper, cloves, anise, and sage. Sometimes the oil extracted from a spice is used to impart the spiced flavor. Among the spiced cheeses are: Caraway, Kuminost or Kommenost, Noekkelost, Leyden, Friesian Clove,

Christian IX, Pepato, and Sage. Bondost, Sapsago, and others are sometimes included in this group. Many of these are of Scandinavian origin and spiced cheeses are especially popular in the Scandinavian countries.

Spiced cheese usually is hard cheese made by the same general method as other hard cheeses, that is, the curd is heated but not excessively, it is stirred while the whey drains off, it is not milled, and the spices usually are added at the same time as the salt before the curd is hooped.

In the United States, Federal definitions and standards for spiced cheese specify that it must either be made from pasteurized milk or be cured for not less than 60 days at a temperature not lower than 35° F.; that it must contain not less than 1½ ounces of spice per 100 pounds of cheese; and that if it is made from whole milk it must contain not less than 50 percent of fat in the solids, and if it is made from partly skimmed milk not less than 20 percent of fat in the solids.

Spitzkäse

Spitzkäse is a small spiced cheese made in Germany from cow's skim milk. It is a Limburger-type cheese similar to Backsteiner and is made in much the same way as Backsteiner except that caraway seed is added to the curd. It is made in two shapes: Rectangular, measuring 1½ by 1⅕ by 4 inches in size; and irregularly cylindrical, about 1½ inches in diameter and 4 inches long. (See Backsteiner.)

Stangenkäse

Stangenkäse, which is a Limburger-type cheese similar to Backsteiner, is made in Germany from partly skimmed cow's milk. It is about 8 inches long, 2¾ inches wide, and 2⅛ inches thick, and weighs about 1¾ pounds. (See Backsteiner.)

Analysis: Fat in the solids, 25 to 40 percent.

Steinbuscher

Steinbuscher, made first in 1860 in Steinbusch, Brandenburg, Germany, is a soft cheese similar to Romadur. The cheeses are about 5 inches square and 2 inches thick. They have a yellow surface, and the interior has a buttery consistency.

The milk, which must be fresh and of high quality, may be partly skimmed but should contain at least 3 percent of fat. It is warmed to a temperature of 86° to 90° F., and cheese color and rennet are added. After a coagulation period of 30 minutes, the curd is cut into cubes about 4 inches in diameter, then stirred and subdivided with a scoop. The curd is warmed gradually to a temperature of 95° and stirring and cutting are continued until the curd particles are the size of cherries. Then the curd is transferred to forms similar to those used in making Limburger. About 2 hours later, the forms of curd are turned, and they are turned again in 6 hours and again in 10 hours. Then the cheeses are removed from the forms and salted on the surface. They are kept in a drying room for a few days;

and then are placed in a humid curing room where they are cured for about 8 weeks in summer and 10 weeks in winter at a temperature not higher than 58°. A layer of white mold forms on the surface of the cheeses during the first 2 weeks. They are washed with salty water and turned frequently, and when the growth of surface mold is sufficient they are rubbed dry and wrapped in parchment.

Steppe

Steppe cheese, first made in Russia by German colonists, is made also in Austria, Denmark, and Germany. It is made in two shapes: (1) Flattened spheres, usually 10 to 12 inches or more in diameter and 4 to 6 inches thick, that weigh from 14 to 25 pounds; and (2) rectangular blocks, about 10 by 5½ by 7 inches, that weigh about 13 pounds. It is a rich, mellow cheese, with a flavor something like Tilsiter, but milder. This cheese usually has small, regular eyes.

Steppe is made from whole milk with color added. The milk is heated to about 90° F., and rennet is added. About 40 to 45 minutes later, the curd is cut into large cubes and some of the whey is removed; then the curd is cut into pieces the size of peas. It is stirred and heated to a temperature of 100° to 104°; after heating ceases, stirring is continued, as the whey drains off, until the curd is firm. Then it is placed in the forms. After the cheeses are removed from the forms, they are turned frequently, salted, and then transferred to a moist curing cellar where they are cured at a temperature of about 55°. They are washed occasionally with salty water while curing.

Stilton

Stilton, considered by many people to be the finest English cheese, is a hard, mild, blue-veined, cow's-milk cheese. It was first made about 1750 in Leicestershire but acquired its name and excellent reputation when it was made and served at Stilton, in Huntingdonshire. It is now made also in other parts of England. High-quality cheese of this type is also made in the United States.

Stilton, which is one of the mold-ripened group of blue-veined cheeses that includes French Roquefort and Italian Gorgonzola, is rich and mellow and has a piquant flavor; however, it is milder than either Roquefort or Gorgonzola. Its distinguishing characteristics are the narrow blue-green veins of mold throughout the curd and the wrinkled, melon-like rind that results from the drying of molds and bacteria that grow on the surface. The open and flaky texture of the curd in Stilton cheese provides conditions suitable for mold growth, so holes are not usually punched in the cheese as in Roquefort and Gorgonzola. At one time the desirable open, flaky texture was obtained by preparing curd in the evening and in the morning and mixing the two curds together. Some dairies still make the cheese twice a day, but the curds are not mixed.

The cheeses usually measure about 8 inches in diameter and from 8 to 12 inches thick, and they weigh from 12 to 15 pounds. However, in some localities, smaller cheeses weighing about 10 pounds and also larger cheeses weighing 16 to 18 pounds are made.

Originally cream was added to the whole milk used in making Stilton, usually cream from one milking being added to whole milk of the next. However, it is now common practice to make "single-cream" Stilton rather than the so-called "double-cream" type. Usually the milk is ripened slightly; if not, a small quantity of lactic starter is added. The temperature in the manufacturing room is maintained at about 65° to 68° F. The milk is warmed to about 85° and enough rennet is added so the curd will be firm enough to dip in about 80 minutes.

The curd is broken carefully, and about 10 minutes later it is dipped in thin slices into cloth-lined draining tins where it remains in the whey for about an hour and a half. Then the whey is drained off, and the cloths are tightened frequently around the curd to aid in draining the whey more completely. Sometimes the curd is removed from the cloths and cut into cubes, and the cubes are turned frequently as the curd develops the desired acidity and firmness. When the curd has drained and matted sufficiently, it is broken into coarse pieces and salted at the rate of 1 pound to 60 pounds of curd. Then it is put into tinned, perforated metal hoops, 8 inches in diameter and 10 inches or more deep. The hoops of cheese rest on cloth-covered drain boards and are turned frequently the first day and then daily for 6 or 7 days. Then the cheeses are removed from the hoops, scraped to smooth the surface, bandaged tightly, and they may be replaced in the hoops. This process is repeated one or more times, until the cheeses are sufficiently firm, at which time the bandaged cheeses are moved to a cool, ventilated room. They are kept in this room until a moldy coating forms on the surface, usually about 2 weeks; then the bandages are removed and the cheeses are transferred to clean shelves in a cool, moist curing room. The mold, said to be *Penicillium roqueforti,* gradually develops in the curd. The cheeses are kept clean and are turned frequently. The usual curing period is 4 to 6 months, but the cheeses may be wrapped and shipped earlier.

Analysis: Moisture, 33.5 to 35 percent; fat, 32 to 34 percent; protein, 23 to 33 percent; and salt, 1.5 percent.

Stracchino

Stracchino is a generic name applied to several types of whole-milk cheeses made in Italy. The best known is Stracchino di Gorgonzola. Others are Stracchino di Milano (also known as Fresco and Quardo), Stracchino Quartirolo, Stracchino Crescenza, and Stracchino Salame or Formaggio Salame. These are described under their specific names.

Analysis: Moisture, 47.5 percent; fat, 26.4 percent; and protein, 22.1 percent.

Styria

Styria cheese is a cow's whole-milk, cylindrical cheese made in the Province of Styria, Austria.

Surati

Surati (or Panir) cheese, which is made from buffalo's milk, is perhaps the best known of the few varieties of cheese made in India. It is named for the town of Surat in the Gujarat district, Bombay Province. The cheese is uncolored and is characterized by the fact that it is kept in whey while it cures and is transported in whey in large earthen containers. It is supposed to have therapeutic properties.

The making process is simple. Lactic starter is added to fresh, whole milk (preferably pasteurized), and rennet is added at a temperature of about 95° F. An hour later the curd is ladled in thin slices into small, clean bamboo baskets that are dressed on the inside with salt. Additional salt is mixed with the curd. The baskets of curd are placed on a draining rack to drain (and shrink) for about an hour, and the cheeses are inverted in the baskets. The whey that drains from the cheeses is strained, and the cheeses are removed from the baskets and ripened by floating them in the whey, at a temperature of 75° to 80°, for 12 to 36 hours. Then they are ready for consumption or shipment. Each cheese weighs about 4 ounces. About 38 pounds of cheese is obtained from 100 pounds of buffalo's milk containing 6 percent of fat.

Sveciaost

Sveciaost is a Swedish cow's-milk cheese, made principally for domestic consumption. It is simpler to make and cure than other Swedish cheeses and often is made when conditions are not just right for making other cheese. It is made from whole, partly skimmed, or skim milk that usually has developed more or less acidity, and there is considerable variation in the composition of the cheese.

Sveciaost is made in much the same way as Gouda, and the cheese resembles Gouda except that it has a more open texture. The curd is cut to about the size of the common bean and is firmed considerably in the vat, the development of acidity is relatively rapid, the drained curd is stirred to prevent matting, sometimes spices are added, and the curd is salted before it is hooped and pressed. When the cheeses are removed from the press, they may be immersed in salt brine at a temperature not over 59° F. for 3 or 4 hours, to harden the rind. The cheeses are cured for several days at a temperature of 59° to 65°, then finally at 50° to 59°. The cheeses are flat, about 15 inches in diameter and 5 to 6 inches thick, and they weigh 26 to 33 pounds. About 9½ pounds of cheese is obtained per 100 pounds of partly skimmed milk.

Analysis: Sveciaost made from partly skimmed milk—moisture, 42 to 43 percent; fat, 26.5 percent; protein, 25.5 percent; and salt, 1.5 percent.

Sweet-curd

Sweet-curd cheese in the United States refers to cheese made by the usual Cheddar process, except that the milk is not ripened and the curd is cut, heated, and drained rather quickly, without waiting for the development of acidity, and the curd is not milled. In other respects, the process is similar to the Cheddar process, and the cured cheese is much like Cheddar cheese but usually contains more moisture and the curd is not so compact. Such varieties as Brick, Münster, Edam, and Gouda are also Sweet-curd cheeses.

Swiss

Swiss (Emmentaler) cheese, which is a large, hard, pressed-curd cheese with an elastic body and a mild, nut-like, sweetish flavor, is best known because of the holes or eyes that develop in the curd as the cheese ripens. The eyes often are ½ to 1 inch in diameter and from 1 to 3 inches apart. The cheeses are about 6 inches thick, frequently more than 36 inches in diameter, and usually weigh between 160 and 230 pounds.

Switzerland is famous for this so-called King of Cheeses, and a large part of the milk produced in Switzerland is used in its production. It was first made, probably about the middle of the 15th century, in the Canton of Bern in the Emmental Valley (which accounts for its native name Emmentaler). The industry was well developed and cheese was being exported by the middle of the 17th century. Only the best cheese is exported, and it is commonly called "Switzerland Swiss."

Swiss cheese is made in many other countries besides Switzerland, including France, Denmark, Germany, Bavaria, Italy, Austria, Finland, Russia, Argentina, and the United States. Allgäuer Emmentaler, Bellunese, Formaggio Dolce, Fontina, Fontine d'Aosta, and Traanen are local names for similar cheeses made in Switzerland and nearby countries. Gruyère, made mostly in France, is similar to Swiss but is smaller and cures somewhat differently. Danish Swiss is called Samso.

The first Swiss cheese in the United States was made about 1850 by Swiss immigrants, and much of it is still being made by their descendants. Among the hard cheeses, Swiss ranks third in the quantity produced each year. About two-thirds of the annual production of 130 million pounds is made in Illinois and Wisconsin. Idaho, Minnesota, Ohio, Utah, and Wyoming also are producers. In the United States, Swiss cheese is often called Schweizer or Sweitzer.

Swiss cheese is one of the most difficult kinds of cheese to make. Control of the quality and composition of the milk, propagation and use of the essential bacterial starters, and the details of manufacture are complicated procedures that require the services of a skilled cheesemaker, and its successful manufacture is a factory operation that requires special equipment.

Three species of bacteria are used as starters: *Streptococcus thermophilus,* called the coccus culture; a lactobacillus—*Lactobacillus bulgaricus* or *L. lactis*—called the rod culture; and *Propionibacterium shermanii* (a propionic-acid-forming micro-organism), called the eye former. The lactobacillus and streptococcus produce lactic acid, which aids in expelling the whey, and they probably contribute to the breakdown of the curd during ripening. The propionic-acid bacteria are largely responsible for the characteristic flavor and eye formation.

Although there are slight differences between the methods used for making Swiss cheese in Switzerland and in the United States, following is a brief description of the general method:

Swiss cheese is made in round copper kettles that hold at least 2,000 pounds of milk, and frequently 3,000 or 3,200 pounds. The kettles are double-jacketed or have a steam chamber in the bottom. Good-quality, fresh milk is essential. It is advisable to clarify and standardize the milk. Clarification increases the elasticity of the curd in the cheese and improves eye formation. Standardizing the fat content of the milk assures cheese of uniform composition; usually slightly more than 10 percent of the fat is removed.

As the milk flows from the clarifier into the kettle, steam is turned on in the jacket or steam chamber under the kettle, and the milk is warmed to setting temperature (88° to 94° F.). Stirring is begun, the starter is added, and shortly thereafter enough rennet extract is added so the curd will be firm enough to cut in 30 minutes (the first indication of thickening appears in from 20 to 22 minutes).

As soon as the curd is firm enough to cut, the surface is "turned under"—that is, the creamy top layer is skimmed off with a wide, flat scoop and pushed to the back of the kettle, in order to mix this creamy layer with the rest of the curd. The curd is cut with a Swiss-cheese harp—from back to front and from side to side—into long rectangular strips about 1 inch square. Then the curd is turned under from top to bottom with a scoop, so that which was underneath will be on the surface, and the pieces are cut into 1-inch cubes. About 5 minutes after cutting is completed, the curd is harped (cut and mixed) until the particles are about ⅛ inch in diameter. This usually requires about 15 minutes.

Then the curd is "foreworked"—that is, stirred slowly, either continuously or at intervals—for 30 minutes to an hour or more as it acquires firmness. When it is sufficiently firm, steam is turned on and the curd is heated, usually in 30 minutes, to a temperature between 120° and 127.5° F. It is stirred continuously while it is being heated, and stirring is continued for at least 25 minutes and sometimes for an hour or longer after the final cooking temperature is reached. This is called "stirring out." As soon as the particles of curd can be broken apart easily without sticking when compressed in the hand, the curd is ready to be dipped. Some cheesemakers add several gallons of cold water at this point. Stirring is discontinued, so the curd will settle, and some of the whey is drawn off.

The curd is enclosed in a large, coarsely woven dipping cloth, and it is hoisted slowly over the kettle with a block and tackle, and the excess whey drains into the kettle. The bag of curd is then lowered into a circular wooden or stainless-steel hoop, which rests on a circular pressboard on a drain table. The curd is pressed gently down into the hoop, the edges of the cloth are smoothed over the curd, a circular pressboard is laid on top of the curd, and the curd is pressed from above with a screw- or lever-press.

About 5 minutes later, the hoop is removed; a clean, light cloth and a clean, heavy burlap cloth are substituted for the dipping cloth; the hoop is replaced; the cheese is turned over and another pressboard is placed on it; and it is pressed again. This process is repeated at definite intervals for 24 hours.

Then the cheese is removed from the press and, still in the hoop, it is taken to the so-called cold room (temperature about 55° F. and relative humidity 80 to 85 percent), where it is salted in brine. The cheese may be removed from the hoop and placed in the salt tank at once; or, still in the hoop, it may be placed on a shelf to cool for a day or so before it is salted. It is left in the salt brine for 2 or 3 days, the time depending on the size of the cheese, the amount of salt absorbed, and the rind formation desired. It is turned over and sprinkled with salt daily. Then it is placed on a circular board on a shelf in the cold room for a week or 10 days; it is washed, turned, and sprinkled with dry salt daily.

Then it is transferred to a clean board on a shelf in the warm room (temperature 65° to 72° F. and relative humidity 80 to 85 percent), where the principal ripening process takes place. The cheese is washed with salty water, it is turned and placed on a clean board, and salt is rubbed on the surface every few days. The eyes begin to form when the cheese is about 3 weeks old; eye formation is controlled to some extent by regulating the temperature of the room. The cheese usually remains in the warm room for 4 to 6 weeks; then it is returned to the cold room for further but slower curing, or to a storage room where it is held at about 40°.

Much of the cheese made in the United States is marketed after curing for 3 or 4 months (the minimum curing period is 2 months). Most of the cheese exported from Switzerland is cured for 6 to 10 months and has a more pronounced flavor.

A cheese weighing between 185 and 210 pounds can be made from a 2,500-pound kettle of milk. Several cheeses are packed in a round, wooden box for shipment; the box may contain more than 1,000 pounds of cheese. Swiss cheese is also made in rectangular blocks, about 28 inches long and 8 inches square, that weigh 25 to 28 pounds.

So-called rindless Swiss cheese is made by a somewhat modified method. The milk (in some instances as much as 20,000 pounds) is set in a rectangular vat, and the curd is prepared in the usual way. The curd and whey are transferred to a so-called press vat. Then, in a procedure similar to that used in making Herrgårdsost, the curd is pressed under the whey into a flat, rectangular block. The block of curd is subdivided into sections, each of which makes a cheese. Each cheese is placed in a cloth-lined box and pressed, then removed from the box, salted in brine, and dried. Then it is wrapped in film and placed in a box to cure.

Analysis (Domestic Swiss): Moisture, 39.4 percent (not more than 41 percent); fat, 27.5 percent (not less than 43 percent in the solids); protein, 27.4 percent; and salt, 1 to 1.6 percent.

Taffelost

Taffelost, a rather sharp-flavored Scandinavian cheese, is said to be a whey cheese resembling Mysost. Small quantities are imported into the United States.

Tafi

Tafi is the name of a cheese made in Tucuman, Argentina.

Taleggio

Taleggio, a soft, surface-ripened, Stracchino (whole-milk) cheese with a moldy rind, was first made in the Taleggio Valley in Lombardy, Italy, after World War I. The cheeses are about 8 inches square and 2 inches thick and weigh from 3½ to 4 pounds.

A starter is added to fresh, whole, cow's milk, and the milk is set with rennet at a temperature between 85° and 90° F. About 30 minutes later, the curd is cut into walnut-size cubes. When the curd is sufficiently firm, it is gathered in a cloth, drained to remove the whey, and then is put into forms.

When the cheeses are firm enough to retain their shape, they are removed from the forms and salted—usually in dry salt but sometimes in brine. They are cured for about 2 months at a temperature between 36° and 40° F.

Tamie

Tamie cheese is made by Trappists in Savoy, France. The exact method of manufacture is a trade secret, but the cheese is similar to Tome de Beaumont. (See Tome de Beaumont.)

Tanzenberger

Tanzenberger is a Limburger-type cheese that is made in Carinthia, in southern Austria.

Teleme

Teleme, also called Brândza de Braila, is a so-called pickled cheese made from goat's or ewe's milk in Rumania, Bulgaria, Greece, and Turkey. It is very much like Greek Feta. Fresh milk is set with rennet at a temperature of about 86° F.; the curd is broken up, collected in a cloth, covered, and pressed with a weight. The pressed curd is cut into pieces about 3 or 4 inches square and 1¼ to 2 inches thick, and they are immersed in salt brine for a day. The cheeses are cured for 8 to 10 days either in dilute salt brine in a cask or packed in layers in a metal container, with salt between the layers. The cured cheese is white and creamy. About 20 pounds of cheese is obtained from 100 pounds of goat's milk and 30 pounds per 100 pounds of ewe's milk.

Analysis: Moisture, 28.3 percent; fat, 37.5 percent; protein, 30.0 percent; and salt, 2.4 percent.

Terzolo

Terzolo is the Italian term used to distinguish Parmesan-type or Grana cheese made in winter from Maggengo, which is made between April and September, and from Quartirolo, which is made between September and November.

Texel

Texel is a ewe's-milk cheese made on the Island of Texel, which is in the North Sea off the coast of the Netherlands. The cheeses weigh between 3 and 4 pounds.

Analysis: Moisture, 54.5 percent; fat, 18.3 percent; protein, 20.1 percent; and salt, 3.4 percent.

Thenay

Thenay is a soft, whole-milk cheese that resembles Camembert and Vendôme. It is made, and most of it is consumed, in the region of Thenay, Department of Loir-et-Cher, France. Rennet is added to a mixture of evening and morning milk at a temperature of about 85° F. About 4 or 5 hours later, the curd is broken up and dipped into hoops about 5 inches in diameter and 4 inches deep. After whey has drained from the curd for about a day, the cheeses are removed from the hoops and salted. They are placed in a well ventilated room for about 20 days, during which time they will become covered with mold. The mold is cleaned off, and the cheeses are moved to a cool, moist cellar to cure for another 15 days.

Analysis: Moisture, 30.1 percent; fat, 15.0 percent; protein, 18.1 percent; and salt, 4.8 percent.

Tibet

Tibet is a hard, grating cheese that is made from ewe's milk in Tibet. The curd is formed into small 2-inch cubes of cheese, and they are hung by strings, 50 to 100 cheeses in a group, to dry and cure.

Tignard

Tignard, which resembles Gex and Sassenage, is a hard, blue-veined cheese made from ewe's or goat's milk in the Tigne Valley in Savoy, France.

Tilsiter

Tilsiter, sometimes called Ragnit, is a cow's-milk cheese that was first made by immigrants from the Netherlands who settled in the vicinity of Tilsit in East Prussia. It is made also in northern Germany, where it is especially popular, and in central Europe. It is a medium-firm, slightly yellow, plastic cheese, similar to Brick cheese, with some mechanical openings, and in some instances small, round eyes. It has a mild to medium-sharp piquant flavor, similar to mild Limburger. Sometimes caraway seed is added to skim-milk Tilsiter.

The cheeses usually are cylindrical and flat, 9 to 10 inches in diameter, 4 to 5½ inches thick, and weigh about 10 pounds. However, in some factories, they are made in rectangular loaf shape.

The milk—preferably whole milk, but frequently skim milk—is warmed in a round, copper kettle to a temperature of 85° to 95° F., the higher temperature being used for whole milk. Lactic starter is added if the milk is pasteurized or if it has not developed enough acidity, and cheese color and rennet are added. About 40 minutes later, when the curd is firm, it is turned with a scoop, cut until the pieces are about half an inch in diameter, and cutting and stirring are continued as the curd is warmed to a temperature of 108° to 115° in 30 to 40 minutes and the curd particles become rather firm and shrink to the size of peas. Then, after the curd settles, much of the whey is removed, and the curd is dipped rapidly into perforated wooden or metal forms that rest on a drain table. The forms of curd, which are covered to keep the curd warm, are turned every 15 minutes the first hour and less frequently the rest of the day. The cheese is not pressed.

When sufficiently firm, the cheeses are removed from the forms and salted. They may be rubbed with dry salt, immersed in brine, or packed in dry salt in small kegs for 2 or 3 days. Then they are dried and cured on clean shelves at a temperature of 54° to 59° F. and a relative humidity of 90 to 92 percent. The shelves are replaced frequently with clean ones, and the cheeses are washed frequently with salty water, wiped practically dry, and turned. They gradually become covered with a yellow smear that changes to a reddish color; the smear is washed off occasionally. The cheese is fully cured in 5 to 6 months but sometimes is marketed in 2 or 3 months. It is wrapped in parchment or tinfoil and packed in octagonal boxes, 10 to 12 cheeses in a box. About 6 pounds of skim-milk cheese and as much as 10 pounds of whole-milk cheese is obtained per 100 pounds of milk.

Analysis: Moisture, from 46 to 56 percent; fat, from 7.2 to 26.8 percent (depending on the fat content of the milk from which the cheese is made).

Tome de Beaumont

Tome de Beaumont is made in France from cow's whole milk. The milk is heated to a temperature of about 80° F. and coagulated with rennet in about 30 minutes. The curd is cut fine, heated to about 100°, stirred, and put into cloth-lined molds that are 7 inches in diameter and 4 inches deep. The cheese is pressed for 6 to 8 hours; the cloths are changed frequently during this period. It is salted and then cured for 5 to 6 weeks.

Topfkäse

Topfkäse, a sour-milk, cooked-curd cheese made in Germany, is a modification of Topfen, the German Cooked cheese. The heated curd is poured into earthen pots (topfe); hence, the name. (See Cooked cheese.)

Analysis: Moisture, 60 to 72 percent; fat, 6 to 7 percent; and protein, 17 to 25 percent.

Toscanello

Toscanello, made in the Department of Tuscany, Italy, is a very hard, ewe's-milk cheese, suitable for grating.

Touareg

Touareg is a skim-milk cheese made by Berber tribes in Africa, from the Barbary States to Lake Chad. Sometimes rennet is used to coagulate the milk, and sometimes a milk-coagulating preparation made from the leaves of the Korourou tree is used. The soft curd is dipped on mats, in very thin layers. When it is firm enough to retain its shape, it is either placed outside in the sunlight for about 10 days or near a fire for about 6 days. It is turned occasionally, and it becomes very hard and dry. It is not salted.

Touloumisio

Touloumisio is a Greek cheese similar to Feta. Curd, which is prepared in the same way as in making Feta, is put into skin bags. After the whey is drained off, the curd is salted on tables, then placed in wooden barrels until it is firm. Then it is washed thoroughly and cut into small pieces which are put into skin bags. Either salt brine or milk is poured into the bags to cover the curd; milk is said to improve the quality of the cheese. The bags of cheese are placed in a cold warehouse to cure; they are opened occasionally to permit gas, which is formed by fermentation, to escape.

Trappist

Trappist cheese was first made in 1885 in a monastery near Banjaluka in Bosnia, Yugoslavia. It is made also in monasteries in Hungary, Czechoslovakia, southern Germany, and other parts of Europe. It is much the same as the Port du Salut cheese made in France and the Oka cheese made in Canada, but there are variations in the manufacturing process.

The cheese is pale yellow and has a mild flavor. Although it is a semisoft cheese, it is cured more like the hard cheeses. It is washed frequently during the curing period, which largely prevents the growth of mold on the surface, and it ripens throughout rather than only from the surface. The size varies, the smallest being about 7 inches in diameter and weighing 2½ to 3 pounds. A larger size is about 10 inches in diameter and weighs about 5 pounds—the usual size of Port du Salut. There are still larger sizes, weighing about 10 pounds or more.

Trappist cheese is made from fresh, whole milk, usually cow's milk but some ewe's or goat's milk may be added. The milk is set with rennet at a temperature of about 82° to 90° F. After a coagulation period of 30 to 40 minutes (or as long as 90 when the setting temperature is low) the curd is cut, stirred, and heated, in some instances to a temperature of 95° to 108°. The whey is removed and the curd is transferred to forms. In Bosnia, the curd is pressed lightly, and the cheese is rather soft and tender. In Hungary and Czechoslovakia, the curd is pressed more heavily, and the cheese is somewhat firmer. The ripening period is from 5 to 6 weeks. The salted cheese is cured initially in a humid room at a temperature of 62° to 68° and later in a cooler cellar. The yield is 9 to 11 pounds of cheese per 100 pounds of cow's milk.

Analysis: Moisture, 45.9 percent; fat, 26.1 percent; protein, 23.3 percent; and salt, 1.3 to 2.5 percent.

Travnik

Travnik, known also as Arnauten and Vlasic, is a soft cheese made from ewe's milk to which a small proportion of goat's milk is added. Usually it is made from whole milk, but sometimes skim milk is used. It was first made more than a century ago in Albania, where it was known as Arnautski Sir or Arnauten cheese. Later the industry spread to Yugoslavia (Bosnia, Herzegovina, and the Vlasic Plain area), and it became known as Travnik for the town of that name in Bosnia, which is the center of trade.

Enough rennet is added to fresh, warm milk to coagulate it in from 1½ to 2 hours, and it is left undisturbed until the curd contracts and whey appears on the surface. Then the curd is put into woolen sacks, and the whey is drained from it for 7 or 8 hours. Then the curd is removed from the sacks and pressed by hand into flattened balls, which are dried for a short time in the open air. When they are sufficiently dry, the balls of cheese are packed in layers in kegs. The kegs are 14 to 28 inches in diameter and about 24 inches deep and hold from 50 to 130 pounds of cheese. Each layer of cheese is salted and pressed to remove air spaces. Usually there is some whey on the surface when the keg is full, and the excess whey is removed. The cheese is covered and pressed lightly. It may be eaten either fresh or after curing for periods ranging from 2 weeks to several months. The fresh, whole-milk cheese is soft, almost white, and mild and pleasing in flavor.

Trecce

Trecce is a small, plastic-curd (pasta filata) Italian cheese. The curd is braided or interlaced. The cheese is eaten fresh. (See Caciocavallo and Scamorze.)

Trouville

Trouville is a soft, ripened cheese, very much like an excellent quality Pont l'Évêque. The two cheeses are made in the same area in Normandy, France, and they are made by almost identical processes except that (1) Trouville is made only from whole milk and Pont l'Évêque is made from either whole or partly skimmed milk; and (2) in making Trouville, the milk is set at a temperature as low as 85° F., as well as at the higher temperatures (90° to 95°) used in making Pont l'Évêque. (See Pont l'Évêque.)

While curing, Trouville is washed frequently with cloths that have been dipped in salty water, to control the development of surface molds and smear.

Troyes

Troyes is the name sometimes used to refer to two kinds of cheese of the Camembert type (Ervy and Barberey) that are made in small quantities near Troyes, France. (See Ervy and Barberey.)

Tschil

Tschil cheese, known also as Leaf, Telpanir, and Zwirn, is made in Armenia from either ewe's or cow's sour skim milk. The milk is heated to a temperature of 122° F. in a kettle over a fire. The whey is removed and the curd is kneaded by hand until it is fairly dry and firm; then it is pressed into cakes. The cakes are placed in a wooden trough, salted, and ripened for 5 to 8 days. When a number of cakes have been made, they are broken up and packed in skins.

Twdr Sir

Twdr Sir cheese is made in Serbia from ewe's skim milk. The milk is set with rennet at a temperature of about 104° F. The curd is cut, dipped in a cloth, salted lightly, and pressed in forms that are from 10 to 12 inches in diameter and about 2 inches deep. When cured, the cheese contains small holes and has a sharp flavor; it is similar to Brick cheese but contains less fat.

Tworog

Tworog, a sour-milk cheese, is made on a large scale by Russian farmers. The milk is set in a warm place for 24 hours; then the whey is removed, and the curd is put into wooden forms and pressed. The cheese is often used in making a bread called Notruschki.

Uri

Uri, a hard, cow's-milk cheese made in the Canton of Uri, Switzerland, is from 8 to 12 inches in diameter, about 8 inches thick, and weighs between 20 and 40 pounds.

Urseren

Urseren (Italian, Orsera) is a mild-flavored cheese made in Switzerland. The milk is coagulated in 30 to 40 minutes at a temperature of 86° to 95° F.; the curd is cooked for 30 minutes at a temperature of 104° to 122°; then it is cut to the size of hemp seeds. The curd is placed in hoops and pressed lightly. After the whey has drained, the cheese is salted and is cured at a temperature of 50° to 54°.

Vacherin

Vacherin is a name common to several different kinds of cheese made in Switzerland and France.

Vacherin à la Main is made in Switzerland and in the Savoy, France. It is ripened cheese with a firm, hard rind and a very soft interior. It is eaten with a spoon or is used as a spread for bread. Cow's whole milk is set with rennet at a temperature of about 85° F., and the coagulated curd is cut fine and pressed in hoops about 12 inches in diameter and 5 to 6 inches deep. The cheeses are salted and ripened. They weigh from 5 to 10 pounds. Similar cheese made in the same region is known as Tome de Montagne.

Vacherin as made in the Canton of Fribourg, Switzerland is a soft cheese.

Vacherin du Mont d'Or is made in France, and is similar to Livarot.

Vacherin Fondu is made in much the same way as Swiss. After it is cured, it is melted and spices are added.

Västgotaöst

Västgotaöst, made in the Province of Västergötland, Sweden, is an open-textured cheese similar to Herrgårdsost. It is made in much the same way as Herrgårdsost except that the curd is broken up and hooped immediately after the whey is removed from the heated curd. This results in cheese with irregular mechanical openings instead of round eyes. (See Herrgårdsost.)

Västerbottensost, made in the Province of Västerbotten, in northern Sweden, is made in the same way except that the curd is stirred for a prolonged period after it is heated which makes it very firm when it is dipped.

Vendôme

Vendôme, which is a soft, ripened cheese similar to Camembert and Thenay, is named for Vendôme in the Department of Loir-et-Cher, France, where it is made. It is cylindrical, about 5 inches in diameter and 4 inches thick. Rennet is added to a mixture of evening and morning milk at a temperature between 75° and 85° F. After a coagulation period of 4 to 5 hours in summer and 5 to 6 hours in winter, the curd is broken up and put into hoops to drain; the hoops are turned frequently. The following day, the cheeses are removed from the hoops, and salt is rubbed on the surface twice daily for several days. They are cured in a cool, moist cellar, sometimes buried in ashes. Most of the cheese is marketed in Paris.

Veneto

Veneto, which is also called Venezza and which is similar to Asiago, is one of the Italian Grana or Parmesan-type cheeses. It is cylindrical and flat, from 8 to 16 inches in diameter and 5 to 8 inches thick, and weighs from 25 to 60 pounds. The surface of the cheese is oiled and may be colored dark. The interior is granular, and usually greenish yellow, but cheese made in the spring may be the color of straw and cheese made in the winter may be nearly white. It usually has a sharp flavor; in some instances, bitter. Usually it does not have eyes. It is cured for 1 to 2 years. When cured, it is very hard and is used for grating. (See Parmesan.)

Analysis: Moisture, 28 to 35 percent; fat in the solids, 25 to 40 percent.

Villiers

Villiers is a square, soft cheese made in the Department of Haute-Marne, France. Each cheese weighs about a pound.

Vizé

Vizé, a hard cheese similar to Romano but smaller, is made in Greece. It is a ewe's-milk cheese suitable for grating.

Void

Void, a soft cheese similar to Pont l'Évêque and Limburger, is made in the Department of Meuse, France. The milk is coagulated with rennet at a relatively high temperature, the whey is removed as rapidly as possible, and the cheeses are washed frequently with salty water while curing. They usually are about 1½ inches thick and weigh about 1¼ pounds.

Vorarlberg Sour-milk

Vorarlberg Sour-milk cheese is a hard, cow's-milk cheese made from either whole or skim milk. Sour (clabbered) milk is added to sweet milk at a temperature of 77° F., and the mixture is then heated with stirring to the coagulating temperature of 95°; or the sour milk is added at the coagulating temperature. After the milk coagulates, the curd and whey are heated with stirring to a temperature of 105°; then the curd is dipped into forms. The curd remains in the forms for about 24 hours, during which time it is turned several times. When the cheeses are removed from the forms, salt is rubbed on the surface and they are held at a temperature of about 67°. Later, the cheeses are placed in a cask for 3 days and salt is sprinkled over the surface daily. Ripening is completed in a cool, moist cellar. The ripe cheese is greasy and has a very strong odor and flavor.

Analysis: Moisture, 33 to 57 percent; fat, 3 to 32 percent; and protein, 26 to 40 percent.

Warwickshire

Warwickshire is an English cheese very similar to Derby. (See Derby.)

Analysis: Moisture, 33 percent; fat, 30 percent; protein, 29 percent; and salt, 2.8 percent.

Washed-curd

Washed-curd (or Soaked-curd) cheese is a semisoft to slightly firm cheese that is made in the same way as Cheddar except that the milled curd is washed with water before it is salted. "Soaked curd" usually indicates a longer washing period than "washed curd."

The curd is matted and milled as in making Cheddar. Then water is added, and the curd is stirred in the water for several minutes, or as long as half an hour, as it cools. Part of the whey is extracted, and water is absorbed by the curd during this process. Then the curd is drained, salted, and pressed (usually in daisy, flat, or print styles), as in the Cheddar process. (See Cheddar.)

Washing the curd increases the moisture content of the cheese, reduces the lactose content and final acidity, decreases body firmness, and increases openness of texture. Washed-curd cheese does not keep as well as Cheddar. Usually it is cured for only 1 or 2 months. If it is made from raw milk it must be cured for at least 60 days unless it is to be used in manufacturing.

Analysis: Moisture, 40 percent (not more than 42 percent); fat in the solids, not less than 50 percent; and salt, 1.4 to 1.8 percent.

Weisslacker

Weisslacker, so named because of its white, smeary, lustrous surface, is a soft, ripened, cow's-milk cheese similar to Limburger and Backsteiner, that is made in Bavaria. In some localities it is well ripened and has a strong flavor and is called Bierkäse. The cheeses are 4 to 5 inches square and 3½ inches or more thick, and they weigh from 2⅔ to 3⅓ pounds.

Usually evening milk is skimmed and mixed with morning whole milk. Enough rennet is added at a temperature of 82° to 86° F. to form curd firm enough to cut in from 60 to 80 minutes. The curd is handled in the same way as in making Limburger except that in making Weisslacker the curd is cut into larger cubes and it is not drained so completely. It is customary to transfer the curd to large molds that are divided into sections to form the individual cheeses. As the curd settles, the molds are turned frequently. When the cheeses are removed from the molds, they are salted on the surface. They are cured at a temperature of about 53° and a high relative humidity; cool, moist conditions are essential for the proper development of surface smear. The cheeses are placed in contact with one another for several days after they are placed in the curing room and then they are separated. They are turned frequently. They are wrapped in parchment after about 3 months, and the flavor is well developed within 4 months. About 12 pounds of cheese is obtained from 100 pounds of milk containing 2.8 percent of fat. (See Limburger.)

Wensleydale

Wensleydale, named for the District of Wensleydale in Yorkshire, England, where it was first made, is a medium hard, blue-veined cheese made from cow's whole milk. The cheeses are similar to Stilton in size and shape; that is, they are cylindrical and weigh 10 to 12 pounds. However, the rind does not have the melon-like network appearance of Stilton; instead, the sides may be somewhat corrugated because of the method of bandaging. The interior is white with blue veins distributed in and between the openings. The cheese has a firm and smooth body, rather than being waxy and crumbly, and is rich and creamy with a stronger flavor than Stilton. The method of making differs considerably on the farms and in the factories. In general it is as follows:

Evening milk is mixed with morning milk and warmed to a temperature of 84° to 90° F. Starter is added, the milk is ripened slightly, and it is set with rennet. After a coagulation period of 90 minutes, the curd is cut coarsely, stirred gently, and allowed to settle for 20 to 30 minutes. Then it is warmed to setting temperature, and stirring and settling are repeated. About 1½ hours after cutting, the whey is drained off. The curd for each cheese is tied tightly in a cloth and either pressed lightly in the vat or left on the draining rack for 20 to 30 minutes. Then the cloth is removed, and the curd is cut into cubes about 4 inches in diameter. Then it is replaced in the cloth and again pressed lightly. This process is repeated until the curd has matted sufficiently and developed the proper acidity; then it is broken into small pieces and salted. Sometimes the salt is added before the curd is put into the forms; sometimes the formed cheeses are immersed in salt brine for 3 or 4 days.

The curd is placed in cloth-lined forms and pressed. The cheeses are turned and redressed several times, and pressed with gradually increasing pressure until the final pressure is about 400 pounds. Then they are removed from the forms and taken to a cool, humid room to cure. They are kept clean and turned daily at first and then every 2 or 3 days. The curing period is about 6 months.

Another type of Wensleydale, which is made from curd that is cut fine and pressed lightly, has a higher moisture content and is marketed before the blue veining appears and before much flavor has developed. The cheeses are 3 to 4 inches in diameter and from 3 to 5 inches thick. This white-curd cheese is marketed sometimes before it is a month old for consumption when it is between 1 and 2 months old.

Analysis: Moisture, 33.5 to 34.7 percent; fat, 31.0 to 33.3 percent; protein, 27.2 percent; and salt, 1.7 to 2.0 percent.

Werder

Werder (or Elbinger) is a semisoft, cow's-milk cheese made on farms in West Prussia, where it is known also as Niederungskäse. The cheeses are shaped like Gouda—that is like a flattened sphere—but the individual cheeses differ greatly in size. They range from 10 to 20 inches in diameter and are 3 to 4 inches thick and weigh from 11 to 26 pounds. Like Tilsiter, Werder is ripened initially by white mold that grows on the surface and later by bacteria that produce a red tint on the surface. However, Werder, which has a mildly acid flavor, is softer and not so sharp as Tilsiter and contains more moisture.

In summer whole milk is used, but in winter the milk is partly skimmed. Cheese color is added. The milk is heated to a temperature of 86° to 90° F., and enough rennet is added so the curd will be firm enough to cut in about 45 minutes. After the curd is cut, it is stirred until the particles are about ½ inch in diameter. Then it is heated gradually, with stirring, to a temperature of 91° to 97°, and it is held at that temperature for about 15 minutes as stirring is continued, after which it is transferred to round, perforated, cloth-lined forms. A follower and weight are laid on the curd in each form, and the forms of curd are turned every few hours. After about 20 hours, the cheeses are removed from the forms. Salting is begun from 36 to 48 hours later, and several applications of salt are rubbed on the surface of the cheeses. After salting, the cheeses are dried. Then they are cured for a month at a temperature of about 60° and a relative humidity no higher than 85 percent; during this initial curing period, they are turned two or three times a week but they are not washed, and white mold grows on the surface. Then they are transferred to a curing room that is maintained at a temperature of 50° and a higher relative humidity. Here the bacteria that produce the red tint on the surface gradually develop over the white mold. The cheeses are fully ripened in about 10 weeks. They are wrapped in parchment and packed in boxes or casks that hold several cheeses. From 10 to 11 pounds of cured cheese is obtained from 100 pounds of milk.

West Friesian

West Friesian cheese is made from cow's skim milk. The milk is put in a copper kettle, and enough rennet is added to coagulate the curd in about an hour. The curd is broken up, placed in a wooden tub, and kneaded. After several hours, salt is added. The curd is pressed for about 3 hours, washed in hot water, wrapped in cloth, and pressed for an additional 12 hours. The cheese is ready to eat when it is about a week old.

Westphalia Sour-milk

Westphalia Sour-milk cheese is a Hand cheese named for Westphalia, Germany, where it is made. Sour milk is heated, with stirring, to a temperature of about 100° F.; the curd is placed in a cloth; salt, butter, and caraway seed or pepper are added. It is molded by hand, dried for a few hours, and ripened in a cool, moist cellar. (See Hand cheese.)

White

White cheese (Fromage Blanc) is a skim-milk cheese made in France in the summer. The milk is set with rennet at a temperature of about 75° F. The curd usually is molded in cylindrical forms. Salt may or may not be added, and the cheese is eaten while it is fresh.

Wilstermarsch

Wilstermarsch, or Holsteiner Marsch, cheese is made from cow's milk in Schleswig-Holstein, Germany. It is similar to Tilsiter in many respects; however, it is made by a considerably different process and is cured for a shorter period. It has a mildy acid flavor and ripens rapidly; in fact, it is often marketed before it has reached the most desirable stage of ripeness.

There are five types of Wilstermarsch, as follows: (1) Rahm, which is made from fresh, whole milk with cream added; (2) Sussmilch, which is made from fresh, whole milk; (3) Zweizeitige, which is made from a mixture of evening skim milk and morning whole milk; (4) Dreizeitige, which is made from a mixture of 24-hour-old skim milk, 12-hour-old skim milk, and fresh whole milk; and (5) Herbst, which is made from a mixture of 36- to 48-hour-old skim milk, 24-hour-old skim milk, 12-hour-old skim milk, and fresh whole milk. Most of the cheese marketed is Zweizeitige; Dreizeitige and Herbst are consumed locally.

The milk is mixed in a copper kettle and curdled with rennet at a temperature of 82° to 86° F. After a coagulation period of 25 to 30 minutes, the curd is cut and stirred with a large scoop or ladle for 25 to 35 minutes. Some of the whey is removed, and the soft curd is transferred to a large curd-drying box that holds enough curd for 3 to 5 cheeses. The box is perforated and has a grating in the bottom and is lined with cloth. The curd is mixed and squeezed in the box until it is rather firm; then the grating is removed, 2 or 3 percent of salt is mixed with the curd, and it is kneaded by hand. The curd is transferred to cylindrical, perforated, cloth-lined forms similar to those used in making Tilsiter. Each form holds between 9 and 11 pounds of curd. The cheese is pressed heavily for 8 to 12 hours; then it is removed from the forms. It is soft at this stage and tends to flatten. If necessary to control flattening, it is bandaged. The cheese is turned daily. After 10 or 12 days, it is transferred to a dry room, and it may be enclosed in a bladder or membrane to protect the surface. The cheese is marketed when 3 to 4 weeks old. From 9½ to 12 pounds of cured cheese is obtained from 100 pounds of milk, depending on the fat content of the milk from which the cheese is made.

Analysis: Whole-milk cheese—moisture, 42.5 to 53.5 percent; fat, 18.9 to 25 percent. Skim-milk cheese—moisture, 59.0 percent; fat, 2.1 percent.

Wiltshire

Wiltshire, which was first made in western Wiltshire, England, is a hard, sweet-curd cheese similar to Derby. One style, which is about 9 inches in diameter and 9 inches thick, is known as Truckles.

Morning milk is added to partly skimmed evening milk, which has been kept cool overnight. The temperature of the milk is adjusted to 80° F., and rennet is added. An hour later the curd is cut with a curd breaker or curd knives. It is warmed, with gentle stirring, to 90°. When it is sufficiently firm, it is removed from the whey, pressed for about 20 minutes, ground in a curd mill, and salted at the rate of about 2¼ pounds of salt per 100 pounds of curd. The curd is pressed overnight in a so-called press vat, which is a wooden form with holes in the bottom to permit drainage of the whey. The following day the cheese is removed from the press, salted on the surface, dressed in cloth, and repressed. This process is repeated once or twice, after which the cheese is pressed continuously for a week. Then it is transferred to the curing room where it is placed on boards. If necessary, the cheeses are bandaged at first to aid in retaining their shape. They may be inverted during curing by means of a revolving rack. The cheese is cured in the same way as Derby cheese. (See Derby.)

Analysis: Moisture, 34 to 40 percent; fat, 25 to 28.7 percent; and salt, 1.4 to 2 percent.

Withania

Withania cheese, made in the East Indies, is so named because the milk is coagulated with rennet obtained from withania berries. The cheese has a desirable flavor if it is ripened to the proper degree, but it will have an acrid flavor if it is ripened too long. Its texture is inferior to that of cheese made with rennet obtained from animals. However, cheese may be made with withania rennet when, for religious or other reasons, it is not desirable to use animal rennet.

Yoghurt

Yoghurt and Acidophilus cheeses are made with the special bacterial-starter cultures that are used in preparing Yoghurt and Acidophilus fermented milks. The starter used in making Yoghurt cheese contains *Streptococcus thermophilus, Thermobacterium bulgaricum,* and *Th. joghurt,* and that used in making Acidophilus cheese contains *S. thermophilus* and *Th. acidophilum*. The starter produces considerable acid in the cheese, which gives it a sharp flavor. Except for the use of the distinctive starters, these cheeses are made in much the same way as either the soft cheeses, such as Cream, Brie, Coulommiers, and Camembert, or the hard cheeses, such as Gouda. The milk is pasteurized to eliminate undesirable micro-organisms. Usually a soft, moist curd is prepared, molded in forms, and consumed while it is fresh. In some instances, the curd is pressed in the forms to make a firmer cheese. Sometimes the cheese is ripened with Camembert mold to make Yoghurt- or Acidophilus-Camembert cheese. If the cheese is ripened, the curd must be well drained.

These cheeses are made mostly in the Mediterranean countries, noted for their use of fermented milks. Yoghurt cheese was first made in Bulgaria from ewe's milk; it is made also in Quebec, Canada, from cow's milk.

In Bulgaria, about 3 percent of Yoghurt starter is added to the pasteurized milk, and it is coagulated with rennet at a temperature of 107° F. After a coagulation period of about 4 hours, the curd is cut, the whey is drained off, and the curd is molded in forms in much the same way as in making Cream cheese.

In Quebec, pasteurized whole milk is coagulated with a Yoghurt starter, the curd is drained in bags, salted, and worked, then packaged in cartons. The cheese has a sharply acid flavor, the consistency of fine-grained Cottage cheese, and good keeping quality for a very soft cheese.

Analysis: Bulgarian method—Moisture, 40 to 50 percent; fat, 25 to 33 percent; and protein, 17 to 21 percent. Quebec method—Moisture, 50 to 55 percent; fat, 23 to 28 percent; protein, 16 to 20 percent; lactose and its derivatives, 2.25 percent; ash, 1 to 1.5 percent; and salt (in the ash), 1 percent.

Ziegel

Ziegel cheese is made in Austria from cow's whole milk or whole milk with as much as 15 percent of cream added. The cheeses are about 3 by 2 by 2½ inches in size and weigh about half a pound.

The milk or milk-and-cream mixture is warmed to a temperature of 95° F., and enough rennet is added to coagulate it in about 30 minutes. The curd is broken up with a harp, loosened from the bottom of the vat, and then left undisturbed for about 30 minutes while the curd mats. The matted curd is cut into pieces and stirred gently for a considerable period. Then, for another 15 minutes, the curd is again left undisturbed while it settles. Then the whey is dipped off, and the curd is dipped into cheesecloth-lined forms, 24 inches long and 5 inches wide, each of which holds the curd obtained from 7½ to 8 gallons of milk. The forms of curd are turned frequently as the whey drains for a day. Then the curd is cut into smaller portions, each of which is placed in a small form that rests on a board. The forms of curd are turned and the board is replaced with a clean one daily for 8 days. Then the cheeses are removed from the forms, salt is rubbed on the surface, and they are washed in salty water and rubbed by hand every day for at least a month. They are ready for market in 2 months.

Ziger

Ziger and Schottenziger are the German names for whey (whey-protein) cheese, which is made by precipitating the albumin in cheese whey with heat and acid. In Italy, where this type of cheese was first made, and also in the United States, it is called Ricotta. It is known also as Albumin cheese. (See Ricotta.)

Cheese of this type made in the Canton of Glarus, Switzerland, is called Hudelziger. Similar cheese made in the Canton of Graubunden, Switzerland, from goat's-milk cheese whey, is called Mascarpone. (In Italy, Mascarpone cheese is made by a similar method but from cream rather than from whey.) Gruau de Montagne is made from a mixture of Ziger and cream in the Savoy (southeastern France).

In the Province of Vorarlberg, Austria, whey cheese is made as follows: The albumin is removed from the hot, acid whey and cooled, drained in cheesecloth, and then pressed in a Swiss-cheese press for 24 hours, with gradually increasing pressure. Then it is salted in a salt bath, to which cider or vinegar is sometimes added.

Analysis: Moisture, 70 percent; fat, 4 percent; and protein, 20 percent.

Zomma

Zomma, made in Turkey, is a plastic-curd, Caciocavallo-type cheese that is very much like Katschkawalj. It is said to contain at least 30 percent of fat. (See Katschkawalj.)

SELECTED REFERENCES

The references listed below contain more complete information on certain cheeses. They, or any portion of this handbook may be obtained in microfilm or photoprint form from the National Agricultural Library, Beltsville, Md. 20705. Copying charges are given at the end of these references, on page 144.

(1) ANONYMOUS.
1943. THE ROMANCE OF CHEESE. 52 pp. Kraft Foods Co., Chicago.

(2) ————
1947. KNOW YOUR CHEESE AND HOW TO SELL IT. 55 pp. The Borden Cheese Co., New York.

(3) ————
1950. NEWER KNOWLEDGE OF CHEESE. 44 pp. National Dairy Council, Chicago.

(4) AGLIO, A. DALL'.
1914. INDUSTRIA CASEARIA. 312 pp. [Robbiolini, pp. 215–216; Robbiole, 217; Mascarpone, 217–219; Crescenza, 219–224; Quartirolo, 225–227; Gorgonzola, 229–240; Cacio fiore, 240–241; Pasta filata, 246–265; Caciocavallo, 248–256; Provolone, 256–262; Scamorze, 262–264; Provole, 264–265; Mozzarelle, 264–265; Bra, 266–268; Asiago, 268–269; Asin, 269–270; Sardo, 270–274; Cotronese, 274–275; Grana, 275–294; Montasio, 302–303; Fontina, 303–304; Bitto, 304–305; Romano, 306–312.] F. lli Marescalchi, Casale Monf., Italy.

(5) BEAU, M., and BOURGAIN, C.
1927. L'INDUSTRIE FROMAGÈRE. PT. 2, LA PRATIQUE FROMAGÈRE. 216 pp. Librairie J.-B. Baillière et Fils, Paris.

(6) BESANA, C.
1923. CASEIFICIO, SCIENZA E TECNOLOGIA. Ed. 2, 312 pp. [Quartirolo, pp. 215–216; Crescenza, 216–217; Gorgonzola, 217–220; Pasta filata, 222–225; Caciocavallo, 222–224; Mozzarella, 224–225; Scamorze, 225; Provole, 225; Provatura, 225; Grana, 225–238; Fontina, 249–250; Montasio, 250; Bitto, 250–251; Cacio fiore, 259–260; Cotronese, 260–261; Romano, 261–264.] Unione, Tipographico—Editrice Torinese, Turin, Italy.

(7) BOCHICCHIO, N.
1911. MANUALE PER L'INDUSTRIA DEL LATTE E DEI LATTICINI. 700 pp. [Crescenza, pp. 475–477; Reblochon, 477–479; Cacio fiore, 483–484; Robbiolini, 487–488; Milano, 494–496; Gorgonzola, 504–509; Mozzarelle, 519–523; Scamorze, 523–528; Provole, 528–530; Trecce, 530–531; Cotronese, 560–563; Romano, 563–569; Grana, 569–585; Fontina, 600–601; Asiago, 601–604; Montasio, 604–607; Caciocavallo, 607–616.] F. Battiato, Catania, Italy.

(8) FARRAR, R. R.
1939. A SOFT CHEESE OF THE BEL PAESE TYPE. U. S. Dept. Agr. Cir. 522, 18 pp.

(9) FASCETTI, G.
1923. CASEIFICIO. Ed. 3, 727 pp. [Robbiolini, p. 521; Robbiole, 521–522; Provole, 522; Mascarpone, 522–524; Crescenza, 528–530; Milano, 530–531; Gorgonzola, 532–536; Pannarone, 536–538; Caciocavallo, 546–549; Provolone, 549; Bra, 549–553; Grana, 559–577; Fontina, 578; Asiago, 578–580; Montasio, 581; Bitto, 581–583; Romano, 583–586.] Ulrico Hoepli, Milan.

(10) Fleischmann, W., and Weigmann, H.
1932. LEHRBUCH DER MILCHWIRTSCHAFT. Ed. 7, 966 pp. [Limburger types, pp. 751–754; Münster, 754–755; Bel Paese, 755–756; Camembert, 756–761; Tilsiter, 773–775; Gouda, 775–777; Edam, 777–778; Emmentaler, 778–784; Roquefort, 789–792; Mysost, 820–821; Ziger, 821–822.] Paul Parey, Berlin.

(11) Funder, S.
1946. THE CHIEF MOLDS IN GAMMELOST. 253 pp. A. W. Brøggers Boktrykkeri A/S, Oslo.

(12) Lochry, H. R.
1948. THE MANUFACTURE OF LOW-ACID RENNET-TYPE COTTAGE CHEESE. U. S. Dept. Agr., Misc. Pub. 119, 14 pp. (Revised.)

(13) ————, Sanders, G. P., Malkames, J. P., Jr., and Walter, H. E.
1951. MAKING AMERICAN CHEDDAR CHEESE OF UNIFORMLY GOOD QUALITY FROM PASTEURIZED MILK. U. S. Dept. Agr. Cir. 880, 39 pp.

(14) Matheson, K. J., and Hall, S. A.
1924. THE MANUFACTURE OF CAMEMBERT CHEESE. U. S. Dept. Agr. Bul. 1171, 28 pp. (Out of print.)

(15) Mengebier, H.
1950. DIE HERSTELLUNG VON LIMBURGER UND ROMADUR. Die Molkerei-Ztg. (Hildesheim), 4 (30): 875–877.

(16) Morelli, L.
1950. MANUALE DEL CASARO. Ed. 7, 277 pp. [Mascarpone, pp. 181–182; Milano, 182–183; Gorgonzola, 183–185; Bernarde, 187; Bel Paese, 187–188; Caciocavallo, 188–190; Grana, 191–210; Sbrinz, 211–215.] Ulrico Hoepli, Milan.

(17) Parisi, O.
1947. IL FORMAGGIO GRANA. (PARMESAN.) 236 pp. Societa Tipografica Modenese, Modena, Italy.

(18) Peter, A., Zollikofer, E., and Hofer, H.
1947. PRAKTISCHE ANLEITUNG ZUR WEICHKÄSEREI (SOFT CHEESE). Ed. 3, 113 pp. K. J. Wyss Erben A.-G., Bern.

(19) ———— and Zollikofer, E.
1942. LEHRBUCH DER EMMENTALERKÄSEREI. Ed. 8, 160 pp. [Emmentaler, pp. 22–121; Gruyère, 122–137; Sbrinz, 138–144.] K. J. Wyss Erben A.-G., Bern.

(20) Phillips, C. A.
1944. THE MANUFACTURE OF MONTEREY CHEESE. Calif. Agr. Ext. Cir. 13, 16 pp. (Rev. ed.)

(21) ————
1944. THE MANUFACTURE OF COTTAGE CHEESE. Calif. Agr. Ext. Cir. 48, 16 pp. (Rev. ed.)

(22) Sammis, J. L.
1948. CHEESE MAKING. Ed. 12, 314 pp. Cheese Maker Book Co., Madison, Wis.

(23) Sanders, G. P.
1951. CHEESE AND CHEESE MAKING. *In* The Encyclopedia Americana, v. 6: pp. 373–375b (5 pp.). Americana Corporation, New York.

(24) ————, Burkey, L. A., and Lochry, H. R.
1950. GENERAL PROCEDURE FOR MANUFACTURING SWISS CHEESE. U. S. Dept. Agr. Cir. 851, 18 pp.

(25) Savini, E.
1937. I FORMAGGI DI PASTA FILATA. 162 pp. [Caciocavallo, pp. 26–44, 66–67; Provolone, 47–57, 68; Mozzarella, 119–122, 131–132; Provole, 136–142; Scamorze, 143–148; Manteca, 149–154.] Soc. An. Arte della Stampa, Rome.

(26) SCHWEIZERISCHE MILCHKOMMISSION.
1948. DIE SCHWEIZERISCHE MILCHWIRTSCHAFT. 943 pp. [Emmentaler, pp. 369–385; Gruyère, 385–390; Sbrinz, 390–394; Tilsiter, 398–401.] Verlags-A.-G., Thun, Switzerland.

(27) SOMMER, H. H., and TEMPLETON, H. L.
1939. THE MAKING OF PROCESSED CHEESE. Wis. Agr. Expt. Sta. Research Bul. 137, 31 pp.

(28) THOM, C., and FISK, W. W.
1938. THE BOOK OF CHEESE. Rev. ed., 415 pp. The Macmillan Co., New York. (Out of print.)

(29) TOSI, E.
1918. MANUALE PRATICO DI CASEIFICIO. Ed. 3, 832 pp. [Grana, pp. 574–613; Fontina, 614–616; Bitto, 616–620; Montasio, 620–628; Asiago, 628–630; Asin, 631–634; Bra, 634–636; Caciocavallo, 637–643; Romano, 643–648; Crescenza, 656–660; Milano, 661–662; Cacio fiore, 662–663; Gorgonzola, 663–673; Robiole, 675–676; Reblochon, 679–681; Mascarpone, 681–683; Mozzarelle, 690; Scamorze, 690–692; Ricotta, 754–756.] Fratelli Ottavi, Casale Monf., Italy.

(30) U. S. FOOD and DRUG ADMINISTRATION.
1952. CHEESES AND CHEESE PRODUCTS. Definitions and standards under the Federal Food, Drug, and Cosmetic Act. Service and Regulatory Announcements; Food, Drug, and Cosmetic No. 2, Part 19, 41 pp. (Title 21, Part 19—cheeses; processed cheeses; cheese foods; cheese spreads, and related foods. Reprinted from the Federal Register.)

(31) VAN SLYKE, L. L., and PRICE, W. V.
1949. CHEESE. Ed. 2, rev. and enl., 522 pp. Orange Judd Pub. Co., Inc., New York.

(32) WEIGMANN, H.
1933. HANDBUCH DER PRAKTISCHEN KÄSEREI. Ed. 4, 422 pp. [Weichkäse (Gervais etc.), pp. 158–172; Yoghurt cheese, 172–173; Neufchâtel etc., 173–176; Bel Paese, 176–177; Milano, 177; Münster, 178–184; Schachtelkäse, 184; Rahmkäse etc., 185–189; Camembert, 189–209; Brie and Coulommiers, 210–217; Roquefort etc., 217–238; Gorgonzola, 238–242; Stilton, 242–245; Limburger (Allgäu), 245–265; Limburger (echte, genuine), 265–267; Stangenkäse, Backstein, etc., 267–268; Weisslacker, 268–269; Romadur, etc., 269–273; Pont l'Évêque, 273–275; Steinbuscher, Broiler, 275–276; Liptauer, 276–280; Tilsiter, 281–289; Werder, 289–290; Wilstermarsch, 290–294; Gouda, 294–305; Edam, 305–312; Trappist, etc., 312–314; Bütten, Leder, 314–316; Emmentaler, 316–343; Allgäuer Emmentaler, etc., 343–345; Herrgårdsost, etc., 345–349; Gruyère, 349–353; Battelmatt, Spalen, 353–355; Chester, 367–368; Parmesan, 368–376; Cantal, 376–377; Caciocavallo, 377–380; Quarg Ziger, 380–389; Harzkäse, Handkäse, etc., 389–398; Kräuterkäse, Schabziger, 398–401; Gammelost, 401–403; Kochkäse, Topfkäse, Schmelzkäse, Schachtelkäse, 403–417.] Paul Parey, Berlin.

(33) WILSON, H. L., and PRICE, W. V.
1935. THE MANUFACTURE OF BRICK CHEESE. U. S. Dept. Agr. Cir. 359, 11 pp.

(34) WILSTER, G. H.
1951. PRACTICAL CHEESE MANUFACTURE AND CHEESE TECHNOLOGY. Ed. 7, 515 pp. Oreg. State College Co-op. Assn., Corvallis.

INDEX

A CATALOGUE OF SELECTED DOVER BOOKS IN ALL FIELDS OF INTEREST

A CATALOGUE OF SELECTED DOVER BOOKS IN ALL FIELDS OF INTEREST

AMERICA'S OLD MASTERS, James T. Flexner. Four men emerged unexpectedly from provincial 18th century America to leadership in European art: Benjamin West, J. S. Copley, C. R. Peale, Gilbert Stuart. Brilliant coverage of lives and contributions. Revised, 1967 edition. 69 plates. 365pp. of text.
21806-6 Paperbound $3.00

FIRST FLOWERS OF OUR WILDERNESS: AMERICAN PAINTING, THE COLONIAL PERIOD, James T. Flexner. Painters, and regional painting traditions from earliest Colonial times up to the emergence of Copley, West and Peale Sr., Foster, Gustavus Hesselius, Feke, John Smibert and many anonymous painters in the primitive manner. Engaging presentation, with 162 illustrations. xxii + 368pp.
22180-6 Paperbound $3.50

THE LIGHT OF DISTANT SKIES: AMERICAN PAINTING, 1760-1835, James T. Flexner. The great generation of early American painters goes to Europe to learn and to teach: West, Copley, Gilbert Stuart and others. Allston, Trumbull, Morse; also contemporary American painters—primitives, derivatives, academics—who remained in America. 102 illustrations. xiii + 306pp. 22179-2 Paperbound $3.00

A HISTORY OF THE RISE AND PROGRESS OF THE ARTS OF DESIGN IN THE UNITED STATES, William Dunlap. Much the richest mine of information on early American painters, sculptors, architects, engravers, miniaturists, etc. The only source of information for scores of artists, the major primary source for many others. Unabridged reprint of rare original 1834 edition, with new introduction by James T. Flexner, and 394 new illustrations. Edited by Rita Weiss. 6⅝ x 9⅝.
21695-0, 21696-9, 21697-7 Three volumes, Paperbound $13.50

EPOCHS OF CHINESE AND JAPANESE ART, Ernest F. Fenollosa. From primitive Chinese art to the 20th century, thorough history, explanation of every important art period and form, including Japanese woodcuts; main stress on China and Japan, but Tibet, Korea also included. Still unexcelled for its detailed, rich coverage of cultural background, aesthetic elements, diffusion studies, particularly of the historical period. 2nd, 1913 edition. 242 illustrations. lii + 439pp. of text.
20364-6, 20365-4 Two volumes, Paperbound $6.00

THE GENTLE ART OF MAKING ENEMIES, James A. M. Whistler. Greatest wit of his day deflates Oscar Wilde, Ruskin, Swinburne; strikes back at inane critics, exhibitions, art journalism; aesthetics of impressionist revolution in most striking form. Highly readable classic by great painter. Reproduction of edition designed by Whistler. Introduction by Alfred Werner. xxxvi + 334pp.
21875-9 Paperbound $2.50

VISUAL ILLUSIONS: THEIR CAUSES, CHARACTERISTICS, AND APPLICATIONS, Matthew Luckiesh. Thorough description and discussion of optical illusion, geometric and perspective, particularly; size and shape distortions, illusions of color, of motion; natural illusions; use of illusion in art and magic, industry, etc. Most useful today with op art, also for classical art. Scores of effects illustrated. Introduction by William H. Ittleson. 100 illustrations. xxi + 252pp.
21530-X Paperbound $2.00

A HANDBOOK OF ANATOMY FOR ART STUDENTS, Arthur Thomson. Thorough, virtually exhaustive coverage of skeletal structure, musculature, etc. Full text, supplemented by anatomical diagrams and drawings and by photographs of undraped figures. Unique in its comparison of male and female forms, pointing out differences of contour, texture, form. 211 figures, 40 drawings, 86 photographs. xx + 459pp. 5⅜ x 8⅜.
21163-0 Paperbound $3.50

150 MASTERPIECES OF DRAWING, Selected by Anthony Toney. Full page reproductions of drawings from the early 16th to the end of the 18th century, all beautifully reproduced: Rembrandt, Michelangelo, Dürer, Fragonard, Urs, Graf, Wouwerman, many others. First-rate browsing book, model book for artists. xviii + 150pp. 8⅜ x 11¼.
21032-4 Paperbound $2.50

THE LATER WORK OF AUBREY BEARDSLEY, Aubrey Beardsley. Exotic, erotic, ironic masterpieces in full maturity: Comedy Ballet, Venus and Tannhauser, Pierrot, Lysistrata, Rape of the Lock, Savoy material, Ali Baba, Volpone, etc. This material revolutionized the art world, and is still powerful, fresh, brilliant. With *The Early Work,* all Beardsley's finest work. 174 plates, 2 in color. xiv + 176pp. 8⅛ x 11.
21817-1 Paperbound $3.00

DRAWINGS OF REMBRANDT, Rembrandt van Rijn. Complete reproduction of fabulously rare edition by Lippmann and Hofstede de Groot, completely reedited, updated, improved by Prof. Seymour Slive, Fogg Museum. Portraits, Biblical sketches, landscapes, Oriental types, nudes, episodes from classical mythology—All Rembrandt's fertile genius. Also selection of drawings by his pupils and followers. "Stunning volumes," *Saturday Review.* 550 illustrations. lxxviii + 552pp. 9⅛ x 12¼.
21485-0, 21486-9 Two volumes, Paperbound $7.00

THE DISASTERS OF WAR, Francisco Goya. One of the masterpieces of Western civilization—83 etchings that record Goya's shattering, bitter reaction to the Napoleonic war that swept through Spain after the insurrection of 1808 and to war in general. Reprint of the first edition, with three additional plates from Boston's Museum of Fine Arts. All plates facsimile size. Introduction by Philip Hofer, Fogg Museum. v + 97pp. 9⅜ x 8¼.
21872-4 Paperbound $2.00

GRAPHIC WORKS OF ODILON REDON. Largest collection of Redon's graphic works ever assembled: 172 lithographs, 28 etchings and engravings, 9 drawings. These include some of his most famous works. All the plates from *Odilon Redon: oeuvre graphique complet,* plus additional plates. New introduction and caption translations by Alfred Werner. 209 illustrations. xxvii + 209pp. 9⅛ x 12¼.
21966-8 Paperbound $4.00

DESIGN BY ACCIDENT; A BOOK OF "ACCIDENTAL EFFECTS" FOR ARTISTS AND DESIGNERS, James F. O'Brien. Create your own unique, striking, imaginative effects by "controlled accident" interaction of materials: paints and lacquers, oil and water based paints, splatter, crackling materials, shatter, similar items. Everything you do will be different; first book on this limitless art, so useful to both fine artist and commercial artist. Full instructions. 192 plates showing "accidents," 8 in color. viii + 215pp. 8⅜ x 11¼. 21942-9 Paperbound $3.50

THE BOOK OF SIGNS, Rudolf Koch. Famed German type designer draws 493 beautiful symbols: religious, mystical, alchemical, imperial, property marks, runes, etc. Remarkable fusion of traditional and modern. Good for suggestions of timelessness, smartness, modernity. Text. vi + 104pp. 6⅛ x 9¼. 20162-7 Paperbound $1.25

HISTORY OF INDIAN AND INDONESIAN ART, Ananda K. Coomaraswamy. An unabridged republication of one of the finest books by a great scholar in Eastern art. Rich in descriptive material, history, social backgrounds; Sunga reliefs, Rajput paintings, Gupta temples, Burmese frescoes, textiles, jewelry, sculpture, etc. 400 photos. viii + 423pp. 6⅜ x 9¾. 21436-2 Paperbound $4.00

PRIMITIVE ART, Franz Boas. America's foremost anthropologist surveys textiles, ceramics, woodcarving, basketry, metalwork, etc.; patterns, technology, creation of symbols, style origins. All areas of world, but very full on Northwest Coast Indians. More than 350 illustrations of baskets, boxes, totem poles, weapons, etc. 378 pp. 20025-6 Paperbound $3.00

THE GENTLEMAN AND CABINET MAKER'S DIRECTOR, Thomas Chippendale. Full reprint (third edition, 1762) of most influential furniture book of all time, by master cabinetmaker. 200 plates, illustrating chairs, sofas, mirrors, tables, cabinets, plus 24 photographs of surviving pieces. Biographical introduction by N. Bienenstock. vi + 249pp. 9⅞ x 12¾. 21601-2 Paperbound $4.00

AMERICAN ANTIQUE FURNITURE, Edgar G. Miller, Jr. The basic coverage of all American furniture before 1840. Individual chapters cover type of furniture—clocks, tables, sideboards, etc.—chronologically, with inexhaustible wealth of data. More than 2100 photographs, all identified, commented on. Essential to all early American collectors. Introduction by H. E. Keyes. vi + 1106pp. 7⅞ x 10¾. 21599-7, 21600-4 Two volumes, Paperbound $11.00

PENNSYLVANIA DUTCH AMERICAN FOLK ART, Henry J. Kauffman. 279 photos, 28 drawings of tulipware, Fraktur script, painted tinware, toys, flowered furniture, quilts, samplers, hex signs, house interiors, etc. Full descriptive text. Excellent for tourist, rewarding for designer, collector. Map. 146pp. 7⅞ x 10¾. 21205-X Paperbound $2.50

EARLY NEW ENGLAND GRAVESTONE RUBBINGS, Edmund V. Gillon, Jr. 43 photographs, 226 carefully reproduced rubbings show heavily symbolic, sometimes macabre early gravestones, up to early 19th century. Remarkable early American primitive art, occasionally strikingly beautiful; always powerful. Text. xxvi + 207pp. 8⅜ x 11¼. 21380-3 Paperbound $3.50

ALPHABETS AND ORNAMENTS, Ernst Lehner. Well-known pictorial source for decorative alphabets, script examples, cartouches, frames, decorative title pages, calligraphic initials, borders, similar material. 14th to 19th century, mostly European. Useful in almost any graphic arts designing, varied styles. 750 illustrations. 256pp. 7 x 10. 21905-4 Paperbound $4.00

PAINTING: A CREATIVE APPROACH, Norman Colquhoun. For the beginner simple guide provides an instructive approach to painting: major stumbling blocks for beginner; overcoming them, technical points; paints and pigments; oil painting; watercolor and other media and color. New section on "plastic" paints. Glossary. Formerly *Paint Your Own Pictures*. 221pp. 22000-1 Paperbound $1.75

THE ENJOYMENT AND USE OF COLOR, Walter Sargent. Explanation of the relations between colors themselves and between colors in nature and art, including hundreds of little-known facts about color values, intensities, effects of high and low illumination, complementary colors. Many practical hints for painters, references to great masters. 7 color plates, 29 illustrations. x + 274pp.
20944-X Paperbound $2.75

THE NOTEBOOKS OF LEONARDO DA VINCI, compiled and edited by Jean Paul Richter. 1566 extracts from original manuscripts reveal the full range of Leonardo's versatile genius: all his writings on painting, sculpture, architecture, anatomy, astronomy, geography, topography, physiology, mining, music, etc., in both Italian and English, with 186 plates of manuscript pages and more than 500 additional drawings. Includes studies for the Last Supper, the lost Sforza monument, and other works. Total of xlvii + 866pp. 7⅞ x 10¾.
22572-0, 22573-9 Two volumes, Paperbound $10.00

MONTGOMERY WARD CATALOGUE OF 1895. Tea gowns, yards of flannel and pillow-case lace, stereoscopes, books of gospel hymns, the New Improved Singer Sewing Machine, side saddles, milk skimmers, straight-edged razors, high-button shoes, spittoons, and on and on . . . listing some 25,000 items, practically all illustrated. Essential to the shoppers of the 1890's, it is our truest record of the spirit of the period. Unaltered reprint of Issue No. 57, Spring and Summer 1895. Introduction by Boris Emmet. Innumerable illustrations. xiii + 624pp. 8½ x 11⅝.
22377-9 Paperbound $6.95

THE CRYSTAL PALACE EXHIBITION ILLUSTRATED CATALOGUE (LONDON, 1851). One of the wonders of the modern world—the Crystal Palace Exhibition in which all the nations of the civilized world exhibited their achievements in the arts and sciences—presented in an equally important illustrated catalogue. More than 1700 items pictured with accompanying text—ceramics, textiles, cast-iron work, carpets, pianos, sleds, razors, wall-papers, billiard tables, beehives, silverware and hundreds of other artifacts—represent the focal point of Victorian culture in the Western World. Probably the largest collection of Victorian decorative art ever assembled—indispensable for antiquarians and designers. Unabridged republication of the Art-Journal Catalogue of the Great Exhibition of 1851, with all terminal essays. New introduction by John Gloag, F.S.A. xxxiv + 426pp. 9 x 12.
22503-8 Paperbound $4.50

A HISTORY OF COSTUME, Carl Köhler. Definitive history, based on surviving pieces of clothing primarily, and paintings, statues, etc. secondarily. Highly readable text, supplemented by 594 illustrations of costumes of the ancient Mediterranean peoples, Greece and Rome, the Teutonic prehistoric period; costumes of the Middle Ages, Renaissance, Baroque, 18th and 19th centuries. Clear, measured patterns are provided for many clothing articles. Approach is practical throughout. Enlarged by Emma von Sichart. 464pp. 21030-8 Paperbound $3.50

ORIENTAL RUGS, ANTIQUE AND MODERN, Walter A. Hawley. A complete and authoritative treatise on the Oriental rug—where they are made, by whom and how, designs and symbols, characteristics in detail of the six major groups, how to distinguish them and how to buy them. Detailed technical data is provided on periods, weaves, warps, wefts, textures, sides, ends and knots, although no technical background is required for an understanding. 11 color plates, 80 halftones, 4 maps. vi + 320pp. 6⅛ x 9⅛. 22366-3 Paperbound $5.00

TEN BOOKS ON ARCHITECTURE, Vitruvius. By any standards the most important book on architecture ever written. Early Roman discussion of aesthetics of building, construction methods, orders, sites, and every other aspect of architecture has inspired, instructed architecture for about 2,000 years. Stands behind Palladio, Michelangelo, Bramante, Wren, countless others. Definitive Morris H. Morgan translation. 68 illustrations. xii + 331pp. 20645-9 Paperbound $2.50

THE FOUR BOOKS OF ARCHITECTURE, Andrea Palladio. Translated into every major Western European language in the two centuries following its publication in 1570, this has been one of the most influential books in the history of architecture. Complete reprint of the 1738 Isaac Ware edition. New introduction by Adolf Placzek, Columbia Univ. 216 plates. xxii + 110pp. of text. 9½ x 12¾. 21308-0 Clothbound $10.00

STICKS AND STONES: A STUDY OF AMERICAN ARCHITECTURE AND CIVILIZATION, Lewis Mumford.One of the great classics of American cultural history. American architecture from the medieval-inspired earliest forms to the early 20th century; evolution of structure and style, and reciprocal influences on environment. 21 photographic illustrations. 238pp. 20202-X Paperbound $2.00

THE AMERICAN BUILDER'S COMPANION, Asher Benjamin. The most widely used early 19th century architectural style and source book, for colonial up into Greek Revival periods. Extensive development of geometry of carpentering, construction of sashes, frames, doors, stairs; plans and elevations of domestic and other buildings. Hundreds of thousands of houses were built according to this book, now invaluable to historians, architects, restorers, etc. 1827 edition. 59 plates. 114pp. 7⅞ x 10¾. 22236-5 Paperbound $3.00

DUTCH HOUSES IN THE HUDSON VALLEY BEFORE 1776, Helen Wilkinson Reynolds. The standard survey of the Dutch colonial house and outbuildings, with constructional features, decoration, and local history associated with individual homesteads. Introduction by Franklin D. Roosevelt. Map. 150 illustrations. 469pp. 6⅝ x 9¼. 21469-9 Paperbound $4.00

THE ARCHITECTURE OF COUNTRY HOUSES, Andrew J. Downing. Together with Vaux's *Villas and Cottages* this is the basic book for Hudson River Gothic architecture of the middle Victorian period. Full, sound discussions of general aspects of housing, architecture, style, decoration, furnishing, together with scores of detailed house plans, illustrations of specific buildings, accompanied by full text. Perhaps the most influential single American architectural book. 1850 edition. Introduction by J. Stewart Johnson. 321 figures, 34 architectural designs. xvi + 560pp.
22003-6 Paperbound $4.00

LOST EXAMPLES OF COLONIAL ARCHITECTURE, John Mead Howells. Full-page photographs of buildings that have disappeared or been so altered as to be denatured, including many designed by major early American architects. 245 plates. xvii + 248pp. 7⅞ x 10¾. 21143-6 Paperbound $3.50

DOMESTIC ARCHITECTURE OF THE AMERICAN COLONIES AND OF THE EARLY REPUBLIC, Fiske Kimball. Foremost architect and restorer of Williamsburg and Monticello covers nearly 200 homes between 1620-1825. Architectural details, construction, style features, special fixtures, floor plans, etc. Generally considered finest work in its area. 219 illustrations of houses, doorways, windows, capital mantels. xx + 314pp. 7⅞ x 10¾. 21743-4 Paperbound $4.00

EARLY AMERICAN ROOMS: 1650-1858, edited by Russell Hawes Kettell. Tour of 12 rooms, each representative of a different era in American history and each furnished, decorated, designed and occupied in the style of the era. 72 plans and elevations, 8-page color section, etc., show fabrics, wall papers, arrangements, etc. Full descriptive text. xvii + 200pp. of text. 8⅜ x 11¼.
21633-0 Paperbound $5.00

THE FITZWILLIAM VIRGINAL BOOK, edited by J. Fuller Maitland and W. B. Squire. Full modern printing of famous early 17th-century ms. volume of 300 works by Morley, Byrd, Bull, Gibbons, etc. For piano or other modern keyboard instrument; easy to read format. xxxvi + 938pp. 8⅜ x 11.
21068-5, 21069-3 Two volumes, Paperbound $10.00

KEYBOARD MUSIC, Johann Sebastian Bach. Bach Gesellschaft edition. A rich selection of Bach's masterpieces for the harpsichord: the six English Suites, six French Suites, the six Partitas (Clavierübung part I), the Goldberg Variations (Clavierübung part IV), the fifteen Two-Part Inventions and the fifteen Three-Part Sinfonias. Clearly reproduced on large sheets with ample margins; eminently playable. vi + 312pp. 8⅛ x 11. 22360-4 Paperbound $5.00

THE MUSIC OF BACH: AN INTRODUCTION, Charles Sanford Terry. A fine, nontechnical introduction to Bach's music, both instrumental and vocal. Covers organ music, chamber music, passion music, other types. Analyzes themes, developments, innovations. x + 114pp. 21075-8 Paperbound $1.25

BEETHOVEN AND HIS NINE SYMPHONIES, Sir George Grove. Noted British musicologist provides best history, analysis, commentary on symphonies. Very thorough, rigorously accurate; necessary to both advanced student and amateur music lover. 436 musical passages. vii + 407 pp. 20334-4 Paperbound $2.75

JOHANN SEBASTIAN BACH, Philipp Spitta. One of the great classics of musicology, this definitive analysis of Bach's music (and life) has never been surpassed. Lucid, nontechnical analyses of hundreds of pieces (30 pages devoted to St. Matthew Passion, 26 to B Minor Mass). Also includes major analysis of 18th-century music. 450 musical examples. 40-page musical supplement. Total of xx + 1799pp.
(EUK) 22278-0, 22279-9 Two volumes, Clothbound $17.50

MOZART AND HIS PIANO CONCERTOS, Cuthbert Girdlestone. The only full-length study of an important area of Mozart's creativity. Provides detailed analyses of all 23 concertos, traces inspirational sources. 417 musical examples. Second edition. 509pp. (USO) 21271-8 Paperbound $3.50

THE PERFECT WAGNERITE: A COMMENTARY ON THE NIBLUNG'S RING, George Bernard Shaw. Brilliant and still relevant criticism in remarkable essays on Wagner's Ring cycle, Shaw's ideas on political and social ideology behind the plots, role of Leitmotifs, vocal requisites, etc. Prefaces. xxi + 136pp.
21707-8 Paperbound $1.50

DON GIOVANNI, W. A. Mozart. Complete libretto, modern English translation; biographies of composer and librettist; accounts of early performances and critical reaction. Lavishly illustrated. All the material you need to understand and appreciate this great work. Dover Opera Guide and Libretto Series; translated and introduced by Ellen Bleiler. 92 illustrations. 209pp.
21134-7 Paperbound $1.50

HIGH FIDELITY SYSTEMS: A LAYMAN'S GUIDE, Roy F. Allison. All the basic information you need for setting up your own audio system: high fidelity and stereo record players, tape records, F.M. Connections, adjusting tone arm, cartridge, checking needle alignment, positioning speakers, phasing speakers, adjusting hums, trouble-shooting, maintenance, and similar topics. Enlarged 1965 edition. More than 50 charts, diagrams, photos. iv + 91pp. 21514-8 Paperbound $1.25

REPRODUCTION OF SOUND, Edgar Villchur. Thorough coverage for laymen of high fidelity systems, reproducing systems in general, needles, amplifiers, preamps, loudspeakers, feedback, explaining physical background. "A rare talent for making technicalities vividly comprehensible," R. Darrell, *High Fidelity*. 69 figures. iv + 92pp. 21515-6 Paperbound $1.25

HEAR ME TALKIN' TO YA: THE STORY OF JAZZ AS TOLD BY THE MEN WHO MADE IT, Nat Shapiro and Nat Hentoff. Louis Armstrong, Fats Waller, Jo Jones, Clarence Williams, Billy Holiday, Duke Ellington, Jelly Roll Morton and dozens of other jazz greats tell how it was in Chicago's South Side, New Orleans, depression Harlem and the modern West Coast as jazz was born and grew. xvi + 429pp.
21726-4 Paperbound $2.50

FABLES OF AESOP, translated by Sir Roger L'Estrange. A reproduction of the very rare 1931 Paris edition; a selection of the most interesting fables, together with 50 imaginative drawings by Alexander Calder. v + 128pp. 6½x9¼.
21780-9 Paperbound $1.50

AGAINST THE GRAIN (A REBOURS), Joris K. Huysmans. Filled with weird images, evidences of a bizarre imagination, exotic experiments with hallucinatory drugs, rich tastes and smells and the diversions of its sybarite hero Duc Jean des Esseintes, this classic novel pushed 19th-century literary decadence to its limits. Full unabridged edition. Do not confuse this with abridged editions generally sold. Introduction by Havelock Ellis. xlix + 206pp. 22190-3 Paperbound $2.00

VARIORUM SHAKESPEARE: HAMLET. Edited by Horace H. Furness; a landmark of American scholarship. Exhaustive footnotes and appendices treat all doubtful words and phrases, as well as suggested critical emendations throughout the play's history. First volume contains editor's own text, collated with all Quartos and Folios. Second volume contains full first Quarto, translations of Shakespeare's sources (Belleforest, and Saxo Grammaticus), Der Bestrafte Brudermord, and many essays on critical and historical points of interest by major authorities of past and present. Includes details of staging and costuming over the years. By far the best edition available for serious students of Shakespeare. Total of xx + 905pp.
21004-9, 21005-7, 2 volumes, Paperbound $7.00

A LIFE OF WILLIAM SHAKESPEARE, Sir Sidney Lee. This is the standard life of Shakespeare, summarizing everything known about Shakespeare and his plays. Incredibly rich in material, broad in coverage, clear and judicious, it has served thousands as the best introduction to Shakespeare. 1931 edition. 9 plates. xxix + 792pp. (USO) 21967-4 Paperbound $3.75

MASTERS OF THE DRAMA, John Gassner. Most comprehensive history of the drama in print, covering every tradition from Greeks to modern Europe and America, including India, Far East, etc. Covers more than 800 dramatists, 2000 plays, with biographical material, plot summaries, theatre history, criticism, etc. "Best of its kind in English," *New Republic.* 77 illustrations. xxii + 890pp.
20100-7 Clothbound $8.50

THE EVOLUTION OF THE ENGLISH LANGUAGE, George McKnight. The growth of English, from the 14th century to the present. Unusual, non-technical account presents basic information in very interesting form: sound shifts, change in grammar and syntax, vocabulary growth, similar topics. Abundantly illustrated with quotations. Formerly *Modern English in the Making.* xii + 590pp.
21932-1 Paperbound $3.50

AN ETYMOLOGICAL DICTIONARY OF MODERN ENGLISH, Ernest Weekley. Fullest, richest work of its sort, by foremost British lexicographer. Detailed word histories, including many colloquial and archaic words; extensive quotations. Do not confuse this with the Concise Etymological Dictionary, which is much abridged. Total of xxvii + 830pp. 6½ x 9¼.
21873-2, 21874-0 Two volumes, Paperbound $6.00

FLATLAND: A ROMANCE OF MANY DIMENSIONS, E. A. Abbott. Classic of science-fiction explores ramifications of life in a two-dimensional world, and what happens when a three-dimensional being intrudes. Amusing reading, but also useful as introduction to thought about hyperspace. Introduction by Banesh Hoffmann. 16 illustrations. xx + 103pp. 20001-9 Paperbound $1.00

POEMS OF ANNE BRADSTREET, edited with an introduction by Robert Hutchinson. A new selection of poems by America's first poet and perhaps the first significant woman poet in the English language. 48 poems display her development in works of considerable variety—love poems, domestic poems, religious meditations, formal elegies, "quaternions," etc. Notes, bibliography. viii + 222pp.
22160-1 Paperbound $2.00

THREE GOTHIC NOVELS: THE CASTLE OF OTRANTO BY HORACE WALPOLE; VATHEK BY WILLIAM BECKFORD; THE VAMPYRE BY JOHN POLIDORI, WITH FRAGMENT OF A NOVEL BY LORD BYRON, edited by E. F. Bleiler. The first Gothic novel, by Walpole; the finest Oriental tale in English, by Beckford; powerful Romantic supernatural story in versions by Polidori and Byron. All extremely important in history of literature; all still exciting, packed with supernatural thrills, ghosts, haunted castles, magic, etc. xl + 291pp.
21232-7 Paperbound $2.00

THE BEST TALES OF HOFFMANN, E. T. A. Hoffmann. 10 of Hoffmann's most important stories, in modern re-editings of standard translations: Nutcracker and the King of Mice, Signor Formica, Automata, The Sandman, Rath Krespel, The Golden Flowerpot, Master Martin the Cooper, The Mines of Falun, The King's Betrothed, A New Year's Eve Adventure. 7 illustrations by Hoffmann. Edited by E. F. Bleiler. xxxix + 419pp. 21793-0 Paperbound $2.50

GHOST AND HORROR STORIES OF AMBROSE BIERCE, Ambrose Bierce. 23 strikingly modern stories of the horrors latent in the human mind: The Eyes of the Panther, The Damned Thing, An Occurrence at Owl Creek Bridge, An Inhabitant of Carcosa, etc., plus the dream-essay, Visions of the Night. Edited by E. F. Bleiler. xxii + 199pp. 20767-6 Paperbound $1.50

BEST GHOST STORIES OF J. S. LEFANU, J. Sheridan LeFanu. Finest stories by Victorian master often considered greatest supernatural writer of all. Carmilla, Green Tea, The Haunted Baronet, The Familiar, and 12 others. Most never before available in the U. S. A. Edited by E. F. Bleiler. 8 illustrations from Victorian publications. xvii + 467pp. 20415-4 Paperbound $3.00

THE TIME STREAM, THE GREATEST ADVENTURE, AND THE PURPLE SAPPHIRE—THREE SCIENCE FICTION NOVELS, John Taine (Eric Temple Bell). Great American mathematician was also foremost science fiction novelist of the 1920's. *The Time Stream,* one of all-time classics, uses concepts of circular time; *The Greatest Adventure,* incredibly ancient biological experiments from Antarctica threaten to escape; The *Purple Sapphire,* superscience, lost races in Central Tibet, survivors of the Great Race. 4 illustrations by Frank R. Paul. v + 532pp.
21180-0 Paperbound $3.00

SEVEN SCIENCE FICTION NOVELS, H. G. Wells. The standard collection of the great novels. Complete, unabridged. *First Men in the Moon, Island of Dr. Moreau, War of the Worlds, Food of the Gods, Invisible Man, Time Machine, In the Days of the Comet.* Not only science fiction fans, but every educated person owes it to himself to read these novels. 1015pp. 20264-X Clothbound $5.00

LAST AND FIRST MEN AND STAR MAKER, TWO SCIENCE FICTION NOVELS, Olaf Stapledon. Greatest future histories in science fiction. In the first, human intelligence is the "hero," through strange paths of evolution, interplanetary invasions, incredible technologies, near extinctions and reemergences. Star Maker describes the quest of a band of star rovers for intelligence itself, through time and space: weird inhuman civilizations, crustacean minds, symbiotic worlds, etc. Complete, unabridged. v + 438pp. 21962-3 Paperbound $2.50

THREE PROPHETIC NOVELS, H. G. WELLS. Stages of a consistently planned future for mankind. *When the Sleeper Wakes,* and *A Story of the Days to Come,* anticipate *Brave New World* and *1984,* in the 21st Century; *The Time Machine,* only complete version in print, shows farther future and the end of mankind. All show Wells's greatest gifts as storyteller and novelist. Edited by E. F. Bleiler. x + 335pp. (USO) 20605-X Paperbound $2.25

THE DEVIL'S DICTIONARY, Ambrose Bierce. America's own Oscar Wilde—Ambrose Bierce—offers his barbed iconoclastic wisdom in over 1,000 definitions hailed by H. L. Mencken as "some of the most gorgeous witticisms in the English language." 145pp. 20487-1 Paperbound $1.25

MAX AND MORITZ, Wilhelm Busch. Great children's classic, father of comic strip, of two bad boys, Max and Moritz. Also Ker and Plunk (Plisch und Plumm), Cat and Mouse, Deceitful Henry, Ice-Peter, The Boy and the Pipe, and five other pieces. Original German, with English translation. Edited by H. Arthur Klein; translations by various hands and H. Arthur Klein. vi + 216pp. 20181-3 Paperbound $2.00

PIGS IS PIGS AND OTHER FAVORITES, Ellis Parker Butler. The title story is one of the best humor short stories, as Mike Flannery obfuscates biology and English. Also included, That Pup of Murchison's, The Great American Pie Company, and Perkins of Portland. 14 illustrations. v + 109pp. 21532-6 Paperbound $1.00

THE PETERKIN PAPERS, Lucretia P. Hale. It takes genius to be as stupidly mad as the Peterkins, as they decide to become wise, celebrate the "Fourth," keep a cow, and otherwise strain the resources of the Lady from Philadelphia. Basic book of American humor. 153 illustrations. 219pp. 20794-3 Paperbound $1.50

PERRAULT'S FAIRY TALES, translated by A. E. Johnson and S. R. Littlewood, with 34 full-page illustrations by Gustave Doré. All the original Perrault stories—Cinderella, Sleeping Beauty, Bluebeard, Little Red Riding Hood, Puss in Boots, Tom Thumb, etc.—with their witty verse morals and the magnificent illustrations of Doré. One of the five or six great books of European fairy tales. viii + 117pp. 8⅛ x 11. 22311-6 Paperbound $2.00

OLD HUNGARIAN FAIRY TALES, Baroness Orczy. Favorites translated and adapted by author of the *Scarlet Pimpernel.* Eight fairy tales include "The Suitors of Princess Fire-Fly," "The Twin Hunchbacks," "Mr. Cuttlefish's Love Story," and "The Enchanted Cat." This little volume of magic and adventure will captivate children as it has for generations. 90 drawings by Montagu Barstow. 96pp. (USO) 22293-4 Paperbound $1.95

THE RED FAIRY BOOK, Andrew Lang. Lang's color fairy books have long been children's favorites. This volume includes Rapunzel, Jack and the Bean-stalk and 35 other stories, familiar and unfamiliar. 4 plates, 93 illustrations x + 367pp.
21673-X Paperbound $2.50

THE BLUE FAIRY BOOK, Andrew Lang. Lang's tales come from all countries and all times. Here are 37 tales from Grimm, the Arabian Nights, Greek Mythology, and other fascinating sources. 8 plates, 130 illustrations. xi + 390pp.
21437-0 Paperbound $2.50

HOUSEHOLD STORIES BY THE BROTHERS GRIMM. Classic English-language edition of the well-known tales — Rumpelstiltskin, Snow White, Hansel and Gretel, The Twelve Brothers, Faithful John, Rapunzel, Tom Thumb (52 stories in all). Translated into simple, straightforward English by Lucy Crane. Ornamented with headpieces, vignettes, elaborate decorative initials and a dozen full-page illustrations by Walter Crane. x + 269pp. 21080-4 Paperbound $2.50

THE MERRY ADVENTURES OF ROBIN HOOD, Howard Pyle. The finest modern versions of the traditional ballads and tales about the great English outlaw. Howard Pyle's complete prose version, with every word, every illustration of the first edition. Do not confuse this facsimile of the original (1883) with modern editions that change text or illustrations. 23 plates plus many page decorations. xxii + 296pp.
22043-5 Paperbound $2.50

THE STORY OF KING ARTHUR AND HIS KNIGHTS, Howard Pyle. The finest children's version of the life of King Arthur; brilliantly retold by Pyle, with 48 of his most imaginative illustrations. xviii + 313pp. 6⅛ x 9¼.
21445-1 Paperbound $2.50

THE WONDERFUL WIZARD OF OZ, L. Frank Baum. America's finest children's book in facsimile of first edition with all Denslow illustrations in full color. The edition a child should have. Introduction by Martin Gardner. 23 color plates, scores of drawings. iv + 267pp. 20691-2 Paperbound $2.25

THE MARVELOUS LAND OF OZ, L. Frank Baum. The second Oz book, every bit as imaginative as the Wizard. The hero is a boy named Tip, but the Scarecrow and the Tin Woodman are back, as is the Oz magic. 16 color plates, 120 drawings by John R. Neill. 287pp. 20692-0 Paperbound $2.50

THE MAGICAL MONARCH OF MO, L. Frank Baum. Remarkable adventures in a land even stranger than Oz. The best of Baum's books not in the Oz series. 15 color plates and dozens of drawings by Frank Verbeck. xviii + 237pp.
21892-9 Paperbound $2.00

THE BAD CHILD'S BOOK OF BEASTS, MORE BEASTS FOR WORSE CHILDREN, A MORAL ALPHABET, Hilaire Belloc. Three complete humor classics in one volume. Be kind to the frog, and do not call him names . . . and 28 other whimsical animals. Familiar favorites and some not so well known. Illustrated by Basil Blackwell. 156pp. (USO) 20749-8 Paperbound $1.25

EAST O' THE SUN AND WEST O' THE MOON, George W. Dasent. Considered the best of all translations of these Norwegian folk tales, this collection has been enjoyed by generations of children (and folklorists too). Includes True and Untrue, Why the Sea is Salt, East O' the Sun and West O' the Moon, Why the Bear is Stumpy-Tailed, Boots and the Troll, The Cock and the Hen, Rich Peter the Pedlar, and 52 more. The only edition with all 59 tales. 77 illustrations by Erik Werenskiold and Theodor Kittelsen. xv + 418pp. 22521-6 Paperbound $3.00

GOOPS AND HOW TO BE THEM, Gelett Burgess. Classic of tongue-in-cheek humor, masquerading as etiquette book. 87 verses, twice as many cartoons, show mischievous Goops as they demonstrate to children virtues of table manners, neatness, courtesy, etc. Favorite for generations. viii + 88pp. 6½ x 9¼. 22233-0 Paperbound $1.25

ALICE'S ADVENTURES UNDER GROUND, Lewis Carroll. The first version, quite different from the final *Alice in Wonderland,* printed out by Carroll himself with his own illustrations. Complete facsimile of the "million dollar" manuscript Carroll gave to Alice Liddell in 1864. Introduction by Martin Gardner. viii + 96pp. Title and dedication pages in color. 21482-6 Paperbound $1.25

THE BROWNIES, THEIR BOOK, Palmer Cox. Small as mice, cunning as foxes, exuberant and full of mischief, the Brownies go to the zoo, toy shop, seashore, circus, etc., in 24 verse adventures and 266 illustrations. Long a favorite, since their first appearance in St. Nicholas Magazine. xi + 144pp. 6⅝ x 9¼. 21265-3 Paperbound $1.75

SONGS OF CHILDHOOD, Walter De La Mare. Published (under the pseudonym Walter Ramal) when De La Mare was only 29, this charming collection has long been a favorite children's book. A facsimile of the first edition in paper, the 47 poems capture the simplicity of the nursery rhyme and the ballad, including such lyrics as I Met Eve, Tartary, The Silver Penny. vii + 106pp. 21972-0 Paperbound $1.25

THE COMPLETE NONSENSE OF EDWARD LEAR, Edward Lear. The finest 19th-century humorist-cartoonist in full: all nonsense limericks, zany alphabets, Owl and Pussycat, songs, nonsense botany, and more than 500 illustrations by Lear himself. Edited by Holbrook Jackson. xxix + 287pp. (USO) 20167-8 Paperbound $2.00

BILLY WHISKERS: THE AUTOBIOGRAPHY OF A GOAT, Frances Trego Montgomery. A favorite of children since the early 20th century, here are the escapades of that rambunctious, irresistible and mischievous goat—Billy Whiskers. Much in the spirit of *Peck's Bad Boy,* this is a book that children never tire of reading or hearing. All the original familiar illustrations by W. H. Fry are included: 6 color plates, 18 black and white drawings. 159pp. 22345-0 Paperbound $2.00

MOTHER GOOSE MELODIES. Faithful republication of the fabulously rare Munroe and Francis "copyright 1833" Boston edition—the most important Mother Goose collection, usually referred to as the "original." Familiar rhymes plus many rare ones, with wonderful old woodcut illustrations. Edited by E. F. Bleiler. 128pp. 4½ x 6⅜. 22577-1 Paperbound $1.25

TWO LITTLE SAVAGES; BEING THE ADVENTURES OF TWO BOYS WHO LIVED AS INDIANS AND WHAT THEY LEARNED, Ernest Thompson Seton. Great classic of nature and boyhood provides a vast range of woodlore in most palatable form, a genuinely entertaining story. Two farm boys build a teepee in woods and live in it for a month, working out Indian solutions to living problems, star lore, birds and animals, plants, etc. 293 illustrations. vii + 286pp.

20985-7 Paperbound $2.50

PETER PIPER'S PRACTICAL PRINCIPLES OF PLAIN & PERFECT PRONUNCIATION. Alliterative jingles and tongue-twisters of surprising charm, that made their first appearance in America about 1830. Republished in full with the spirited woodcut illustrations from this earliest American edition. 32pp. 4½ x 6⅜.

22560-7 Paperbound $1.00

SCIENCE EXPERIMENTS AND AMUSEMENTS FOR CHILDREN, Charles Vivian. 73 easy experiments, requiring only materials found at home or easily available, such as candles, coins, steel wool, etc.; illustrate basic phenomena like vacuum, simple chemical reaction, etc. All safe. Modern, well-planned. Formerly *Science Games for Children.* 102 photos, numerous drawings. 96pp. 6⅛ x 9¼.

21856-2 Paperbound $1.25

AN INTRODUCTION TO CHESS MOVES AND TACTICS SIMPLY EXPLAINED, Leonard Barden. Informal intermediate introduction, quite strong in explaining reasons for moves. Covers basic material, tactics, important openings, traps, positional play in middle game, end game. Attempts to isolate patterns and recurrent configurations. Formerly *Chess*. 58 figures. 102pp. (USO) 21210-6 Paperbound $1.25

LASKER'S MANUAL OF CHESS, Dr. Emanuel Lasker. Lasker was not only one of the five great World Champions, he was also one of the ablest expositors, theorists, and analysts. In many ways, his Manual, permeated with his philosophy of battle, filled with keen insights, is one of the greatest works ever written on chess. Filled with analyzed games by the great players. A single-volume library that will profit almost any chess player, beginner or master. 308 diagrams. xli x 349pp.

20640-8 Paperbound $2.75

THE MASTER BOOK OF MATHEMATICAL RECREATIONS, Fred Schuh. In opinion of many the finest work ever prepared on mathematical puzzles, stunts, recreations; exhaustively thorough explanations of mathematics involved, analysis of effects, citation of puzzles and games. Mathematics involved is elementary. Translated by F. Göbel. 194 figures. xxiv + 430pp. 22134-2 Paperbound $3.00

MATHEMATICS, MAGIC AND MYSTERY, Martin Gardner. Puzzle editor for Scientific American explains mathematics behind various mystifying tricks: card tricks, stage "mind reading," coin and match tricks, counting out games, geometric dissections, etc. Probability sets, theory of numbers clearly explained. Also provides more than 400 tricks, guaranteed to work, that you can do. 135 illustrations. xii + 176pp.

20338-2 Paperbound $1.50